The Emergence of Dialectical Theory

The Emergence of Dialectical Theory

Philosophy and Political Inquiry

Scott Warren

The University of Chicago Press
Chicago and London

SCOTT WARREN is assistant professor of government at
Pomona College.

The following works of T. S. Eliot are quoted in chapter
seven: *The Rock,* copyright 1934 by Harcourt, Brace and
Co., Inc.; *Collected Poems 1909–1935,* copyright 1936 by
Harcourt, Brace and Co., Inc.; and *Four Quartets,* copyright
1943 by T. S. Eliot.

The University of Chicago Press, Chicago 60637
The University of Chicago Press, Ltd., London

Library of Congress Cataloging in Publication Data

Warren, Scott.
    The emergence of dialectical theory.

    Bibliography: p.
    Includes index.
    1. Political science—History. 2. Dialectic—
History. I. Title.
JA83.W28 1984   320'.01   83-24300
ISBN 0-226-87390-0
ISBN 0-226-87391-9 (pbk.)

Contents

v

To my parents, Cal and Merlene

Preface

A book is never finished. Both the excitement and the frustration of writing one are derived from that very sense of incompletion. There is always something of the arbitrary in choosing where to begin and end a book and in filling up the pages in between. A book presents us with the illusion of the finite, as if somehow it were a self-contained whole. In fact, it is simply a moment of expression, wrested from the flow and fullness of our experience and reflection and frozen for a time. And like all expression, as Merleau-Ponty once said of Cézanne's view of his own art, one often wonders whether it contains meaning, or at least whether it contains the meaning one thinks one intended to convey. We are never quite sure whether our expression leads anywhere, whether it points in the direction we had hoped, or to what extent it has moved beyond our control. Nonetheless, we know that we must continually make the effort.

This book is just such an effort. As a page out of the diary of my intellectual journey through political theory, it represents one possible attempt to locate and reorient our current position within the long history of political inquiry. In one sense, it mirrors the path I have traveled in trying to discover and understand that position. It is nevertheless a path that I believe, and hope, many other students of political theory are traveling, and I trust that there are others eager to begin the voyage.

My account of the evolution of dialectical theory, a perspective I hope can enrich and nourish our view of political inquiry, actually gets under way in chapter 2. Chapter 1 covers some fairly well-known ground in recent political science, and the issues should be familiar to most serious students of politics—that is, the debate during the past few decades between positivist-inspired, behavioralist political science and the revival of the tradition of political theory. I think it is important, however, that we recollect some aspects of that debate in order to make more intelligible the meaning and promise of the alternative of dialectical theory and to provide a current context for the beginning of our journey in chapter 2, which requires a return to Kant, Hegel, and Marx. The subsequent chapters represent the various major stations along the way of our expedition to the present. The final chapter points a hopeful finger in the direction of one possible, humanistic future for political inquiry. This is 1984, and we can be thankful to whatever remains of open, humanistic, and critical thinking in our society that the world depicted in Orwell's novel has not yet been completely brought into existence.

If a book is never finished, the same holds true for any list of people to whom one ultimately owes thanks for assistance in writing one—people both living and dead, known either face-to-face or only through words. But a few significant debts have to be acknowledged. My first gesture of gratitude is to Dante Germino, who introduced me to the seductive world of political theory when I was a student at the University of Virginia. My life was irrevocably altered in those days, and I think often of his singular influence on my thought. He should not, of course, be held responsible for the use I have made out of his introduction. I can only hope that I have not violated the spirit of the quest he shared with me.

Gratitude needs to be extended also to three of my teachers during my sojourn at the Claremont Graduate School, each of whom continually renewed my enthusiasm for political and philosophical inquiry. Lee Cameron McDonald, whom I consider to be one of the finest historians of political theory in our country today, guided me with a calm and critical hand. In his thoughtfulness, he always refused to let me get too carried away with my occasional flights of imagination. Gerald I. Jordan and Lucian C. Marquis are two of the most Socratic teachers a student of politics and philosophy could ever want. I received a critical and stimulating education at their hands that I could never hope to repay or replace. Each in his own way guided me judiciously through a labyrinth of philosophical questions and scholarly tasks.

A different variety of appreciation is in order for Nancy Burson, who typed two versions of the manuscript and who demonstrated the kind of zeal for perfection and attention to detail, not to mention the good humor and humanity, that no word processor will ever match.

Finally, I am grateful to Kay Koeninger, my wife, who steadfastly contributed absolutely nothing but her existence to this work (since art is her world), and who for that very reason has cheerfully agreed to accept all blame for any errors of fact or interpretation. This book is dedicated to my parents, Cal and Merlene, whose importance extends beyond the obvious.

1   The Recent History of Political Inquiry

Two Leading Views in Political Science

These are exciting times for students of political theory. It is possible that we are riding the crest of a wave of what Richard Bernstein has recently called "the restructuring of social and political theory."[1] Whether or not we are really on the verge of something so radical as a new era for the self-understanding of political science is an open question, but it is certainly an important and promising one. At the very least, it is a question which reveals an ongoing concern over how we are to understand the nature of political knowledge and reality. It is essential that political science continue to address itself to questions concerning its proper epistemological orientation and the appropriate domain of its interest.

Seventeen years ago, Dante Germino addressed these questions in a work that helped to clarify the major debate that had emerged in political science regarding the nature of authentic political theory.[2] In those days he correctly isolated the two dominant antagonists as the positivists of the behavioral movement and the revivalists of the classical tradition of political theory. After witnessing the numerous ways in which that debate has taken shape over the past decades, I decided it was necessary to bring to the fore and clarify a third voice often unheard in contemporary political science. It is my intention to offer some ideas that emerge from the development of post-Kantian Continental philosophy, in its particularly dialectical expressions, that might provide insight into the continuing debates over the epistemological foundations of political inquiry. I hope to reconstruct this development of a broad "dialectical theory" in a new light which places a sensitivity to the concept of "dialectic" at the center of such varied post-Kantian movements as phenomenology, marxism, existentialism, and critical theory.[3] In other words, I believe we can isolate the "dialectic" at the epistemological level as a key unifying principle of a new philosophical orientation for political science.

It is furthermore my belief that political inquiry is continuously shaped and nourished by broad philosophical traditions. Even if we are not on the verge of a radical restructuring of political theory, there is a philosophical tradition about which our discipline needs to be clearer and more understanding. This means we can detect and interpret certain developments and thinkers within a broad dialectical tradition, which can be related to and clarify the philosophical problems that condition yet are often hidden to the field of political science.

At the same time, it may be possible to detect a kind of dialectic at work in the "metatheoretical" debates in recent political science, such as in that between positivist and classical political theory. We might imagine a dialogue of sorts which can lead beyond the conflict of such positions to a new and, one hopes, more appropriate understanding of the nature of political inquiry. This kind of dialectical interaction, which usually exists in a rather implicit and perhaps unintentional manner, forms the background of this work. But what I want to focus upon is the actual development of a broad dialectical tradition in philosophical inquiry, and I offer one possible interpretation of that tradition so that it might yield a clearer alternative to the epistemological debates in political science. Furthermore, I should perhaps emphasize that this enterprise takes its bearings and its point of departure from within political science, not from within the history of philosophy, and is intended to speak to political scientists in hopes of broadening the philosophical nature and concerns of contemporary political science.

The Plan of This Volume

This work was conceived in an attempt to understand the juncture at which we stand in the history of political inquiry. The source of this interest can be seen in the light of two important problems for contemporary political theory. First, political science still labors under the spell of behavioralism and of the many attempts to criticize it. Second, the perennial question of the proper role of epistemology in political inquiry is still far from being resolved. Both of these problems form for me a concern over the appropriate epistemological roots of political theory and the philosophical status of that question today.

As is well known, twentieth-century political science has spawned an approach to political understanding based on a criticism of all previous "traditional political philosophy," from Plato onward, as hopelessly "metaphysical," scientifically imprecise, unfounded, and confused.[4] This mood or movement, known as "behavioralism," strongly infused with the positivism of the late nineteenth century and inspired by the empirical-analytical methods of the "natural" sciences, came to be seen by many concerned observers in political science as a threat to the existence of critical and open thought and to the breadth and depth of vision of classical political theory. The resulting conflict gave birth to the numerous debates which have come to dominate the metatheoretical and methodological level of discourse—debates over the proper relation of fact and value, "is" and "ought," description and prescription, empirical theory and normative theory, noncognitivism and cognitivism, and so forth.[5]

In response to the gaining momentum of the behavioral persuasion, around the middle of the century and into its second half, advocates of the revival of political theory came to the fore.[6] Those political thinkers and historians of political philosophy dissatisfied with the inadequacies of behavioralism criticized both its theoretical assumptions and the spirit of its research. Their critique quite often involved an attempt to return to and revive the great tradition of political theory from Plato to Hegel. The ranks of what we might call these "traditionalist" critics of behavioralism include such figures as Hannah Arendt, Carl Friedrich, Dante Germino, Bertrand de Jouvenel, Lee McDonald, Michael Oakeshott, Eric Voegelin, and Sheldon Wolin.[7] Perhaps one of the most influential of these critics, especially in the United States, was Leo Strauss. His work has become a symbol of the philosophical "counterrevolution" against the behavioral revolution. To a certain extent, one can represent the essential points of the traditionalist critique by way of a summary of Strauss's criticism of behavioralist political science.

Like many others who have reflected on the recent history of political inquiry, I found myself standing on the threshold of this critique of behavioralism. It is a critique that, in light of the rich and varied tradition of political theory, attacks the epistemological and methodological reductionism often found in the empiricist assumptions of behavioralism. It is a critique that attacks the essential ontological myopia of "factualism" and the historical parochialism implied by behavioralism. And it is a critique that attacks the dual and contradictory attitudes of behavioralism toward political life: on the one hand, one finds a strict adherence to the positivist segregation of fact and value, which supports a liberal-egalitarian conception of "values"; and on the other hand, one finds a technocratic, manipulative attitude toward politics.

Yet this critique begins to appear inadequate if one looks beyond its negative value to the positive assumptions contained within it. The epistemological emphasis on the authority of reason implies a depreciation of the cognitive importance of unreason as well as the prerational, prereflective dimension of human and political life. This assumption can often culminate in a form of "rationalism," even if not to the extreme of the narrow, formalistic rationalism of the Enlightenment. The ontological emphasis on an absolute, or at least objectively structured, reality existing independently of human knowledge implies a depreciation of the importance of a creative epistemological and practical subjectivity in shaping the knowledge and structure of reality itself. This in turn can culminate in a reified metaphysical realism. In terms of a theory-practice relationship, a predominantly contemplative stance toward political practice is often assumed, which may lead to a rigidification of the Platonic alternatives of *vita activa* and *vita contemplativa* and to the vitiation of a vital theory-practice relationship through epistemological impotence and practical quiescence, if not metaphysical quietism.

All of these assumptions can be found to share something with the inadequate implicit metaphysical assumptions of behavioralism itself. For example, both orientations to political inquiry accept a nondialectical separation of the epistemological subject and object, although subject and object are defined differently for each. For another example, both orientations share an objectivistic view of a well-ordered (one might say "preordered") reality. And for yet another example, both approaches to understanding political reality possess an abstract quality in their respective endeavors. Behavioralism abstracts itself from the totality of human experience, while traditional political theory often abstracts itself from the concrete, lived world in which we participate every day. Throughout the following investigation, I hope to explore more of the crucial similarities between behavioralism and the revived tradition of political theory.

At this point in reflecting on the debate between the behavioral revolution and the revival of "normative theory," it appeared to me that an alternative approach to political inquiry could be evoked. The convergence of inadequate nondialectical, objectivistic, and abstract qualities in both positivist behavioralism and traditional or classical theory elicits the possibility of an alternative self-understanding of political inquiry based on a dialectical critique of both of these dominant understandings. Such an approach could transcend any mere "combination" of the epistemological claims of rationalism and empiricism. We can locate such an alternative in the very complex and diverse movement of post-Kantian thought which has often been branded rather monolithically as "historicism," or even more loosely as "relativism," especially insofar as we can find there a stance taken against any transcendent or immanent objectivism.[8]

From this diverse and often seemingly incoherent "realm of thought," one can detect two interrelated philosophical developments which seem interesting and important for a dialectical self-understanding of political inquiry. On the one hand, one notes an important epistemological development which, if interpreted in a certain way, moves from Kant's theory of knowledge through the reflections of Hegel and Marx to certain expressions of contemporary "critical theory" and "neomarxism." On the other hand, one notes a philosophical development, also post-Kantian and Continental, which involves the emergence of transcendental phenomenology with Husserl and moves through such figures as Heidegger and Sartre to the dialectical existential phenomenology of Merleau-Ponty. If we examine these interrelated developments, we may be able to glean from them some principles and perspectives which point toward an alternative epistemological framework and orientation for political inquiry—an orientation which we might tentatively label, without too much encumbrance, "dialectical theory."

These preliminary reflections have elicited my interest in unearthing the philosophical roots and nature of dialectical theory in general. To pursue this interest requires in part the historical reconstruction of ideas which lead to, and give meaning to, such general propositions as "knowledge and reality are dialectically related, as well as historically relative and relational." This kind of proposition in itself is neither new nor terribly helpful. Yet what I hope to suggest is that what separates a *dialectical* theory of knowledge and reality from other variants of historicism and relativism is a particular kind of radical "openness"— a dialectical openness which preserves the tension between the relative and the absolute, the historical and the universal, and which prevents a degeneration into the mindless and vulgar relativism (especially of the moral sort) which can characterize much of historicist and relativist thought. I hope also to suggest that it is the dialectical, open quality of such an orientation which gives coherence to the argument that knowing the world and changing the world can no longer be separated epistemologically. Philosophy can become engaged and interested in a world in the making. Political theory can become critically and concretely creative, without deteriorating into unreflective ideology.

In the following chapters, then, I trace the movement of ideas which give shape to an alternative epistemological orientation for political inquiry. Beginning briefly with a review of behavioralism and of the largely representative critique that Leo Strauss offers on behalf of the revival of political theory, I then move to a reconstruction of the eighteenth- and nineteenth-century philosophical roots of the epistemological development of dialectical theory in the major figures of Kant, Hegel, and Marx. It is this development that begins to clarify an alternative to both behavioralism and classical theory. This leads us to what I believe are the most important twentieth-century philosophical movements embodying a dialectical orientation capable of offering a new understanding of the nature of political inquiry: dialectical, as opposed to positivistic, marxism; existential phenomenology; and critical theory. Our journey through this evolution of a dialectical orientation for political inquiry should also shed some light on the classical topics of political theory: the questions of human nature, political order, and history.

The purpose of this volume is thus actually twofold. First, it is simply to make students of political science more aware of an underrepresented philosophical tradition which can assist us in our efforts to clarify the nature of our theoretical endeavors. By giving some shape to a different tradition, I try to suggest a possible future for contemporary political inquiry. Second, I want to reconstruct what I perceive as the history of dialectical theory, in the hope of illuminating a number of insights into the proper efforts and interests of political theory. And one always hopes that the most serious and important undertaking of political theory is the understanding and creation of a social and political world which, to paraphrase Hegel, is worthy of the human spirit to inhabit.

The Fact-Value Dichotomy:
The Behavioralist Quest for a Value-Free Political Science

The emergence in our century of behavioralism as a dominant movement or mood in political science can be seen as a successful culmination of the positivist spirit of the late nineteenth century—perhaps even of the general movement toward a scientistic culture in the West since the Renaissance. The relative success of the "behavioral persuasion" in political inquiry has had at least two aspects. On the one hand, it has succeeded, at least in broad terms, in defining much of the debate over the nature of political inquiry during the past thirty years or so. On the other hand, to the extent that the debate between behavioralism and classical political theory has subsided in intensity and publicity in recent years, one could argue that the spirit of a positivist-inspired attitude has "settled into" the common sense and daily routine of political inquiry. The relative silence, in contrast to the uproar of the nineteen fifties, sixties, and early seventies, may indicate not so much an overt victory of principle as a quiet supremacy of endurance by default.

It is not my intention in this brief section to reconstruct the complex evolution of behavioralism, or to offer a lengthy summary of its various elements. There already exist several judicious treatments of the subject, and it is quite well known to most students of politics.[9] Nonetheless, it is important here to recollect at least in general outline form some of the origins, inspirations, and central arguments of a behavioralist view of political inquiry. Keeping in mind that behavioralism does not present itself as a rigid body of doctrine and that there is great variety among its various proponents, we are still able to glean a common epistemological thread running through its foundations, orientation, and concerns.[10]

The birth of behavioralism was in large measure the expression of a disenchantment with the tradition of political theory. Nowhere is this made clearer than in the work of David Easton. In an early classic statement of the behavioralist position, Easton bemoans the "disappointing results of a discipline already twenty-five hundred years old." It is a disappointment largely caused by the "reluctance in American political science" to emulate the "scientific method," and by the attendant imprecision and confusion in political knowledge.[11] It becomes necessary to transcend such a "malaise of political science" by moving away from an outmoded form of thought toward a quest for "reliable knowledge."[12] Thus we find a burgeoning hope in the early behavioralist movement of leaving behind an unscientific and largely useless age of inquiry.

Eugene Meehan, another champion of the behavioral persuasion, echoes the spirit of Comte's original formulation of positivism when he exhorts political science to abandon the "older, theologically-oriented, and 'traditional' " system of thought in favor of the "modern, scientific, empirical, logical, and antimetaphysical" system of thought.[13] It is only in this fashion that political science can cure its malaise and disenchantment with the classical tradition of political theory. And it is only in this fashion that political science can get over its "inferiority complex" in the face not only of the natural sciences, but of the other social sciences as well. Here we discover one of the leading inspirations of the new "scientific" political science:

> If the condition of political science represented the exhaustion of its present potentialities, then there would be little justification in voicing any concern about it. But comparison with the level of achievement of other social sciences demonstrates what political science could be doing. However much students of political life may seek to escape the taint, if they were to eavesdrop on the whisperings of their fellow social scientists, they would find that they are almost generally stigmatized as the least advanced. They could present society, they would hear, with at least a slice of bread but they offer it only a crumb.[14]

Thus the beginnings of the movement have a clear sociological and situational foundation, and one that is partially related to the issue of professional pride.

Of course the roots and concerns of behavioralism and positivist-inspired political inquiry lie beyond and beneath the sociological conditions and state of political science in the middle of the twentieth century. Underlying the behavioralist rebellion is a profound epistemological concern: the quest for "reliable knowledge" of political behavior and events, guided by an empiricist-oriented theory of knowledge and aimed at formulation of nomological propositions about political reality. Or in the words of the author of one of the most balanced and reasoned cases for scientific political theory, our goal is to augment, through use of the scientific method, "objective knowledge of an intersubjectively transmissible character in the social sciences."[15] The behavioralist quest for reliable and objective knowledge is thus counterposed against the unreliable, subjective outpourings of political theory, which itself has degenerated into a form of "historicism" and a mere history of ideas.[16] Such a state of affairs, argues Easton, has resulted in an exclusive interest in "learning what others have said and meant" in the long history of "value theory."[17] In the meantime, the production of objective and serious knowledge in the present is inhibited.

The alternative to overly subjective, "historicist," relativistic, and outmoded forms of political theory lies in a clear awareness of the appropriate epistemological orientation for political inquiry. The epistemological roots of behavioralism are discernible in what Easton calls the "empirical revolution" in nineteenth-century Europe. Although he decries the extremes of "hyperfactualism" in a political science infused by this revolution, Easton nonetheless praises the horizon it opens up to the political inquirer.[18] In a more exhuberant and straightforward proclamation, Meehan argues that empiricism is "the only epistemic base for human knowledge."[19] In later work, he sticks to his guns regarding the empiricist foundation of political inquiry: "In very general terms, the approach to inquiry accepted here combines empiricism, naturalism, instrumentalism, and pragmatism, but without dogmatism. The prime assumption is that man can acquire information about the environment *only* through the sensory apparatus."[20] Regardless of varying degrees of enthusiasm and focus, defenders of the behavioral persuasion are clear about the proper general orientation for the process of political inquiry.

With these concerns in mind, the goals of behavioralist political science become more intelligible. The more immediate, less grandiose, task of behavioralism lies in the area of describing and explaining political behavior. In Easton's words, "the task of the political scientist is to describe the way in which people act politically together with the determinants of this activity." He goes on to list such objects of study as how and why people vote as they do, how a bill gets through Congress, and other areas about which we can collect "objective facts."

In their search for a causal theory, political scientists are interested in discovering "new variables to explain more fully why political activity takes any given form."[21] For Heinz Eulau, in our attempt to arrive at an "empirical discipline," we must "return to the behavior of man as the root of politics."[22]

Such a return compels political inquiry to attain a greater degree of precision and clarity in its language and concepts. This requires expunging such traditional concepts as freedom, equality, justice, and democracy from the vocabulary of political science, for they are simply too inadequate for scientific purposes. In Meehan's eyes, "such concepts are vague, ambiguous, difficult or impossible to operationalize, useless as a guide to empirical choice."[23] For Easton, such concepts bear the burden of being too "value-laden" for clear scientific use or empirical research; they "provide the additional difficulty of conveying both factual and distinctly evaluative meanings in research which presumably seeks to be primarily empirical."[24] Political science needs to be raised above the muddled, ambiguous language of common sense and everyday insight to the level of greater technical sophistication, scientific precision, and empirically verifiable propositions.

Beyond the goal of linguistic and conceptual clarification lies the even greater goal of universal, generalized knowledge of political reality. The objectives of "pure science" in political inquiry lie in "the discovery of uniformities in political life." Without the "search for uniformities in political relations," and for "various levels of generalizations," the "development of research towards theory is . . . retarded."[25] The end of a pure science of politics, then, is to generate nomological propositions about the uniformities of political behavior within a developed general theoretical framework that lends a universal meaning or truth to those propositions. Or, to cite Easton's view of the goal of universal knowledge and of the relation between fact and theory, political science needs to develop a "general framework within which . . . facts [can] acquire meaning to transcend any particular time and place."[26] Any question of historicism or relativism is settled in the bargain.

The new political science thus requires a substantial reorientation of the epistemological base and emphasis of inquiry, as well as substantial changes in the language, concepts, and character of universal meaning appropriate to scientific knowledge. All of these changes are ultimately part and parcel of the overarching quest for a "value-free" science of politics and society. The "scientific study of man," as Eulau phrases it, must focus its efforts on deciding the validity of theoretical propositions about human behavior, derived from empirical observation. Questions of ultimate value, such as human nature, belong outside our domain. To the question of whether man is a democratic being, a power-seeking or self-interested being, or a just being, Eulau has a reply: "These are philosophical questions better left to the philosophers."[27] Although Eulau is cautious about the possibility of a thorough-going value-free science of politics, he is certain about its desirability: "[It] does not follow that a value-free science of politics is undesirable because it may be difficult to achieve."[28]

Thus we arrive at the crux of a behavioralist and positivist-inspired approach to political inquiry, which is to say, at the issue of value-free social science and the relationship between facts and values. Without a logical separation of facts from values, of objective reality from subjective preferences about reality, a true science of politics would be impossible. Even if we look at one of the more cautious of axiological positivists such as Easton, we discover the centrality of the fact-value dichotomy to the pursuit of the scientific study of man. It is worth citing at length Easton's comment, since even today it often operates as a silent working hypothesis in much of political inquiry. For Easton, our primary working assumption must be that

> values can ultimately be reduced to emotional responses conditioned by the individual's total life-experiences. In this interpretation, although in practice no one proposition need express either a pure fact or a pure value, facts and values are logically heterogeneous. The factual aspect of a proposition refers to a part of reality; hence it can be tested by reference to the facts. In this way we check its truth. The moral aspect of a proposition, however, expresses only the emotional response of an individual to a state of real or presumed facts.[29]

The framework is clear. Values or "moral aspects" are emotions and desires; facts refer to reality and can be verified in reference to it. Therefore facts can be true or false, while values are meaningless in terms of truth or falsity.

Although values are nothing more than expressions of our preferences, Easton allows the possibility of studying them as observable empirical facts insofar as people do "hold values." This axiological positivist moderation, which permits us to study values scientifically as "social facts" but not as values, has survived much of the storm of opposition to behavioralism during the past few decades. Nonetheless, it remains that values in and of themselves can tell us nothing about objective truth. Indeed, a more recent and less cautious champion of a positivist political science goes so far as to equate the terms "objectivity," "empirical," and "scientific," while equating the terms "subjectivity," "value," and "normative."[30] The aversion to lending a cognitive status to values, then, is fueled by the desire to construct a value-free science—one in which value-judgments have been purged and objective knowledge can reign.

While most proponents of behavioralism, or empirical theory, recognize the impossibility of totally value-free research and science, they nonetheless admit their desirability. Easton, who as an early and sensitive observer is aware of how values underlie research, still holds his ground on the issue: "The mere statement, however, that values underlie all research, does not in itself lead to the inevitable conclusion that these values must, by virtue of their presence, influence this research. Conceivably they could be there, but remain quite innocuous and even irrelevant."[31] We have already noted Eulau's declaration for such a goal. The same sentiment is discernible in the influential political scientist Robert Dahl, who divides political scientists into two camps: the "Empirical Theorists" and the "Transempirical Theorists." The former, of course, argue in favor of pursuing "neutral" and "objective" political analysis, while the latter, whom Dahl argues are led by Leo Strauss, oppose such a project. Now Dahl, who is a cautious observer like Easton, tries to build a bridge between the two positions by moderating the extremes of the Empirical Theorists (especially of logical positivism) while defending their position. So his conclusion still calls for the goal of a value-free science, and for the development of "a neutral and objective body of empirical theory" in political science.[32]

What we therefore discover at the heart of the behavioralist movement even among its most modest proponents, such as the axiological or "Weberian" positivists, is an unshaken commitment to value-free social science and an inability or unwillingness to transcend the positivist dogma of the fact-value dichotomy. As Easton puts it, regardless of the role and influence of values in political inquiry, "validity still is determined by the correspondence of a statement to reality," and thus by the empiricist criterion of verifiability.[33] An objectivist view of both knowledge and reality is proclaimed. In the words of a less subtle or modest follower of the behavioral persuasion: "Knowledge is not knowledge until it has been substantiated, using the procedures which have been labeled 'scientific method.' "[34] Such a sentiment is the logical, extreme implication of the fact-value dichotomy, despite the various attempts within behavioralism to moderate the implications of the quest for a value-free political science.

The past ten years or so have seen a lessening of strenuous efforts to establish a strict behavioralist or positivist science of politics. The flurry of intellectual activity represented by the numerous articles and books that dotted the academic landscape during the fifties and sixties has subsided. To a certain extent this silence has meant that many political scientists have simply turned their research efforts elsewhere, in most cases quietly accepting, I would suggest, the basic thrust and assumptions of the behavioral persuasion.[35] Lest one think, however, that all attempts at developing a positivist framework for social and political inquiry have ceased, a couple of brief examples will quickly dispel the notion.

As already noted, many early proponents of behavioralism have continued to develop its theoretical insights in more moderate and sophisticated fashion. Meehan writes of the need to salvage a version of scientific political science by rejecting the rigid empiricism and scientism of the past. In so doing, he wants to retain the positivist distinction of fact and value, and the notion of "value judgment," and to demonstrate that value judgments can be treated "rationally and empirically."[36] The point becomes to find a way to combine explanation of empirical reality with evaluation of that reality and the choices that arise within it: "Explanation and evaluation must prosper together or they will not prosper and man will be the loser for it."[37]

In order to carry out this plan, Meehan defines value judgments as "reasoned choices" and proceeds to examine the logic of how we can and do make those choices. Admitting an "instrumentalist" approach, Meehan translates the issue of values into a procedural one whereby we are interested in *how* to make rational (or rationalized) choices among various alternatives. He further admits that his approach is ultimately one of "social engineering," an approach to value judgment which "must be empirical, experimental, and rational or calculative, *if we are to control it and improve its quality.*"[38] By understanding the various steps involved in making a value judgment, the process and structure of which are "invariant" regardless of the context or content of the choice, we are able to make the "best" judgment possible in any situation.

While logically interesting in its detail, Meehan's argument does not abandon the assumptions of earlier behavioralist theory. He retains the assumption that "man can acquire information about the environment only through the sensory apparatus." His view of value judgment as a reasoned choice boils down to applying a calculus of some sort to alternatives placed on a "preference continuum," or what amounts to "a kind of cost-benefit analysis." Thus Meehan has a highly objectivist and calculative view of reason itself. And finally, he still refuses to lend any cognitive status to value judgments, which are viewed as having nothing to say about "reality" and which cannot be proved by reference to factual data.[39] Despite his expressed desire to combine explanation and evaluation, Meehan ultimately holds tightly to the dichotomy of fact and value.

A more recent attempt to save the science in social science is found in the work of David Papineau, who argues that "the social sciences can and ought to conform to the standards set by the natural sciences."[40] While eschewing the term "positivism," which he suggests is in low repute in academic circles, Papineau nonetheless wants to rescue and advance the general thrust of the positivist spirit in social inquiry. Thus he rejects the extreme empiricism of vulgar positivism but maintains that there is a general methodological unity between the natural and social sciences. Indeed, Papineau argues what is becoming an increasingly popular theme: that social scientists have for too long operated with a mistaken conception of what the natural sciences are. For this reason he tries to accommodate the work of such postempiricist and relativist philosophers of science as T. S. Kuhn and Paul Feyerabend. Both Kuhn, with his theory of paradigms, and Feyerabend, with his "epistemological anarchism," argue for the contingency of "reality" on the nature of theoretical frameworks. In other words, what counts as the reality to be observed depends on the paradigm or theoretical perspective of the scientist. In Papineau's words this means "that scientific conclusions are at bottom relative to the scientist's theoretical preferences rather than the empirical evidence."[41]

Regardless of Papineau's concessions to attempts like Kuhn's and Feyerabend's to get beyond the overly objectivist view of reality and knowledge in positivism, he will not concede all objectivism in science; neither will he surrender the idea of an "independent reality." Science, writes Papineau, "is still an objective process in which observation plays some part in directing scientific theorising towards ever-improving representations of reality."[42] Characterizing his own view of science as a "realist" one, Papineau wants us to hold onto the idea of a qualified objective correspondence between knowledge and reality:

> For this view does nothing to deny that there is an articulated reality 'out there,' that our scientific theories are trying to represent that reality as it is, and that our scientific practice selects those theories that do this most satisfactorily. That there need be nothing in reality corresponding neatly to the concepts we use does not preclude this. . . . So there is a perfectly good sense in which our theoretical frameworks should be taken as answerable to an independent reality.[43]

Thus one of the crucial positivist tenets is kept intact.

Now what does Papineau do about the dichotomy of fact and value? His solution is to redefine the distinction in terms of "beliefs" and "desires" as two basic kinds of "mental states." Recast in this way, the argument about the dichotomy proceeds as follows. Beliefs are what we hold about what "is," or about the "facts." Desires are what we hold about what "ought" to be, or about what we want or "value." Beliefs are manifested as assertions about what exists, some of which are justified and others of which are not. Desires are expressed as evaluations, and justification is not an issue in making them.[44] Although Papineau believes that we can distinguish assertions and evaluations in social science research, he recognizes the inevitable intrusion of evaluations into research in the form of value-loaded terms, the structuring of the research project, and the like. Nonetheless, he recommends that we not abandon whatever hope we might have for achieving value-free social science: "The existence of processes by which values affect beliefs does not imply that beliefs are always so affected. Even if these processes do at present operate in the social sciences, there are good reasons for thinking that we can avoid them if we try, and also good reasons for making the effort to do so."[45] In spite of his sophistication and moderation, Papineau's quest is still one for a value-free social science, values are still understood as desires, and the question of justification is not seen as an important one regarding issues of evaluation or of what "ought to be." In this sense, the original spirit of positivism survives.

One need not look very far to discover the continuing currency of the issues raised and the mood set by the behavioral revolution. Just a few years ago, in his presidential address to the American Political Science Association, Warren Miller spoke of the "beginning of a new era" in which political science would become a "unified discipline."[46] What allows for such a hope? The answer is clear, for it lies in the growing clarity and acceptance of the "basic logic of social inquiry," which will allow the discipline to become truly scientific:

> The increasing unification of our discipline as a scientific enterprise has been made possible largely because of the development of new methods of social research. In particular, the post-World War II growth of methods and techniques, often associated with the behavioral mode, has been vitally important, less because of the intellectual ferment surrounding questions of epistemology and more because those methods and techniques have increased our powers of observation.[47]

Pushing aside the kinds of issues which concern us here, Miller quietly accepts the basic thrust and logic of a positivist-inspired political science. Sounding very much like the early Easton, he lauds the new methods for allowing us to "create evidence that is needed to establish empirical regularities and to test the explanatory theories that transform those regularities . . . into matters of important intellectual concern."[48]

Throughout his address, Miller reiterates the concerns and language of the behavioral persuasion. He speaks of the need to beware of serving "value-laden ends" and praises the new "sophisticated elaborations of classical experimental design" which help us create new knowledge. He exhorts us to work for the goal of a "unified social

science discipline." Indeed, Miller conceives one of our biggest problems in political science today in terms of how little time we are spend-
ing generating new data, in contrast to the time spent on the analysis
and manipulation of empirical data.[49] It is interesting that throughout
his argument for fulfilling much of the early behavioralist dream, and
in his call for unifying the whole discipline of political science, Miller
does not once cite or even mention the name of a so-called normative
theorist. It is an omission which reveals much about the planned future
of a newly unified political science.

Needless to say, it would be a mistake to assume that the influence
of the spirit and substance of behavioralism in particular, and of positivism in general, is no longer exerted or felt in the process of political
inquiry. The relative silence in political science about the nature of that
influence should not be taken as a sign of its demise. It is necessary
to understand the general character of this leading view of political
inquiry in order to consider adequately the problems and promises that
await the further evolution of political science. It is against the background of this view of political inquiry that we can better evaluate the
emergence of a second, competing view in political science—one which
can best be described as the revival of political theory.

The Fiction of the Fact-Value Dichotomy: Strauss's Critique of Behavioralism

The revival of political theory is essentially the revival of the traditional concept of theory and a return to the prepositivist conception
of political inquiry. As such, it primarily marks a return to the classical
Platonic-Aristotelian conception of political science and to the partial
survival of that conception in the modern tradition from Hobbes to
Hegel.[50] This revival, so important to the survival of critical thinking,
involves a response to two major developments in the recent history
of political science.

On the one hand, the revivalists of the tradition of political theory
have responded to the often heard pronouncement of the death or dying
of political theory.[51] Thus we have witnessed over the past decades
various attempts to prove false the proclamation of political theory's
demise, and to a certain extent the proof has become self-validating.[52]
On the other hand, we have witnessed a response to the intrusion of
positivist theoretical dogma into the tradition of political theory involving debates over the meaning of "science" and "theory" in political science, the validity of the fact-value dichotomy, and the notion
of value freedom in research. Thus the revival has also produced transcendental reflections on the roots and claims of positivist social science
and behavioralism, or the "new political science," in the face of what

for over two thousand years has been called "political theory." The result has been a number of works concerning the proper self-under-standing of political inquiry.[53]

One of the leading exponents of the revival of political theory was Leo Strauss. The critique Strauss brings to bear on the positivist and empiricist self-understanding of political inquiry is, I believe, largely representative of the revived tradition in general. It would certainly be an unforgivable oversimplification to claim that all the critics of behavioralism who emerge from the revival of political theory—Arendt, Oakeshott, Voegelin, Wolin, and others—could take Strauss as their spokesman; the differences among these figures on some issues are often substantial. Yet it seems that the salient points of Strauss's criticism of behavioralism are shared by most critics who take their lead from the classical tradition of political philosophy. And in the debate between the behavioralists and the revivalists, Strauss's singular influence and importance appears unmistakable.

As is well known, the basis of Strauss's critique lies in his return to the Western birth of a critical science of politics in Plato and Aristotle. As Strauss notes, Aristotle never made the distinction between political science and political philosophy that is commonplace today, but instead made one between the theoretical sciences (natural sciences, metaphysics) and the practical or political sciences (ethics, economics, politics). There was for Aristotle an innate connection between political knowledge and ethical practice. That connection was severed in the seventeenth century, if not in the Renaissance, with the divorce of science and philosophy, propelled by the "metaphysically neutral" physics of Copernicus and Newton. Thus the separation of political science from political philosophy began to take shape. The result of this process was the displacement of the independence of the practical sciences (involving the principles of right human action) from the theoretical sciences by the temporal and positional priority of the theoretical sciences over the so-called applied sciences.

"Scientific knowledge" understood on the model of the theoretical natural sciences alone becomes genuine knowledge, a status denied to the awareness inherent in practice. Thus, according to Strauss, the new political science is based on a "scientific psychology" rather than on political experience. The new political scientist is the neutral observer rather than the political citizen. The latter Aristotelian perspective necessarily involves evaluation of political things while the former "scientific" perspective conceives of principles of action, or values, as unscientifically subjective, if meaningful at all. Furthermore, Strauss insists upon distinguishing the divergent views of "is" and "ought" which are accepted by the two conceptions of political science. The Aristotelian conception claims that man is a being sui generis with a dignity of his own based upon an awareness of how he ought to live, resulting in a necessary connection of morality and law, the dignity of man and of the public order: hence a necessary connection between "is" and "ought." The new political science admits of no such connection, viewing man only in a behavioral manner, and thus denies the facticity of the "common good" as something that is, insisting that at most it only ought to be.

The basis of Strauss's critique of "value freedom," therefore, rests in the assertion of the essential nonneutrality of political things. Since an understanding of political things demands that we take seriously their claim to be judged in terms of justice or injustice, good or bad, then knowledge of the standards of judgment becomes a requirement in political science: "all knowledge of political things implies assumptions concerning the nature of political things, i.e., assumptions which concern not merely the given political situation but political life or human life as such."[54] A philosophic or truly scientific approach to politics can emerge only when these assumptions are made the theme of critical and coherent analysis. An example is the study of voting behavior: " 'voting behavior' as it is now studied would be impossible if there were not in the first place the universal right to vote."[55] The right itself is an ingredient of behavior and a science of politics must include a critical standard of judgment by which to study the very assumption and nature of a "right."

The controversiality of political knowledge and the ambiguity of politics, due to its comprehensive nature,[56] prevent the compartmentalization of political science as just one among many natural sciences. Man is unique, hence politics is unique, and hence political knowledge is unique. Compartmentalization of politics in the natural world by degree involves a failure to face our whole situation as human beings.

Strauss attacks the reductionist epistemology of behavioralism. A science of politics must stand or fall by the truth of a prescientific knowledge of political things, an empirical but not necessarily scientific knowledge. Certainty of the truth of prescientific empirical statements, insofar as it is possible, lies in a kind of "natural awareness" or common sense. Every epistemology presupposes the truth of empirical statements, but behavioralism explicitly elaborates an exclusive empiricist epistemological base. By ultimately reducing our way of knowing to the reception of sense data, empiricism confuses the perception of sense data (colors, shapes) with that of things (chairs, political regimes), the latter requiring "extrasensory" perception: this is the claim of "common sense."

Empiricist political science must perforce reject the results of prescientific political understanding and political experience as such, especially ascriptive emotive human properties which can never become sense data. Therefore, "since the political things are given to us in political understanding and political experience, the new political science cannot be helpful for the deeper understanding of political things: it must reduce the political things to non-political data."[57] But behavioralism's attempted break from common sense is doomed to inconsistency because the truth of "empiricism cannot be established empirically: it is not known through sense data that the only possible objects of perception are sense data." Furthermore, "sense data as sense data become known only through an act of abstraction or disregard which presupposes the legitimacy of our primary awareness of things as things and of people as people."[58] To the charge of imperfections residing in prescientific political experience and common sense, Strauss responds that we must accept a certain unavoidable naivete in human thought.

Strauss draws two major conclusions from these epistemological and methodological considerations concerning the premises of the new political science. First, behavioralism is constantly compelled to borrow from common-sense knowledge, thus "unwittingly testifying to the truth that there is a genuine pre-scientific knowledge of political things which is the basis of all scientific knowledge of them."[59] Second, the foundational logic of the new political science provides sufficient criteria of exactness but does not provide objective criteria of relevance which "are inherent in the pre-scientific understanding of political things; intelligent and informed citizens distinguish soundly between important and unimportant political matters."[60]

The new empiricist-behavioralist political science replaces the universals of classical political science (classification of regimes and their purposes) with new universals, predicated upon the discovery of homogeneity in all existing regimes. Strauss outlines this process in three steps. First, behavioral political science focuses on the relation between freedom and coercion as common to all regimes in varying proportions. Second, it conceptualizes political societies in terms of groups. Third, it underpins and guides researches regarding groups with a general behavioral theory of personality.

The first step not only involves a degree of arbitrariness but also begs the crucial definitional question concerning freedom, presumably blindly accepting the liberal-bourgeois prejudice. Hence the described "is" necessarily leads to an "ought." The second step requires a theory of groups and thereby reduces political science to political sociology. The third step further reduces the process of inquiry to the level of psychology. Hence the new universals of behavioralism are subsumed under the psychologistic empiricist-positivist framework of the "laws of human behavior." The logic of this methodological reduction leads to a great disparity between the broad goal of a general theory of social change and the petty researches undertaken to achieve the goal. The disproportionality is a necessary result of the lack of objective criteria of relevance.[61] The new political science faces a dilemma of its claim and method. The claim to discover universal laws of human behavior is confronted by the method of empirical reference to particular regimes. Ultimately the new political science absolutizes the relative and peculiar, and thus historically parochializes itself.

Strauss further criticizes as unwarranted behavioralism's claim to an unambiguous and precise language, distinct from that of political men: "political life would be altogether impossible if its language were unqualifiedly vague," and, moreover, "the alleged vagueness of political language is primarily due to the fact that it corresponds to the complexity of political life, or that it is nourished by long experience with political things in a great variety of circumstances."[62] "Scientific" definitions are limited in ignoring those things which exist in the penumbra of experience. Reductionist and sterile expressions such as "politics equals power" and "power relations" originate not in political life but in academic reaction to understanding political life only in terms of lawlike relations.

The use of terms in hypothesis formulation is also subjected to Strauss's criticism: "The allegedly provisional or hypothetical terms are never questioned in the process of research, for their implications channel the research in such directions that the 'data' which might reveal the inadequacy of the hypotheses never turn up."[63] Ultimately, however, Strauss's criticism lies not in a substantive analysis of language but in a chastisement of behavioralist abuses of language:

> To the extent to which the new political science is not formalistic, it is vulgarian. This vulgarianism shows itself particularly in the 'value-free' manner in which it uses and thus debases terms that originally were meant only for indicating things of a noble character—terms like 'culture,' 'personality,' 'values,' 'charismatic,' and 'civilization'.[64]

When we turn more specifically to the problem of the fact-value distinction, we discover in behavioralist political science an unreflective ontological ambiguity and an epistemological-methodological reductionism. These problems may be reflected in the following series of questions. First, is the linguistic distinction itself an accurate reflection of the nature of reality? What are its ontological presuppositions? The response usually involves an unadmitted reductionist materialism. Second, if the distinction possesses a valid ontological basis, why should values be ignored in favor of the "facts of behavior" in the process of research? One response has been the more sophisticated axiological positivism. Where the logical positivist strand still exists, political science remains epistemologically bound to empiricism, and "intersubjectively transmissible knowledge" (what we can agree upon) becomes the criterion for the truth and quality of our discoveries. Third, does forcing the distinction of fact and value at the fundamental level of human reality produce a fiction about human life? Does behavioralism tacitly recognize the whole of reality, yet diminish it in order to obtain "scientific knowledge" of it and therefore obtain understanding of a truncated reality, that is, no real understanding at all? Finally, does a social scientific method based on the dogma of the fact-value distinction possess values beneath and around it to which it blinds itself? This is the problem of a value-free social science with which Strauss begins his critique of the fact-value dichotomy.

A value-free social science attempts to expel so-called value judgments from the process of inquiry. The result is the conceptualization of values merely as preferences, the postulation of "ethical neutrality," and hence "moral obtuseness is the necessary condition for scientific analysis."[65] The social scientist is dedicated to one and only one value—ethically neutral truth. But Strauss offers at least four considerations against the possibility of value-free social science positivism.

First, inquiry into social phenomena necessarily involves evaluation, or value judgment. Any attempt otherwise merely conceals evaluation, and values enter as it were through the back door of research.[66] Furthermore, since the scientist necessarily makes the assumption that a healthy social life is good (note Karl Deutsch's metaphor of behavioralism as a social physician), then factual assertions are based on conditions which remain unquestionable as long as we deal with facts qua facts.[67] Second, the rejection of value judgments is based on the assumption that value conflicts are essentially insoluble for human reason, which has never been proven. Third, Strauss again returns to the contention that empiricist-scientific method gravely depreciates prescientific knowledge, that is, it neglects the prescientific presuppositions upon which it is based. And there are certain areas in the whole of political reality where phenomena can only be perceived as what they are with the unarmed, "unscientific" eye of the citizen.

Finally, Strauss attacks the incipient historicism of positivistic social science, or the translation of temporal and spatial peculiarities into the essential character of human society. Although valid factual answers to our questions about "human society" may be judged by rules of logic, the questions depend on value-oriented interests. For Strauss, there can be no divorce of subjective and objective elements: "the objective answers receive their meaning from the subjective question."[68] And if the value orientations of social science are socially and historically dependent, then social science itself is relativized. Positivism becomes historicism and further subverts the superiority of a rational, philosophical understanding of politics. Thus historicism rejects the paradigmatic question of "*the* good society," preferring to await the judgment of a completed history.

The classical question in political theory of the common good is essential to Strauss's criticism of the fact-value dichotomy assumed by the scientific study of politics, especially regarding the is-ought relation. Owing to the lack of a socially agreed upon objective, the new political science denies the concept of a "substantive public interest." The denial derives from the fact-value distinction according to which only factual judgments can be true or objective.[69] Hence justification of values, which involves the illegitimate derivation of an "ought" from an "is," is bequeathed to the nonscientific endeavors of political philosophy, ethics, or ideology. The behavioralist position leads thus to the implicit notion of a rational society. But the quest after a nonideological regime in this sense seems to express a concealed liberal ideology itself. Strauss's conclusion here seems poignantly penetrating:

> Since this understanding implies that before the tribunal of reason all values are equal, the rational society will be egalitarian or democratic and permissive or liberal: the rational doctrine regarding the difference between facts and values rationally justifies the preference for liberal democracy—contrary to what is intended by that distinction itself.[70]

The modern liberal *Geist* which gives birth to behavioralism is reciprocally justified by it.

Strauss's criticism of the positivist-behavioralist view of the is-ought relation flows from the following observation: "Man possesses a certain latitude; he can choose not only from among various ways of overt behavior . . . but from among various values; this latitude, this possibility has the character of a fact." But value must be distinguished from mere desire; the former involves choice of ends, a positing of values, which is peculiar to man, and "this positing is taken to be a fact."[71] Further, "the view that the pertinent Is is our positing of values, in contradistinction to the yielding to mere desires, necessarily leads to Oughts of a radically different character from the so-called Oughts corresponding to mere desires." Hence we may conclude that

> the 'relativism' accepted by the new political science according to which values are nothing but objects of desire is based on an insufficient analysis of the Is, that is, of the pertinent Is; and furthermore, that one's opinion regarding the character of the Is settles one's opinion regarding the character of the Ought.[72]

Behavioralism must posit an equal dignity for all desires since no factual standard of judgment is possible. Therefore, a consistent behavioralism reveals a concealed opinion concerning the treatment of desires—namely, permissive egalitarianism.

We are thus able to recognize the concealed values assumed by behavioralism, particularly the fact that there is "more than a mysterious preestablished harmony between the new political science and a particular version of liberal democracy."[73] Value-free political inquiry is governed by an inherent, unavowed, and unquestioned commitment to liberal democracy, that is, by an ideology of democratism. Scientifically discoverable laws of human behavior are laws about democratically molded human beings, and hence a Benthamite underpinning to inquiry emerges at the base of behavioralism. By declaring that no value judgments are rational, the new political science can reconcile the doubt of any compelling case for liberalism with an unfaltering commitment to liberal democracy. Thus it conceals the crisis of liberal democracy with a ritual which calls itself methodology or logic.[74] On the one hand, the discouragement of "oughts" implies the sterile and stagnant preservation of the existent "is." On the other hand, any future political attempt to manipulate human society need not fear critical opposition from political science.

Is there a coherent and comprehensive Straussian solution to the problems raised by Strauss's critique of behavioralism? Is there a systematic counterposition in Strauss's counterrevolution against the behavioral revolution? As we have seen, it is the return to the Socratic-Platonic-Aristotelian origins of the classical tradition of political inquiry that forms the essence of Strauss's response to the behavioralist problem. The "classical solution" to the question of political philosophy and political science is guided by the thematic question of regime (political order). Regime is the character-giving form of social life. In Platonic fashion, the regime is the "whole": "the form of life of a society, its style of life, its moral taste, form of society, form of state, form of government, spirit of laws."[75] Furthermore, the regime (politeia) is characterized by teleological social life-activity. Social organization and constitution must exist in accordance with the goal of society, and thus classical political philosophy is guided by the question of the best regime.[76] The actualization of the best regime (good society) is vitiated, however, by human nature, although an individual solution is possible: the good man (not the good citizen) may exist in transcendence from immanent to best regime. Strauss adheres to the classical ontological separation of form and matter; regime is form and "nation" matter. Form possesses the higher dignity, and hence Strauss accepts the appellation "idealism."

Political philosophy for Strauss becomes a kind of quest for cosmology—that is, a quest for knowledge of the whole. Therefore it exists in tension between the parts and the whole. Political philosophy must resist the dual temptations of the "charm of competence" to absolutize knowledge of the parts and of the "charm of humble awe" to absolutize knowledge of the whole, developed by meditation on the human soul.[77] Thus it must participate in a dialogue between the parts and the whole, hoping to arrive at a more complete knowledge of both through continual illumination of each with the character of the other. However, absolute knowledge of the whole requires a coincidence of both kinds of knowledge, which is impossible. In this sense, the Socratic-Platonic dialectic never ends.

There is another interesting interpretation which suggests that Strauss's position is a form of Latin Averroism: a position which "presupposes the radical separation, not of fact and value, but of reason and faith."[78] Political philosophy based on reason is distinguished from political theology based on revelation, although the two are never explicitly related to form a distinct, comprehensive political science. Rather, the authority of knowledge rests in a notion akin to the Aristotelian *spoudaios*. However, the *spoudaios* derives no spiritual claim of authority from a transcendent-divine ground of being; rather, he remains allied with the claims of Reason. This is the direction of Strauss's quest for the ground of truth and the nature of political knowledge.

In the final analysis, however, there is no Straussian system with which to appose systematic, positivistic behavioralism. Indeed, Strauss's primary effort involves the interpretation of important texts rather than the elaboration of a new or alternative epistemological orientation for political inquiry.[79] His critique of the residual nineteenth-century positivist invention of the fact-value dichotomy is motivated and underpinned by empathetic textual interpretation of the classical political philosophers. Here Strauss's sensitivity is important, for the interpretive distortion of classical texts which usually results from reading through the lenses of the fact-value dichotomy and the empiricist framework of political science is often substantial.[80]

Thus in light of our attempt to glimpse an alternative epistemological orientation for political inquiry, Strauss's legacy is an ambiguous one. On the one hand, the critique of positivist behavioralism which emerges from the revival of political theory and is exemplified by his reflections reveals the narrowness and closure of most contemporary political science. To a certain extent, Strauss's criticisms of behavioralism are sufficient. On the other hand, however, one feels the need to push beyond the position offered to us by the revival of political theory, especially as represented by Strauss, to a different level which submits both positivism and the revival of classical theory to critical scrutiny.

To be sure, there is much more that could be (and indeed has been) written on the debate between contemporary political science and the tradition of political philosophy. But the intention here is simply to put forth one important form of that debate and then to turn our attention to a different tradition altogether, one which may shed some new light on the debate. As we have seen, Strauss ultimately translates the problem of the elaboration of a new critical-epistemological orientation for political inquiry into a primarily cosmological and hermeneutical one. Thus it remains for the incipient critique of both positivism and traditional theory, which lies in the evolution of dialectical theory, to offer new insights into the possible future of political inquiry. It is this modern dialectical tradition to which we turn in the next chapter, after a brief interlude concerning some philosophical and historical sources of the current debate.

A Note on Rationalism and Empiricism

I have suggested that the stage of the recent debate over the proper nature of political science has been dominated by two actors: positivist behavioralism and the revived tradition of political theory. We have seen briefly one form that the debate has taken, where behavioralism, which has produced a certain orthodoxy in political science, has found itself under fire from an older tradition of theory. Now both of these movements understand themselves primarily as competing approaches to the process of political inquiry, not essentially as competing epistemologies. Yet it would seem that each of the two approaches has discernible epistemological presuppositions and orientations, which in turn have older roots in the history of philosophy. A brief mention of these will help to clarify the context and purpose of the next chapter.

The classical roots of the revival of political theory lie with Plato and Aristotle and the birth of political philosophy. Since Plato, political theory has usually understood itself as a noetic enterprise, guided first and foremost by the faculty of reflective reason rather than by empirical sensation and observation. This has naturally lent a formal and contemplative character to the efforts of political theorizing. The implicit epistemological emphasis on reason—or the existence of a kind of rationalist, as opposed to empiricist, "impulse" discernible at the birth of political philosophy—appears to endure the entire tradition of political theory from Plato to Hegel. Although there are crucial divergences within the great tradition of political inquiry, one can still detect in all the major figures (even in a so-called empiricist such as Locke) a certain allegiance to the epistemological primacy of reflective reason, which clearly sets this tradition apart from the positivist tradition that shapes much of contemporary political science.[81]

Two factors make it difficult to sustain the argument for a general unity of the entire tradition of political theory based on a shared epistemological emphasis and orientation. First, in our reviews of the history of political thought, we usually tend to emphasize the break between ancient (or ancient-medieval) and modern political theory—whether that break is understood as resulting from the rejection of nature as the source of right, or the "gnostic" flight from a transcendental, divine ground of Being, or the move from a theocentric to an anthropocentric humanism.[82] Thus we often tend to neglect the enormous coherence of that tradition. Second, and this is particularly true of classical theory, epistemological concerns have often been subordinated to ontological concerns, the quest after the nature of Being, leaving questions involved in theory of knowledge at a more implicit level of interest. Thus it is unsurprising that major leaders of the revival of that tradition, such as Strauss and Voegelin, focus more attention on ontology than they do on epistemology.[83] Nonetheless, it seems appropriate to note the epistemological orientation which underlies the revival of political theory, even though it precedes the invention of "epistemology" as a subject matter in modern philosophy, and even though it often remains implicit.

In a sense, the roots of the positivist view of knowledge in political science are not as old or deep as those of the revival of political theory. Although one might cite such ancient, distant progenitors as Leucippus, Protagoras, Democritus, Pyrrho, or Epicurus, it is really not until David Hume in the eighteenth century that we begin to discover the foundations of a scientific empiricism. Earlier, in the seventeenth century, we can find the philosophical rumblings which gave birth to modern philosophy in the debate between "Continental rationalism" and "British empiricism." With Descartes and Spinoza standing in stark opposition to Bacon and Locke, we discover in that century the first truly clear-cut polarization of the rational and empirical modes of knowing. Along with the development of "scientific method," the empiricist tradition has proven itself to have a long arm, reaching into the debates in the political science of the twentieth century.

For contemporary political science, the most important development took place in the nineteenth century with the emergence of two major forms of empiricism: pragmatism with C. S. Peirce and, especially, positivism with Auguste Comte. It was positivism, which was developed further by Ernst Mach and later sophisticated by the "logical positivism" of Moritz Schlick, Rudolph Carnap, and others of the Vienna Circle, that served as the impetus for the burgeoning behavioralist movement in the middle of the twentieth century.[84] The general hostility of positivism to all metaphysics and traditional philosophy became a cornerstone of the behavioral revolution in political science. One must also take note of the old philosophical tradition of naturalism, which in its narrowest moments bequeathed to our century a physicalist conception of consciousness.[85] It was such a conception that helped form the foundation of John Watson's "behaviorism" in psychology, which in turn has had no little impact on behavioralist political science.

There is, finally, one more movement in contemporary philosophy about which brief mention should be made: the development of "ordinary-" or "contextual" language philosophy, which has had considerable influence in Anglo-American thought. Linguistic philosophy grew out of the Vienna Circle as a revolt against logical positivism, although its proponents still accepted a central positivist tenet that a priori statements reveal nothing about reality and value judgments have no cognitive validity. As a movement dedicated to clarifying the previously confused language about reality, the investigations begun by G. E. Moore, the later Wittgenstein, and John Austin emerged in opposition to both positivism and traditional philosophy, especially since linguistic philosophy's extreme contextualism rejected any general epistemology at all. Although not nearly so influential in recent political science as positivism, this movement is probably still best exemplified in political theory by T. D. Weldon.[86]

There is much more to be said concerning the roots of the epistemological orientations of the two dominant participants in political science's recent internal debates, but this is not our purpose. I have simply wanted to indicate briefly some contours in the history of philosophy which have helped to shape the general epistemological directions of the revived tradition of political theory and the movement of positivist political science. Two warnings are thus in order. First, I have obviously omitted much of importance in this brief summary, and to deal adequately with the developments raised in the previous pages would require a detailed history of philosophy.

The second warning concerns my hope that I have not attributed some kind of monolithic and simplistic unity to the revival of political theory or to the related movements of positivism and behavioralism. These movements are extremely sophisticated and diverse, and the debates between them are too complex to treat summarily. My purpose has been to bring into stark relief the overall conception of the nature of knowledge and inquiry loosely shared by those on both sides of the debate, without being too unfair to either side. With this general picture of political science's two competing spokesmen in mind, we can turn our attention to a third voice which is straining to be heard.

The remainder of this book is devoted to the contention that there is a tradition of inquiry, resting under a broad cloak of "dialectical theory," which deserves greater attention and investigation on the part of scholars interested in the nature of authentic political science. The point of departure in the next chapter is the uncovering of what I believe are the clearest origins of a dialectical tradition in philosophy, the development of which can help in shaping our view of contemporary political inquiry. The evolution of this tradition, beginning with Kant, Hegel, and Marx, can illuminate for us an epistemological view which often parts company from those of the two major contestants for the "true" mantle of political science. Finally, although much has been written about the relation of these three thinkers to political science, I intend to focus upon a specific epistemological development that takes place in their thought and that may prove to be important for political scientists today.

2   The Roots of Contemporary Dialectical Theory

Kant, Hegel, and Marx

Kant: The Synthesis Begun

Although it is not unusual for political scientists to return occasionally to Kant in order to investigate the political relevance of his writings, attention is not usually directed toward his *Critique of Pure Reason*.[1] For good reason, our focus is most often directed at his insights into the relations of morality and politics found in such works as the *Critique of Practical Reason, Metaphysical Elements of Justice, Foundations of the Metaphysics of Morals,* and the like. But it may be that political science also has much to learn from Kant as an important harbinger of a dialectical theory of knowledge. In light of the previous philosophical debates between proponents of rationalism and empiricism, Kant clearly sets us off on a new "epistemological journey."

As is well known, the *Critique of Pure Reason* is a response to both rationalism and empiricism, and in particular it entails a criticism of Hume's radical empiricism.[2] For Hume, reality implicitly possesses an independent status, separate from the knower, and is grasped immediately through sense experience prior to reflection. Observation of reality involves the passive reception of sense impressions.[3] In response to this view, Kant formulates a central problem of modern philosophy by refusing to accept the world as something that has arisen independently of the knowing subject. For Kant, a radical divorce and independence of the subject that knows from the object that is known entails an illusion. The radical empiricist restriction of "knowledge" to mere sensation, to the reception of a complex, endless stream of impressions, leads to a denial of the creative activity of the mind and of the epistemological use of concepts to understand the "external" world. This kind of extreme sensationism, which denies the validity of abstract concepts, has dire consequences regarding the nature of knowledge. It prevents any possibility for the unity of knowledge or even any concept of knowledge itself. Thus, for Kant, a consistent radical empiricism denies the very possibility of knowledge.[4]

Kant's argument against Hume, then, consists of demonstrating that knowledge is possible and cannot be restricted to the passive reception of sense data. Rather than being perceived immediately through sense observation, reality is apprehended in a mediated fashion by means of a priori categories of the mind. The mind appears as creative and active. This is not to say that reality is a pure construct of mind, but to postulate the active, synthetic function of the mind. It is this notion that becomes important for the dialectical criticism of rationalism and empiricism. The form that the argument takes in Kant's effort to elicit the transcendental conditions for the possibility of knowledge in the *Critique of Pure Reason* is the demonstration of the possibility and legitimacy of synthetic a priori judgments about reality. Unlike analytic a priori or synthetic a posteriori judgments, synthetic a priori judgments tell us something that is both new and universally valid about reality.[5] This marks a revolutionary and dialectical moment in Kant's thought, since we are no longer forced to choose exclusively between the superiority of analytic reason, as Leibniz did, or the superiority of sense experience, as Hume did.

At the heart of the *Critique of Pure Reason,* the section entitled "Transcendental Analytic," we are introduced to Kant's famous invention of the Transcendental Logic and the categories of the mind. Unlike formal logic, which is concerned with the logical consistency of conclusions deduced from premises, transcendental logic is concerned with the fundamental concepts of the understanding which form necessary conditions for making judgments about reality, or for comprehending what we intuit in time and space.[6] The search for these necessary conditions leads us to the a priori categories of the mind. It is precisely this transcendental-logical interest that gives epistemology a new dimension and sets the stage for the possible transcendence of the debate between rationalism and empiricism.

In order to demonstrate the legitimacy of a priori categories for knowledge, Kant turns to the necessity of the unity of consciousness, which is revealed by what he calls the "subjective deduction." Here he argues that in order to know a series of sense impressions as an object in space and time, there must be a synthetic process at work in consciousness that involves simultaneously the apprehension of unconnected sense impressions as a unity, the imaginative reproduction of that unity for conscious retention, and the recognition of sense impressions as sense impressions.[7] This threefold process is nonempirical and expresses the necessary unity of consciousness. Without such a synthesis, there could be no self-consciousness (no "memory of experience") and thus no knowledge of an object as an object.

What, then, precisely is this unity of consciousness? Kant argues, through the "objective deduction," that there can be no objective empirical experience without the prior possession of the nonempirical concept itself of "object," which is not identical with any sense experience of it.[8] This concept precedes and conditions experience and again reflects the necessary unity of consciousness, which Kant calls "transcendental apperception," or the transcendental "I."[9] Furthermore, this transcendental "I," which has experience and holds consciousness together, can never be objectified as an object of knowledge, for that would simply push the question back a step further and require yet another subject or "I" which knows. This is the point where Kant's transcendental deduction must stop; all that can be known about transcendental apperception is that it is the fundamental logical condition of knowledge and expresses the unity of consciousness.

Throughout the transcendental deduction, there is a hint of another dialectical moment in Kant's reflections. Nowhere in the argument does Kant suggest that a priori categories of the mind absolutely determine or create the object of experience. The object (which is actually a synthesis of sense impressions made possible by the unity of consciousness) is indeed dependent on the rules set forth by the categories. But there is a sense in which the object and consciousness determine each other. In terms of epistemological subject and object, one can discover a hint of dialectical, nonlinear codetermination. Therefore, if it is the case that without the use of categories our intuition of reality through sense experience is blind, it is no less the case that without sensory intuition the categories are empty.[10]

Although Kant criticizes the excesses of empiricism, there is nonetheless an empiricist and objectivist strain in his thought—a strain which may somewhat vitiate his appearance as a consistent dialectical theorist. This emerges in the argument that for anything to exist it must be verified by sense experience. A concept is not veridical unless it is decided by sense experience: only "that which is bound up with the material conditions of experience, that is, with sensation, is actual."[11] Kant is interested in rescuing the objectivity of reality from extreme skepticism, and in establishing the indubitability of our experience of external objects. This is why he calls himself an "empirical realist."

Now admittedly Kant argues that it is in the very nature of reason (Vernunft) to want to answer metaphysical questions about nonempirical objects—which is to say, we try to employ the categories of the understanding (Verstand) beyond objective phenomena given in space and time.[12] But such an effort results in an illusion, since metaphysical ideas (such as the proof of God's existence) have no empirical corre-

spondence and objective reality. Thus metaphysical questions are un-
avoidably in the interest of reason, but are nonetheless illegitimate.[13]
We can only understand (apply the categories to) empirical external
objects which appear in space and time and about whose existence
there is no doubt. This is the position of empirical realism, or "transcendental idealism," as opposed to that of empirical idealism, or
"transcendental realism." The latter position assumes the existence of
transcendental objects, outside space and time, which are ultimately
"real" and of which empirical objects are merely inferred sense representations. Kant rather wants to argue the transcendental idealist
position against any such quasi-Platonic view and to restrict knowledge
to the objective realm of external phenomena.[14]

The objectivism which makes Kant's "dialectic" problematical becomes clearer in light of the distinction between phenomenon and noumenon.[15] As is well known, a phenomenon, the only possible object
of knowledge, is what we intuit in space and time. The categories of
the mind have only an empirical applicability. The concept of "noumenon" (*Ding an sich,* or "thing-in-itself") refers to what is not an
object of intuition, or that which has no logical possibility of ever being
known. Thus it refers only to the limits of possible knowledge, and
not, as is often mistakenly supposed, to a transcendental object known
through nonsensory intuition.[16] Noumenon is a "negative" or limiting
concept for which there is no empirical or objective correspondence,
and it would be erroneous, Kant argues, to postulate in the spirit of
idealism or rationalism a dualism of empirical objects and transcendental objects. The error of metaphysics lies in treating the *Ding an
sich* as an object of knowledge.[17] When the error is committed, one
arrives at the usual metaphysical antinomies (for example, "the world
is unconditionally either finite or infinite") in which both sides or claims
may be false.[18] In our example, both claims are false because the world
is not a *Ding an sich:* "it exists *in itself* neither as an *infinite* whole
nor as a *finite* whole. It exists only in the empirical regress of the series
of appearances, and is not to be met with as something in itself."[19] The
world is not an unconditioned whole; it can only be "indeterminate."

This last statement is important, for it exhibits the kind of openness
that we shall see is central to authentic dialectical theory. Indeed, Kant
goes so far as to assert that although the ideas of pure reason lead us
to transcendental illusions, those ideas are nonetheless important in a
"regulative" way. They can be helpful in correcting our judgments
about metaphysical concerns, thus avoiding dogmatic rationalist or
empiricist assertions, if we refrain from arguing that they "constitute"
our knowledge of reality. The transcendental ideas of reason "have
their own good, proper, and therefore *immanent* use" as long as they
are not "taken for concepts of real things."[20] Again, if the metaphysical

ideas of reason are transformed into metaphysical objects that lie beyond the possibility of experience and are asserted a priori to exist, then those ideas are being employed constitutively. But since it is necessary to seek unity in our knowledge, we may use transcendental ideas to regulate our process of inquiry. We may proceed as if such ideas were transcendental objects in order to organize and understand what lies within our experience, and to "secure an empirical criterion" of our knowledge.[21] This is precisely what Kant does, for example, with such ideas as transcendental freedom and the immortality of the soul, in the *Critique of Practical Reason*.

It is this openness of the regulative employment of the ideas of pure reason that saves Kant from the kind of empiricist and dogmatic anti-metaphysical attitude which dominates positivism and much of contemporary political science. Kant avoids the extremes of empiricism by arguing for the theory of categories of mind, and of dogmatic rationalism by arguing against the illusions of metaphysics. Yet the notion of the regulative use of the ideas of pure reason saves metaphysical assertions from total meaninglessness and uselessness, and thus the dialectical character of Kantian epistemology leaves open the question of the existence of metaphysical objects.

What, then, does Kant bequeath to us regarding the evolution of dialectical theory? First of all, Kantian epistemology introduces the concept of the synthetic activity of mind, which as we shall see, opens the door to the development of a critical and dialectical theory of knowledge. Knowledge is seen to take a creative stance toward reality, although not the manipulative attitude later taken in positivism. (It is interesting to note that while the centuries after Kant witnessed the recession of his approach in favor of positivism, there is today an interest in returning to Kantian foundations.)[22] In terms of bridging the age-old gap between epistemological subject and object, Kant offers the suggestion that the "object of thought" be viewed as something creatively conditioned by categories of the understanding or consciousness. The object becomes a mediated construct of the subject. Thus Kant "dialectically" closes the gap between subject and object, and between consciousness and reality, without denying the integrity of either side. This project becomes important for dialectical theory.

There are some other problems in Kant, however, that prevent us from depicting him as a thoroughly consistent dialectical theorist. First, his attempted resolution of the abstract dualities plaguing knowledge is primarily a logical one. Although he appears to overcome the duality of subject and object, he introduces a new duality of phenomenon and noumenon which effectively expresses the fundamental problem of existence itself outside the realm of human knowledge as the mysterious *Ding an sich*. This new dualism reveals how the empiricist and rationalist strains in Kant's thought are still too clearly separated. The view that knowledge is possible only of phenomena given in sense experience is still too strongly influenced by empiricism. In this sense, a critic like Habermas can claim that Kant assumes a normative concept of science, with physics taken as the model of legitimate "scientific knowledge."[23] The rationalist influence appears in the argument for a priori categories of the mind, which presupposes a "transcendental ego" about which we can know nothing.

Second, Kant maintains an abstract distinction between theoretical and practical reason. The "subject" of the *Critique of Pure Reason* is merely the theoretic, knowing subject, not the concrete, whole subject in whom knowing and acting, thinking and existing, are dialectically united. Although Kant emphasizes the activity of subjectivity, he deals separately with the epistemologically active subject (in the *Critique of Pure Reason*) and the ethically, practically active subject (in the *Critique of Practical Reason*). The distinction prohibits the establishment of a concrete dialectical theory of knowledge; the synthetic activity of consciousness remains an abstract, contemplative activity.

We must remember that Kant's attempt to synthesize subjectivity and objectivity was essentially undertaken to rescue the objectivity of knowledge. Nonetheless, the insights provided by his reflections leave the door open for eventual resistance to the lure of "objectivity" and indeed reveal to us some of the errors and illusions involved in the debate between rationalism and empiricism. When we turn to the critique begun by Hegel and continued by Marx, we can see more clearly the emergence of a dialectical theory of knowledge which can inform contemporary social and political theory.

Hegel: The Synthesis Made Radical and Absolute

With Hegel we encounter an important thinker who both advances and inhibits the evolution of dialectical theory. The advances lie in his uncovering of the circular presuppositions of Kantian epistemology and in his concepts of the historicity and totality of experience and knowledge. The hindrances, as we shall see, result from Hegel's reliance upon the "philosophy of identity," the presupposition of absolute knowledge, the overspiritualization of human consciousness, and his view of philosophy as retrospective.

The Critique of Kant

In Hegel's *Phenomenology of Mind,* the propaedeutic to his entire philosophical system, we discover a critical alternative to Kant's theory of knowledge.[24] Hegel begins by criticizing Kant's failure to justify the conditions which make possible the transcendental critique of knowledge, thus claiming that Kantian epistemology is not "radical" enough:

> Meanwhile, if the fear of falling into error introduces an element of distrust into science, which without any scruples of that sort goes to work and actually does know, it is not easy to understand why, conversely, a distrust should not be placed in this very distrust, and why we should not take care lest the fear of error is not just the initial error. As a matter of fact, this fear presupposes something, indeed a great deal, as truth, and supports its scruples and consequences on what should itself be examined beforehand to see whether it is truth.[25]

Thus Kant's epistemology is caught in a vicious circle; it can never establish itself as the desired presuppositionless "First Philosophy" *(Ursprungsphilosophie)* since it relies upon that which is given in experience as already known. Furthermore, the "bad infinity" of having to explain how the preconditions of knowledge are themselves already knowledge leads to Hegel's criticism in the *Logic:*

> [Kant] demanded a criticism of the faculty of cognition as preliminary to its exercise. That is a fair demand, if it mean that even the forms of thought must be made an object of investigation. Unfortunately there soon creeps in the misconception of already knowing before you know—the error of refusing to enter the water until you have learnt to swim. True, indeed, the forms of thought should be subjected to a scrutiny before they are used: yet what is this scrutiny but *ipso facto* a cognition?[26]

To escape this bad infinity requires recognizing that the forms of thought are also in action, so that the "application" of the action of thought (which is the "dialectic") to the "categories" is not performed transcendentally but is immanent in their own action.[27]

Hegel goes beyond the disclosure of this unavowed, circular presupposition to reinterpret the epistemological relation of subject and object. He recoils at the sight of a theory of knowledge which separates knowledge of phenomena from the thing-in-itself. We see this in his reference to Kant's *Critique of Pure Reason:*

> It starts with ideas of knowledge as an instrument and as a medium; and presupposes a distinction of ourselves from this knowledge. More especially it takes for granted that the Absolute stands on one side, and that knowledge on the other side, by itself and cut off from the Absolute, is still something real; in other words, that knowledge, which, by being outside the Absolute, is certainly also outside truth, is nevertheless true—a position which, while calling itself fear of error, makes itself known rather as fear of the truth.[28]

The division of phenomenon and noumenon results in an unwarranted subjectivism, or subjective idealism, with subjectivity coming to embrace the ensemble of experience, "and nothing remains on the other side but the 'thing-in-itself.' "[29] To separate knowledge of phenomena gained through the understanding from the unknowable object-in-itself, which reason can only indicate, is to prevent the possibility of absolute knowledge—the only true knowledge for Hegel. Absolute knowledge is only attained when subject and object become totally identical and the opposition between knowing and all objecthood is superseded. To argue with Kant that knowledge of the *Ding an sich* is impossible is to restrict reason: "It degrades Reason to a finite and conditioned thing, to identify it with a mere stepping beyond the finite and conditioned range of the understanding." For Hegel, the truly infinite is more than transcendence of the finite. It involves the absorption of the finite into itself, making the whole of reality, and thus Hegel reads with surprise Kant's claim not to know the thing-in-itself: "On the contrary there is nothing we can know so easily."[30]

Hegel is further bothered by Kant's argument for the staticity of the epistemological subject, which derives from his view that the ultimate logical condition for objective knowledge and self-consciousness is a static or fixed transcendental unity of apperception that holds experience together. For Hegel, the epistemological subject, self-consciousness, exhibits historical movement, and indeed it is only through such movement that consciousness is able to permeate objectivity as it follows the pathway to absolute knowledge.[31] Instead of a static, logical faculty, the epistemological subject is a dynamically unfolding phenomenological movement, which is consciousness traveling the road of experience. And experience is nothing but the dialectical process "which consciousness executes on itself," where the gradual interpenetration of subject and object culminates in the absolute identity of subject and object.[32] The *Phenomenology of Mind* represents the mapping out of this experiential route of consciousness from beginning to final destiny.

Thus Hegel contributes a "historic-genetic," or "phenomenological," dimension to Kant's logical analysis.[33] He insists that any epistemological inquiry begin with consideration of the genesis of knowledge itself. Although Hegel too wants to prove the objectivity of knowledge, he sees this as requiring a phenomenological reconstructive method of consciousness that can demonstrate the process of coming to knowledge presupposed by Kant's critique. What is dialectically radical about Hegel's project is his insistence on demonstrating the formative process of reflection leading up to the confrontation of consciousness with the object, while Kant takes this confrontation as his starting point.[34] The self-knowledge that Kant presupposes as immediately given, Hegel takes as the goal of knowledge. Hegel wants to end where Kant begins.

The Phenomenology

In the eight chapters of the *Phenomenology*, which make up the comprehensive survey of the various modes in which experience appears, Hegel reconstructs and develops the experience of consciousness from immediate sense experience through self-consciousness to the ultimate self-consciousness of spirit in absolute knowledge. Although Hegel purports to trace the path of spirit to its complete self-consciousness, he already presupposes spirit as a whole and single movement and as the supreme reality or principle which connects all forms of experience. In other words, absolute knowledge is the end which dominates the movement of experience from its beginning; absolute knowledge gives unity and meaning to the movement of experience. There is something complete, already finished, about even the first stage of the experience of consciousness. Indeed, this notion is consistent with Hegel's view that philosophy is no longer the loving pursuit of wisdom *(philosophia)* but the actual possession of absolute knowledge, with every bit of "partial knowledge" merely a stage on the road to absolute knowledge.[35] As will become more evident, it is precisely this postulation of absolute knowledge as both the goal and the presupposition of all experience which poses a problem for Hegel as a consistent dialectical thinker.

In any event, Hegel's purpose in the *Phenomenology* is to treat self-consciousness, or Kant's synthetic unity of apperception, not as a given but as something to be demonstrated, and thus as a result rather than a precondition of experience.[36] Thus he introduces a radically historicist critique of Kant's theory of knowledge and of the knowing subject. For Hegel, the process by which the subject comes to complete self-consciousness is a self-formative process which involves substantive changes. The practice of phenomenological reflection demonstrates that at every stage in the reconstruction of the self-formative process of consciousness, the standards of knowledge contained in the previous stage disintegrate and new ones arise. By thus historicizing the view of consciousness proposed by Kant, Hegel tries to abolish the Kantian distinction between theoretical and practical reason. He argues that the critique of knowledge necessarily entails a critique of rational action or forms of life. At each new stage in the self-development of consciousness, the subject reconstructs its self-understanding in relation to its past. This reconstruction involves the "negation" of the old forms of consciousness, which are forms of, *and* attitudes toward, concrete life. There is, then, an inherent ethical and practical dimension to the theoretical subject's coming to know itself. Thus in the *Phenomenol-*

ogy, there is a direct correspondence between the theoretical elements or attitudes of sensation, perception, and understanding, and respectively, the practical attitudes of desire, the struggle for recognition, and freedom.[37] This represents Hegel's attempt to unite theory and practice dialectically.

One could pose a Kantian objection at this point: if the self-formation of consciousness requires the destruction of past stages and forms of consciousness, what maintains the unity of self-consciousness? Without the continuity provided by an unchanging transcendental ego, what holds experience together? How do we have memory? Hegel's response introduces the dialectical concept of *Aufhebung:* the continuity or unity of self-consciousness is provided by the simultaneous negation and retention of past forms of consciousness within a radical recomprehension of the totality. We shall return later to this concept of *Aufhebung* which is so important for dialectical theory.

In the face of Kant's theory of knowledge, therefore, Hegel argues for the historicity of the knowing subject (consciousness) and for the epistemological connection between knowledge and moral life, or theory and practice. He leads us beyond the view that a theory of knowledge can rest content with a consideration of the a priori principles of the knowing subject and argues that the critique of knowledge itself must extend into the relation of the knowing subject to the moral community. For example, in the well-known fourth chapter of the *Phenomenology,* we find a correspondence drawn between a particular epistemological stage in the evolution of self-consciousness (regarding the struggle between subject and object) and the historical-moral stage of master-slave relations in the evolution of mankind (the struggle between lord and bondsman).[38] This argument not only dissolves the Kantian distinction between theoretical and practical reason but suggests also that history is epistemological and epistemology historical. In other words, the phenomenological critique of knowledge must include the reconstruction of the constitutive experience of the history of mankind.[39]

Thus we are led from epistemology as a categorization of a priori principles to epistemology as a philosophy of history. Since history for Hegel is the history of spirit, that supreme guiding and consummating principle, we are further led inexorably to absolute knowledge, the end of spirit: the "last embodiment of spirit—spirit which at once gives its complete and true content the form of self, and thereby realizes its notion and in doing so remains within its own notion—this is *Absolute Knowledge.*"[40] In order to understand the meaning of this development for dialectical theory, we must turn to the dialectic of logic and history in Hegel's theory. First, however, it may prove helpful to devote a moment to Hegel's view of the "absolute."

The Absolute

As already noted, the absolute is the object or goal of philosophy; it is what is ultimately real as an object, yet it also expresses itself variously as a subject. Since philosophy is that "peculiar mode of thinking" which becomes knowledge through notions,[41] the absolute, as the ultimate "notion," proceeds like all other logical concepts through a triadic dialectical process of self-identity (the absolute-in-itself), otherness (for-itself), and the return to complete union with itself (in-and-for-itself). These three moments of the notion of the absolute and united yet distinguishable, and each expresses the absolute's single concrete reality from a particular perspective.

The three corresponding sciences of these moments, to which Hegel devotes three separate works, make up the whole of philosophy. Thus Hegel's *Logic* deals with the absolute-in-itself, as "pure idea" or abstract self-identity.[42] As the science of the pure universal principles of the absolute, the *Logic* provides the master plan of reality, which is capped by the absolute idea. Hegel's *Philosophy of Nature,* the science of the idea in its "otherness," traces the notion of the absolute for-itself into its self-externalized and self-estranged expression in nature and its particularity in time and space, which is capped by organic death. Finally, we are led to the *Philosophy of Mind,* the "science of the Idea come back to itself out of that otherness," where we encounter the explicit union of the pure universality of logical idea and the pure particularity of nature into a synthetic expression of the concreteness of the absolute—the absolute-in-and-for-itself.[43] Here the self-conscious "idea" of logic becomes living spirit, which presupposes the logical idea and nature yet is ontologically prior to both, and the absolute is fully realized. It is capped by the glory of free spirit.

This journey of the notion of the absolute to the *Philosophy of Mind,* which is primarily a systematic and embellished restatement of the *Phenomenology,* brings us back to the beginning. Spirit (or mind) is the ultimate source of both logic and nature, yet is also the goal of their developments. The absolute, which is "essentially a result," only true at its end, is thus also the beginning of that of which it is the end.[44] The major difference between the "identical" beginning and end of the absolute idea, as Hegel notes, "may be compared to the old man who utters the same creed as the child, but for whom it is pregnant with the significance of a lifetime."[45] We might now better understand how for Hegel the world is both a unified self-contained whole and a self-contained process. This self-contained whole, the absolute, is both constituted and understood by the principle of spirit. Furthermore, reason, which ultimately becomes self-conscious spirit and has spirit as its infinite concrete content, is both the source and object of reality and that which understands and explains reality.[46] Here we can catch a glimmer of how the "philosophy of identity" is so fundamental to Hegel.

It is recalled that in the first two "sections" of the triadic-structured *Phenomenology* ("Consciousness" and "Self-Consciousness"), Hegel tries to establish the fact that all conscious experience occurs within the distinction of thought and being, or subject and object. He goes further, however, to claim that this distinction exists within a larger single unity, the highest expression of which takes place in the form of absolute self-consciousness. Thus we are introduced to the philosophy of identity *(Identitätsphilosophie),* which posits the absolute identity of thought and being.[47] By establishing this unity as the single self functioning simultaneously in both subject and object, Hegel hopes to avoid the subjective idealism of Kant and Fichte as well as the abstract, objective union of subject and object in Schelling, which separates this unity from the self, placing it beyond expression.

Subject and object thus stand in a relation which constitutes the totality of experience. No longer is the object par excellence (the *Ding an sich*) beyond the reach of the knowing and experiencing subject. The principle which unifies this relation is *thought,* which becomes for Hegel both the function of the knowing subject and the governing nucleus of the reality of the object. Thought becomes profoundly ontological as well as epistemological. And as the *Phenomenology* demonstrates, the apparent opposition of subject and object at our lower, more immediate forms of experience begins to dissipate in the light of the analysis of experience to its higher, more self-conscious forms. The goal of experience emerges at the end of the *Phenomenology* where subject and object become transparent to one another and the self-conscious unity of the two is established and comprehended.[48] In other words, the "transparency" of subject and object to one another is reached when the subject (consciousness) becomes aware of itself in the object, and the object corresponds to the activity of the subject. As the process of the evolving consciousness of self, experience culminates when the subject achieves total awareness of itself in the object and as the object, and conversely, when it "sets up the object as its self." At this final stage of reconciliation and union with the object, the subject is finally "at home" with itself in its otherness; consciousness is no longer self-alienated from, but at home in, its world.[49]

In the form of, and because of, this philosophy of identity, reason is freed from pure subjectivity and is capable of union with its object. The Kantian prohibition is lifted and reason can now know the "secret" of the thing-in-itself because ultimately it is in the thing-in-itself. Reason creates the world in its image because it finds its likeness in the face of the world.[50] This ontological-epistemological relationship is a statement of the philosophy of identity, and it helps to explain why our examination of Hegel's concept of the absolute is so important. With this discussion in mind, we can turn finally to two major points in Hegel's development of dialectical theory: the two meanings of the term "dialectical" in Hegel's conception of logic and the stages of the transcendence of the subject-object distinction in his view of the unity of logic and history.

Logic and History

Hegel believed that he was completely overthrowing all previous views of formal logic. Rather than view logic as concerned with the formal operation of thinking,[51] Hegel's critique of Kantian logic attempts to free logic from the confines of the "understanding" so it can proceed through reason to the domain of the thing-in-itself. Logic, which is "the science of the pure Idea" and "Speculative Philosophy," comes now to have a direct relation to truth and reality: "The term 'logical' is equivalent to 'truthful'; logic is truth in the form of truth."[52]

Furthermore, in Hegel's new dialectical logic, "dialectical" has two meanings, a narrow and a broad one.[53] Every thought which is logically real or true has three aspects or moments to it: (1) the abstract, rational form of the understanding; (2) the negative, dialectical form of reason; and (3) the speculative, positive form of reason, or "concrete comprehension." These inseparable moments of logical doctrine taken together are the dialectic in its broad sense, while the second moment is the dialectic in its "proper" sense. Hegel makes this clear:

> These three aspects do not constitute there *parts* of logic, but are stages or 'moments' of everything that is logically real or true.
> They belong to every philosophical Concept (Notion). Every Concept is rational, is abstractly opposed to another, and is united in comprehension together with its opposites. *This is the definition of dialectic.*[54]

If we understand the dialectic not as the whole process of logic but simply as the second moment, negation, seen from the perspective of the understanding, then we can be led to mere skepticism. Thus the dialectic understood broadly leads beyond reason to become implanted as the "law of things and of the finite as a whole," and as the principle which constitutes "the real and true."[55] Hegel's conception of the dialectic has moved a long way from Kant's view of it as "transcendental illusion."

Hegel's definition of the dialectic supplies it with a new ontological status and allows for the union of logic and history. Let us recall that his radicalization of Kant's theory of knowledge centers around Kant's divorce of theoretical and practical reason and postulates instead a critique of knowledge that must include a phenomenological recon-struction of the constituting experience of mankind's history. Hegel's own reconstruction of the stages of experience in the *Phenomenology* yields three ultimately identical moments. We discover, then, a recon-struction of the moments constituting the self-formation of the indi-vidual, of the universal history of mankind, and of the consciousness of experience expressed in absolute spirit—which culminate, respec-tively, in self-consciousness, freedom, and absolute knowledge. From the perspective of this one work alone, it is evident how the devel-opment of consciousness becomes dialectically related to that of the historical world spirit. Logic and history come together as the single source of all forms of experience, logic providing a coherent expression of the whole of experience by connecting all universals required for its ordered totality, and history providing the "facts" of experience which manifest the process and content of conscious experience grounded in time.

To the eye searching for a full dialectical theory of knowledge, some-thing is amiss here. Hegel's discussion of the logical dialectic and its three moments indicates that these moments are not primarily meth-odological or epistemological; they are fundamentally ontological. In other words, it appears to be the dialectical structure of Being, or the ontological dialectic, that determines the structure of thought. Philos-ophy seems to lose some creative power since it can in no way trans-form Being itself; logical thought, or knowledge, is dialectical only because Being is dialectical. If history is both the source and content of dialectical reality, philosophical thought is simply its "reflective" language. Epistemological method is not truly dialectical in the pow-erful and creative sense that Being is. Method and knowledge, as Hegel repeatedly has it, are contemplative and passive, or phenomenological in the sense of the reflective reconstruction of experience. It appears that knowledge has been relegated to a kind of passive description: "True scientific knowledge, on the contrary, demands abandonment to the very life of the object, or, which means the same thing, claims to have before it the inner necessity controlling the object, and to express this only." Knowledge "steeps itself" in its object, and

> being sunk into the material in hand, and following the course that such material takes, true knowledge returns back into itself, yet not before the content in its fullness is taken into itself, is reduced to the simplicity of being a determinate characteristic, drops to the level of being one aspect of an existing entity, and passes over into its higher truth.[56]

It is in this sense that Kojève has a point in speaking of the "posi-tivism" of Hegel's method.[57] The Owl of Minerva appears to be a rather positivist bird, although a keen-sighted and noble one. The philosopher finds himself having experience dictated to him by the dialectic of real Being: the "dialectic process which consciousness executes on itself—on its knowledge as well as on its object—in the sense that out of it the new and true object arises, is precisely what is termed Experience."[58] The philosopher at his best "experiences" revealed dialectical Being, which is to say Being reflects itself on him, and he describes it in its dialectical movement without "deforming" or changing it.

This interpretation makes sense in light of how Hegel understood his position in the history of philosophy. He was fond of the Socratic-Platonic dialectical method of inquiry, which involved human inter-locutors dialoguing their way to truth, although in Plato it led to a nondialectical ontological totality. That dialectical method began to fade in Aristotle's aporetic dialectic, which became more scholastic and monologic in character, and by the time of medieval philosophy the only interlocutor available to the inquirer was God. Saint Augustine, for example, could only direct dialogue inwardly toward his soul, the source of divine discourse. Thus dialogic dialectic became meditative dialectic, or meditation. With the emergence of modern philosophy, then, we find Descartes's "meditations" and the meditative form of method of systematic philosophers from Kant to Fichte and Schelling.[59]

Although Hegel sees this development as a retreat from the classical dialectic, he recognizes that it carries the implicit Platonic dialectic through history, mediated by the philosophers after Plato. These philosophers reflect the real dialectic of Being as it comes to completion before the eyes of Hegel. In a sense, Hegel can now abandon the dialectic as method, and simply "reflect" in "positivist" fashion the dialectic of Being moving through history. To reflect and know the history of philosophy is to reflect and know the movement of real history itself. Consciousness and history have "come together." Such a transformation, abandoning the dialectic as method, assumes completion of the "dialectical Real," which is "proven" by Hegel's very recognition of it. Any epistemological dialectic is resolved into onto-logical dialectic, to which knowledge surrenders, and which it can only describe.

Subject and Object

Ultimately, though, it is too simplistic to apprehend Hegel's epistemological method as positivist. Although Being reveals itself to reflection objectively, Hegel is trying to be both subjective and objective.[60] This becomes clearer if we look closely at the self-generating dialectic of the subject in the stages of reflection. It is well known that dialectical movement involves an immediate positing, which is negated so that the implicit contents of the positing are heightened as contradictions, which in turn are pushed to their extremes and further sublated to a unity that is more complete than the original position. For Hegel, this movement is not only necessary but normative; it is liberating and ethical. In the *Phenomenology,* dialectical movement results in the unity of subjective and objective spirit, which is the "essential nature of ethical life." Spirit is the unity of subject and "ethical substance" as the objective side of spirit.[61]

This dialectical process takes place epistemologically in the stages of reflection. Reflection begins with the subject unfolding itself as an immediate positing. Here the knowing subject and the object are one in the primordial form of immediate identity, as reality's fixed and permanent self-identity. Yet this identity is a tautological "immediate universality" empty of all concrete content.[62] The first stage of reflection carries within it its own negativity, and as the subject experiences growing self-consciousness it begins to mediate its relation with the object.[63] A split emerges between subject and object as the subject begins to see the object in its otherness, as alien and beyond its power. This is the beginning of the second stage where the subject "forgets" that the object only arose in the positing by the subject. The dialectical negativity contained in reality is revealed and threatens the original identity. Subject and object stand in contrast to one another, and the object-world is diversified and counterposed to the unified subject, as in Kant's view of the understanding confronting phenomena. The third stage emerges when reason moves beyond the understanding to recover the totality of Being. By becoming aware that the existence of the object is owed to the posited externalization of the self (spiritual subject) in the world, the subject rediscovers itself in its objectivity and thus returns to itself through this objectivity.[64] The whole dialectical process of reflection, therefore, reveals Being as a totality of identity and negativity through speculative or positive reason. Being is a dialectical totality which is "becoming," an identity achieved through negativity: "it is affirmation by negation."[65]

It is thus that the subject-object distinction is "overcome" by the process of reflection. The apparent independence of the object assumed by Kant and expressed by Newtonian science is revealed as an illusion at the second stage of reflection. Also an illusion is the first stage of immediate subject-object identity in a primordial ontology. Reflection reveals a mediated unity of subject and object, which can only be grasped once the subject returns to itself after the historical experience of its alienation from the object, and establishes a unity full of the experiential content of that journey:

> True reality is merely this process of reinstating self-identity, of reflecting into its own self in and from its other, and is not an orig-

inal and primal unity as such, not an immediate unity as such. It is the process of its own becoming, the circle which presupposes its end as its purpose, and has its end for its beginning; it becomes concrete and actual only by being carried out, and by the end it involves.[66]

At the end of this process, Hegel sees the subject of knowledge and the substance of reality united. The substance of reality is posited and moved by "thinking," that is, by Being revealing itself in the dialectical movement of reflection. The substance of reality comes alive as the subject of reality; spirit becomes the absolute subject-and-substance. Still, what appears truly dialectical in the transcendence of subject and object is not so much the human process of inquiry, but the "concrete Real." What is dialectical is the totality of spirit which reveals itself on the human phenomenal level as historicity and is mirrored by the experiential stages of reflection.

It is clear by now how Hegel has radically broadened the realm of possible knowledge and experience in the face of Kant. In doing so, however, he has transformed Kant's human knowing subject into spirit reflected in the forms and laws of nature and phenomenal experience. The subject is ultimately the ordering objective spirit of ethical life. Furthermore, the forms of experience are not produced by human mind, but discovered in the order of Being. Here Hegel seems to retreat behind Kant in terms of a concrete dialectic of subject and object, for the Hegelian human subject never gives order to the formless or in any way "deforms" Being in the process of knowing. Knowledge is a becoming self-conscious and manifestation of the movement of Logos already resident in the world. Rationality is never really put in the world by the knowing subject. Spirit as absolute subject-substance is dialectical, but at the level of human inquiry and exposition the dialectic deflates. The dialectic becomes description of the dialectical structure of Being and the self-realization of spirit. There is an ontological but not a human epistemological dialectic in Hegel. In this sense, the human mind for Hegel becomes less powerful and creative than it was for Kant, albeit for Kant it operated in a much more limited realm.

Hegel's Legacy

We can now summarize how Hegel both advances and inhibits the emergence of a dialectical theory of knowledge. First of all, we have seen how he uncovers some nondialectical assumptions in Kant's view of the relationship between the knowing subject and knowledge: a normative and progressivist conception of science; a view of the knowing subject as static or fixed; and the distinction between theoretical and practical reason.[67] In their place, he has offered the following contributions: (1) the notion that all criteria of knowledge continually undergo a historical and dialectical *Aufhebung;* (2) the argument for an immanent phenomenological reconstruction of the knowing subject's experience; and (3) a dialectical phenomenological mode of reflection where theoretical and practical attitudes are united. Kant's view on this last issue had offered us two different "egos"—a knowing self of consciousness and an acting self of free will—which Hegel wants to reunite in the process of reflection as a simultaneously moral and knowing subject.[68] As one critic has it:

> The affirmative moment that is contained in the very negation of an existing organization of consciousness becomes plausible when we consider that in this consciousness categories of apprehending the world and norms of action are connected. A *form of life* that has become an abstraction cannot be negated without leaving a trace, or overthrown without practical consequences.[69]

Hegel's contribution also includes the recovery of reality as an interrelated and dialectically mediated totality, which has important methodological implications for political science. There is a "philosophy of internal relations" in Hegel's theory which militates against ontological and methodological atomism. The whole of reality is a totality that is mediated to itself by its relations with its parts, so that the "whole" itself is a mediated relation.[70] In this sense, the whole

> is the whole Relation and the independent totality; but for this very reason it is only a relative term, for that which makes it a totality is precisely its Other, the Parts; and it has its consistence not in itself but in its other.
> Thus the Parts are also the whole Relation. . . . Further, they have this Whole in themselves as their moment.[71]

This is a crucial observation, for it offers us a view of reality as an interdependent and related totality whereby the truth and reality of each part is contained in the whole, and the whole in each part. It is impossible to understand any aspect of reality apart from its relations to each other part and the whole; such understanding is only possible in terms of relations. It is neither the whole nor the parts which is ontologically fundamental, but the relations among them. This notion is essential for grounding a dialectical theory of knowledge. Henceforth inquiry should delve into neither an abstract whole nor apparently independent and separate parts of the whole. What "holds together" the parts and the whole is this manner is a "mediated negativity" where the part is both what it is and what it is not.[72] Thus Hegel's recovery of "totality" not only expands the limits of knowledge but offers a view of reality where the "concrete" is the mediated whole of relations and the "abstract" is the immediate specificity of separated parts of the whole. It is this view of reality that seems appropriate to a dialectical theory of knowledge.

Another of Hegel's contributions lies in his argument for the historicity of knowledge and experience. The Kantian logical analysis of knowledge requiring a fixed foundation of transcendental consciousness is replaced by a phenomenological reconstruction of the genesis and history of knowledge. Yet the historicity of knowledge does not for Hegel indicate the mere temporality or linear process of the experience of consciousness; it is also a matter of eruptions or "reversals" in time which occur through the labor of negativity and preserve the past in new forms. In a sense, history is not absolutely relativized to exclude standards of knowledge, but dialectically relativized to reconstruct the emergence of new standards at every stage of the self-formative process of consciousness. Thus the very possibility of a knowing subject rests upon its historical self-formation, which has to be recounted in reflective reconstruction. This process of consciousness is linked through the dialectical totality of absolute spirit to both the history of mankind, and the history of philosophy.[73] The histories of individual mind, mankind, and philosophy become one as spirit labors historically to its self-reconciliation in absolute knowledge. Reality is knowable only in its historicity, at every stage of its development. This is how Hegel tries to establish the historical immanence and determination of truth:

> The truth is the whole. The whole, however, is merely the essential nature reaching its completeness through the process of its own development. Of the Absolute it must be said that it is essentially a result, that only at the end is it what it is in very truth; and just in that consists its nature, which is to be actual, subject, or self-becoming, self-development.[74]

There is yet another contribution from Hegel that may be important to dialectical theory, but it is an ambivalent one. It is the suggestion that history is created or "made" by a "metasubject," or universal subject, something beyond the isolated efforts of particular individuals. On the one hand, the notion of a universal subject (in this case, spirit) above all individual subjects which both knows and creates the world of reality seems to support a dialectical view. For Hegel, spirit *is* reality, and it is the epistemological and practical subject confronting reality. The notion of a metasubject which continually creates that which it is argues against any nondialectical, positivist view of an ahistorical, objective, "natural" reality. On the other hand, it would be easy to mystify and objectify such a metasubject and thereby take the powers of creation and knowledge out of human hands altogether. In this case, philosophy becomes merely the vehicle for the self-realization of spirit, and in terms of creating the world, human subjectivity takes a back seat to an objectified metasubject. Furthermore, the singularism of Hegel's view of spirit gives us a metasubject which is both monistic and deterministic, allowing for no plurality and ambiguity. The creation of reality by a laboring metasubject beyond the reach of real human effort is what makes Hegel's philosophy of history appear as a kind of theophany.

The criticism of Kant and the introduction of the concepts of totality, internal relations, historicity of knowledge, and laboring metasubject in history all to some extent advance the emergence of dialectical theory. Where Hegel hinders this evolution is in the assumption of absolute knowledge, the philosophy of identity, and the view of philosophy as retrospective. On the first count, Hegel seems guilty of the same charge he levels against Kant: the problem of "knowing before we know."[75] The end of our experiential route in the *Phenomenology* is also our radically presupposed beginning: absolute knowledge. Indeed, the undertaking of the *Phenomenology* is only possible given the necessity of absolute knowledge. According to Hegel's own criterion in criticizing Kant, it is the very possibility of absolute knowledge that needs to be justified. Instead, we find that we possess absolute knowledge in the end only because it is what guides us from the beginning.[76] But if absolute knowledge is the goal of philosophical experience only because it is the presupposition for such experience, then its phenomenological justification is unforceful and unnecessary.[77]

Absolute knowledge is thus not something we achieve in human inquiry, but the philosophical incarnation of an ontological metasubject. It is the "last embodiment of spirit," which "reaches its beginning only at the end."[78] This marvelous tautology is not meaningless, since the return to the beginning is mediated by the rich historical experience of spirit. Still, human history is relegated to the status of a "medium" for spirit's task of knowing itself.[79] With the presupposition of absolute knowledge, the dialectic is circumscribed by the absolute.

Hegel's reliance upon the philosophy of identity again rears its head. To be sure, the absolute identity of subject and object overcomes the feared opposition between knowing and objecthood, but it does so in a way which eliminates any serious dialectic of subject and object.[80] What occurs is a conflation of subject and object that establishes the ontological superiority of the subject, with the object being the self-externalization of absolute subjectivity. The object is only a form of the subject, which is why it is so easy for spirit to be at home with itself at the end of its journey.[81] Any epistemological dialectic of subject and object is overshadowed by an ontological dialectic: "Or, truth is the known presence of the ontological dialectic in the subject."[82] What we find here is a kind of disintegration of epistemology as Hegel finds refuge in the presupposition of absolute knowledge in an "absolute idealism," which derails critical philosophy and hinders the development of dialectical theory.[83]

Finally, Hegel retreats from a thorough dialectical theory of knowledge by establishing philosophy as a passive and retrospective enterprise. Philosophy cannot intervene in reality without "perturbing" and distorting it. Thought is dialectical only to the extent that it mirrors the dialectic of Being: "Process in philosophy mirrors the absolute Idea," and "true knowledge lies rather in the seeming inactivity which merely watches how what is distinguished is self-moved by its very nature and returns again into its own unity."[84] Whatever activity is involved in philosophy (the Owl of Minerva does, after all, spread its wings) is confined to retrospective activity (the wings are spread only with the falling of dusk). The labor of the mind is only a kind of reflective recollection, while the "labor of the negative" involved in real creation lies in reality itself. Such a view of philosophy undermines the development of a conception of knowledge as real constructive and creative activity.

We have spent quite some time with Hegel because he is such a champion of the dialectic, and his influence on developments in the nineteenth and twentieth centuries has been considerable and central. We have noted how certain aspects of his thought have advanced, while others have inhibited, a consistent dialectical theory. The elements involved in his radicalization of Kant's synthesis of rationalism and empiricism move us forward, but when Hegel proceeds to absolutize the synthesis by way of absolute knowledge and the philosophy of identity, we retreat from the openness of the dialectic. The certainty with which he presupposes absolute knowledge contradicts the spirit of his original, radical phenomenological project. When Hegel substitutes the metasubject spirit for the importance of human epistemological activity and hence resolves the transcendental tension in Kant's theory into a philosophy of identity, the dialectical character of his thought falters. When we turn to Marx, we find an attempt to dissolve that philosophy of identity, and to reawaken and make concrete the openness of dialectical theory.

Marx: The Synthesis Made Practical and Human

Marx presents us with an incipient theory of knowledge that seems to presuppose the importance of the synthesis sought by Kant and Hegel, especially in his debates against idealism and materialism.[85] For Marx, however, the overcoming of the subject-object distinction is not guaranteed by a philosophy of identity; it requires an open-ended synthesis of man and nature produced by human labor, or praxis. In this regard, there are two ways in which Marx tries to move beyond Kant and Hegel.

First, although Marx agrees with Kant that human consciousness is synthetic creative activity and thus that knowledge is the product of this synthetic activity, he refuses to accept the idea that the synthesis takes place solely at the level of consciousness. It occurs rather at the level of the concrete totality of human life. There are not, as in Kant, two distinct human consciousnesses or subjects: the theoretic subject of knowledge and the practical subject of ethical life. For Marx, the activity of consciousness supersedes the distinction between theoretical and practical reason. Consciousness is not simply the synthetic activity which creatively orders the manifold of sense experience, but becomes the practical process of humanly created reality itself. Not only is knowledge active, it is concretely and socially active as a social creation: "Consciousness is, therefore, from the very beginning a social product, and remains so as long as men exist at all."[86] Consciousness becomes social consciousness, and epistemology becomes a kind of "socioepistemology," which is to say that theory of knowledge becomes social theory.

Second, knowledge conceived as concrete and social activity includes the supersession of subject and object. Once the two actively interpenetrating "poles" of knowledge—subjective human consciousness and objectively active "being"—are seen as grounded in the dialectical totality of human life, then the overcoming of the distinction between subject and object is no longer just a problem for traditional philosophy or logical thought; it becomes a problem for, and a presupposition of, practical life.

> It is only in a social context that subjectivism and objectivism, spiritualism and materialism, activity and passivity, cease to be antinomies and thus cease to exist as such antinomies. The resolution of the *theoretical* contradictions is possible *only* through practical means, only through the *practical* energy of man. Their resolution is not by any means, therefore, only a problem of knowledge, but is a *real* problem of life which philosophy was unable to solve precisely because it saw there a purely theoretical problem.[87]

The overcoming of the alienation of subject and object through a synthesis of labor takes place at the level of human practical life but does not exclude the efforts and activity of theoretical consciousness. For Marx, our general relationship to reality is still our consciousness, which becomes powerful, colorful and important.[88] As with Hegel before, consciousness is capable of penetrating the thing-in-itself, but now human consciousness is no longer restricted to the mere cognitive reflection of an ontological dialectic. It is directly and inherently involved in the creation and transformation of that dialectic, which is to say, human knowledge has a critical and negative role in reality. The resolution of the subject-object distinction in human praxis simultaneously argues against any view of knowledge as reflective cognition as well as any view of practice as independent from the conditions of knowledge. This does not mean for Marx that knowledge itself is reduced to the material transformation of reality, but that it is dialectically and inextricably bound up with such transformation.

We have already seen how Kant laid the foundation for a dialectical theory of knowledge based on the synthetic activity of consciousness, and how Hegel's radicalization of Kant introduced the historicity of consciousness and the dialectical totality of reality. Marx accepts these developments as his starting point but is upset by where they often lead. In particular, he finds Hegel's argument for the transcendence of subject and object through the movement of self-consciousness to be inadequate, since the object is posited as an externalized form of the subject. In other words, when the object returns to the subject in synthesis, it is really the subject returning to itself in its complete self-consciousness. Because this synthesis is based on a philosophy of identity, the duality of subject and object is ultimately transcended only in "thought," or in the self-consciousness of spirit. For Marx, this robs the object of its reality and dignity and essentially relegates real human historical development to the level of a mirror reflection or predication of the superior reality of spirit.

Perhaps what bothers Marx most about the way in which Kant and Hegel deal with the epistemological dilemma of subject and object is that they remain imprisoned by traditional philosophy. Kant escapes the dilemma by recreating it at the level of phenomenon and noumenon, and Hegel avoids it in a circular ontology based on a philosophy of identity. Marx argues that maybe this is the best we can do if we persist with traditional philosophy and try to overcome the duality of thought and existence dialectically in logic. Logic, as Marx has it, "is the *money* of the mind," and no matter how dialectical, it always expresses a reified and alienated mediation of man and reality.[89]

In response to Kant and Hegel, Marx evokes the possibility of a concrete union of subject and object which is based in part on Kant's notion of creative, active consciousness and in part on Hegel's ontology of dialectical totality. He posits a dialectical identity of consciousness and existence which is historically contingent, rather than assume as Hegel does that history itself is contingent upon a prior identity. For Marx, the identity must be achieved and reachieved continually by new generations of human beings creating history. Furthermore, this identity of thought and existence means that the two are aspects of "one and the same real historical and dialectical process."[90] Thus for Marx, the union of subject and object is accomplished epistemologically as the union of man and nature in praxis. Such a union cannot be achieved ahistorically (Kant) or on the basis of a philosophy of identity (Hegel). It can only be achieved by means of a self-consciously constructive historical, identical subject-object—the human species in the process of its historical self-formation through labor. Helpful to an understanding of this position is a closer examination of Marx's specific critique of Hegel's dialectic, where we can find Marx trying to introduce a concrete epistemological-practical human dialectic.

The Critique of Hegel's Dialectic

Marx's criticism of Hegel's epistemological views, especially as they evolve in the *Phenomenology* and the *Logic,* appears in his "Critique of Hegel's Dialectic and General Philosophy." There he considers the "*essential* question" of philosophy in his own time to be "how do we now stand with regard to the Hegelian *dialectic?*"[91] And while he undertakes a direct critique of Hegel's position, he never wavers in his own thought from the general framework of the dialectic, the notion of a dialectical totality, and the philosophy of internal relations which he finds in Hegel.[92] Indeed, partial evidence of this lies in Marx's heavy reliance upon Feuerbach, "the only person who has a *serious* and *critical* relation to Hegel's dialectic."[93] Perhaps what so strongly attracts Marx to Hegel's phenomenological dialectic is its discovery, although in an abstract way, of man as the potential subject of history, or of the historical self-genesis of man. Hence Marx sets out to criticize the abstract form of this discovery and to recover from Hegel the epistemological-practical function of the human subject—the notion that human beings can really change the world in the act of knowing it.[94]

Marx outlines the process of the dialectic of spirit in Hegel's *Phenomenology* to the point where it becomes self-validated by relating to itself as absolute spirit in absolute knowledge. Here he detects a "double error" in Hegel. First, reality is conceived only in the form of thought, as objects of thought and therefore as the alienation of pure thought. The philosopher, as man alienated from existence, becomes the measure of the alienated world. Thus the history of philosophy becomes the history of alienated thought. The nature of this alienation and its supersession lies in the opposition of subject and object as an opposition in thought itself between abstract thought (in the *Logic*) and sensible reality (in "nature").[95] Therefore, the overcoming of the alienation of subject and object occurs through the appropriation by the subject of the object (by man of his objectified, alienated faculties).

But this is an appropriation only of objects "as *thoughts*" and "as *movements of thought,*" and thus is an abstract, alienated appropriation. This is what Marx calls the error of Hegel's concealed "uncritical positivism," which leaves the real world untouched.[96]

Second, Hegel's vindication of the objective world in the overcoming of subject and object needs to be humanized. With Hegel, the vindication is that of abstract thought, a mental vindication, since he views man as essentially self-consciousness. The human character of nature lies only in the positing of nature by thought itself. Although Hegel thus comprehends the alienation of man in the opposition of subject and object (man and nature) and is critical of it, it remains an abstract criticism. And it will remain abstract as long as the philosophy of identity is presupposed, where the subject is self-consciousness and the object is merely an object of abstract consciousness:

> Since abstract consciousness (the form in which the object is conceived) is in *itself* merely a distinctive moment of self-consciousness, the outcome of the movement is the identity of self-consciousness and consciousness—absolute knowledge—the movement of abstract thought not directed outwards but proceeding within itself; i.e. the dialectic of pure thought is the result.[97]

The humanization of the synthesis of subject and object requires the abolition of the philosophy of identity.

For Marx, the great achievement of the *Phenomenology* lies in the discovery of "the dialectic of negativity as the moving and creating principle."[98] Man is posited as a process of self-creation, and through the dialect of negativity, Hegel "grasps the nature of *labour*" whereby man appears as the result of labor. Although it is not so clear in Hegel that man is the result of his own, rather than spirit's, labor, Marx still sees the germ of the idea that man's complete self-affirmation lies in the historical and communal realization of all of his "species-powers."[99] Hegel's achievement lies in awakening the laboring negativity and historicity of the dialectic.

Hegel's limitations, however, are glaring. Although labor is presupposed as the nature of man's self-development, the process is alienated within the duality of subject and object. Labor is only "mental,"[100] and the process of man's "coming to be" is the process of laboring spirit expressing itself in philosophy. Therefore, the essence of philosophy is the essence of labor, which is "*alienated* science *thinking* itself." Since Hegel's philosophical science claims to be absolute science, based on the presupposition of absolute knowledge, it is the last chapter of the *Phenomenology,* containing its "concentrated spirit," against which Marx directs his most sustained criticism.[101]

Marx's critique of absolute knowledge reflects a concern for the resulting "nonobjectivity" of man and natural life. For Hegel, the object of consciousness is self-consciousness, or objectified self-consciousness. Hegel's target of attack is objectivity itself as the alienation of man or self-consciousness. The only way he sees to overcome alienation is to overcome objectivity qua objectivity. The result is man conceived as a nonobjective, spiritual being—as self-consciousness. Marx counters that self-consciousness is only a quality of human nature; human nature is not a quality of self-consciousness.[102] If we agree with Hegel, man becomes an abstract egoist. Since for Hegel, human life is essentially self-consciousness, then the alienation of human life is the alienation of self-consciousness, and can be overcome only in self-consciousness. The target of Marx's attack is not the human-as-subject or even "spirit"; rather, it is the overspiritualization of the human subject which negates all objective life and equates alienation with objectivity as such. He wants the recovery of objective man.

Marx is thus worried about the way Hegel construes the supersession of the object, or the overcoming of the alienation of subject and object. In Hegel's view, the result of the alienation of self-consciousness is "thinghood" *(Dingheit),* or objectivity *(Gegenständlichkeit).* But this alienation is dialectical and thus has a "positive" meaning for self-consciousness as well. How is this possible? Since self-consciousness knows the "nullity" of the object by alienating (externalizing) itself as the object, then the object actually is itself; the object is self-consciousness. In this manner, the object comes back to the subject and the subject is at home in the "object" as *its* object.[103] Here the philosophy of internal relations comes into play in a positive sense for Marx, but the dialectical totality thusly conceived transforms the object into a "spiritual"object, or just another form of the subject.

What Marx wants is the recovery of "thinghood" and the restitution of the concrete objective subject. For Hegel, objectivity per se is conceived as the product of alienation. But for Marx, objectivity cannot simply be alienated self-consciousness if we recognize that the real subject is not the abstraction of man but human nature understood as the synthesis of man and nature. Otherwise, the "thinghood" established by the Hegelian alienation of self-consciousness would be the creation of an abstract, and profoundly unreal, "thing." Marx's dialectic emerges as robust and complex in his desire to re-establish the independence or "being" of objectivity as something more than a construct of self-consciousness. Yet this move is not a return to naturalism or materialism in an objectivistic sense. The dialectic for Marx establishes both the subjectivity of objectivity (nature) and the objectivity of subjectivity (man).

Thus we are brought to Marx's attempted dialectical rehabilitation of both nature and the objectivity of the human subject. Man is no longer seen as simply self-consciousness; he is also corporeal *(leibliche),* or embodied. The expression of human nature is the positing of man's faculties or powers as a human being (his *Wesenkräfte).* That positing itself is not the subject, however, but only the subjective aspect of man's objective expression:

> When real, corporeal man, with his feet firmly planted on the solid ground, inhaling and exhaling all the powers of nature, *posits* his real objective faculties, as a result of his alienation, as alien objects, the *positing* is not the subject of this act but the subjectivity of *objective* faculties whose action must also, therefore, be objective.[104]

Man is an objective being, and that objectivity as such is not alienation, but part of his nature. Indeed, not only does man create and establish objects by his nature, but he too "is established by objects." Man is thus a *natural* being, understood as the dialectical union of subject and object. In this broad sense, mind or self-consciousness is no longer the ground of nature, but nature becomes the ground of mind. Marx despiritualizes human consciousness and reinstates both the subjectivity and objectivity of nature. It is in this sense, and not as an environmental determinism, that the response to both idealism and materialism must be a thoroughgoing and dialectical naturalism or humanism.[105]

The dialectic of subject and object now emerges in a new light. Its locus is man as the creator and creature of nature. As "living being" he is subject, and as "embodied being" he is object. Man now appears as the subject-object. In other words, man as an objective, natural, sentient being is an object for nature and for others. But he also has object, nature, and "sense" outside himself, which is to say, he is also a subject of nature and others. If one accepts this dialectic of subject and object, then one approaches the understanding of anything in terms of the relations between subject and object, since the nature of something lies neither inside it nor outside it alone, but in the relation between inner and outer, subjectivity and objectivity.[106] Marx's point is that any being which is not objective, nor has a real object, is a nonbeing. Otherwise we recur to a kind of ontological solipsism. In this sense, the dialectic truly becomes concrete and total. For if "I have an object, this object has me for its object," which is to say, the object itself has a subjective character.[107] To be real is both to be an object (admitting the subjectivity of nature and others) and to have objects of sensuous expression, or to "experience" (admitting the subjectivity of self).

The reason that this recovery of the sensuous objectivity of man and reality does not lead to either empiricism or simple naturalism is that "man is not merely a natural being."[108] He is also human and as such is a subjective natural being. Therefore man is a being with self-consciousness (a species-being) who expresses himself in both thought and nature.[109] Human objects are never direct natural objects, and human sense is never immediate, given sensibility. Marx is no empiricist. The human being never confronts directly either objective or subjective nature. The relation is always a mediated one; human nature is a mediation of subject and object, which is to say, the process of its own genesis as the synthetic process of social labor and the conscious process of history. Thus historically contingent social labor is the synthesis which mediates objective and subjective nature.[110]

The labor about which Marx speaks is not the unidirectional, instrumental, material transformation of nature or reality by men. If labor transforms the world, so also labor transforms men as subjects, and thus labor itself contains a dialectic of subject and object. Human nature appears as the historically mediated subject-object created by labor; human nature is never "fixed," whether transcendentally or empirically. At each stage in history there appears

> a sum of productive forces, an historically created relation of individuals to nature and to one another, which is handed down to each generation from its predecessor; a mass of productive forces, capital funds and conditions, which on the one hand, is indeed modified by the new generation, but also, on the other, prescribes for it its conditions of life and gives it a definite development, a special character. It shows that the circumstances make men as well as that men make the circumstances [dass also die Umstände ebensosehr die Menschen, wie die Menschen die Umstände machen].
>
> This sum of productive forces, capital funds, and social forms of intercourse, which every individual and generation finds in existence as something given, is the real basis of what the philosophers have conceived as 'substance' and 'essence of man,' and what they have deified (apotheosiert) and attacked; a real basis which is not in the least disturbed, in its effect and influence on the development of men, by the fact that these philosophers rebel against it as 'self-consciousness' and the 'Unique.'[111]

Although Marx's recovery of the objectivity of the human subject aims at the practical resolution of alienated subject and object in laboring praxis and history, one could also interpret this move in terms of the epistemological objectivity of man. Knowing, for Marx, is a twofold act: it involves the activity of both consciousness and that which is *for* consciousness; knowledge is the joint creation of subject

and object, or a synthesis through labor. Man possesses an epistemological objectivity precisely because of his activity; the fact that he
is objectively active makes him also an objective knowing subject.[112]
The objective epistemological subject for Marx is neither Kantian transcendental consciousness nor Hegelian spirit. It is the concrete human
species in the laboring process of its self-formation as a natural, objective species. The new knowing subject, therefore, is concrete human
being constituted by and as labor. This point bears emphasis because
it indicates that labor is not only the practical mediation of man with
nature; it is also the epistemological mediation of the knowing subject
with reality.

We have seen that for Hegel the only way for consciousness to know
an object is to know its nullity, or to know that it has no objectivity
outside the subject's knowing of it.[113] This clarifies for Marx the illusions at which Hegel arrives. Because of the philosophy of identity,
consciousness does not simply "know" the object, it must directly be
the object. The Hegelian knowing subject is offended by objectivity
itself, while the Marxian knowing subject is offended only by *alienated*
objectivity.[114] Thus the philosophy of identity leads to a false positivism
and false criticism. This becomes clear with the example of religion.
For Hegel, the criticism of religion qua self-alienation leads to the
overcoming of that alienation by establishing the self (spirit) in religion
qua religion. This is also why the critical struggle for freedom is achieved
in the consciousness of freedom.[115]

The critical function in Hegel's epistemology does not lead to real
transformation. For Marx, however, if one knows religion as alienated
self-consciousness, then the alienation is overcome only with the
supersession of religion itself and not simply of the alienated self-
consciousness of religion.[116] Hegel's dialectic as negation, then, is not
the positive affirmation and confirmation of "true being" *(des wahren
Wesens)* that it pretends to be, but it is the transformation of illusory
being into an absolute subject. Such a move culminates in equating
true human existence with philosophy, true political existence with
philosophy of right, and so on.[117] This view denies what Marx considers
to be actual political man, actual religious man, and so forth.

Thus there is a return in Marx to a concrete epistemological dialectic.
For example, in Hegel "private property *as thought* is superseded in
the *thought* of morality."[118] Marx demands more of philosophy and
epistemology. Overcoming private property in thought is a "false overcoming" since the real, sensuous object remains in existence in the
world. Or from another perspective, since the object is simply a moment of thought, for Hegel, its real existence confirms thought itself.
Again, we are confronted with what Marx sees as a *practically* uncritical epistemology. Knowledge must be grounded in the criticism of

real, sensuous existence. Hence Hegel's supersession is not of the real or of the object, but of the thought of the real or of the object as knowledge.

Finally, we arrive at Marx's concept of "real supersession" *(Aufheben)* which rests upon the concrete epistemological-practical human dialectic. For Marx, Hegel's notion of supersession as a movement which overcomes alienation contains an important but alienated insight. It is the alienated insight into supersession as the appropriation of objective being and into the real objectification of man. Supersession now appears as man's appropriation of his objective being by way of the destruction of the alienated character of the objective world or of an alienated mode of existence.[119] In this light, atheism as the *Aufhebung* of God results only in theoretical humanism, while communism as the supersession of private property results in practical humanism.[120] Put another way, humanism is the mediated negation of religion and private property. Marx's concept of real supersession recovers the concrete dialectic of human being. For now supersession does not mean the loss of the objective world, but the emergence of human nature as something real, created by man himself.

Therefore, although Hegel conceives labor as man's self-formative act, he conceives it abstractly and formally; the self-generative act is formal and logical since man is self-consciousness.[121] Thus the synthesis of subject and object which overcomes alienation results in a mere formal overcoming of alienation, which is to say a confirmation of real alienation. For Marx, this synthesis is not formal, whether it be the achievement of Kant's transcendental apperception or the movement of absolute spirit. Rather, the synthesis of subject and object (man and nature) lies in social labor, and thus is an achievement of the human species-subject producing itself in history. The synthesis does not take place in the medium of the dialectical movement of concepts, but in that of labor broadly understood. It thus expresses itself not in philosophy alone but in various historical systems of social labor.[122]

With this conception, Marx introduces a new "metasubject" in history. With Hegel, the movement of self-creation (the dialectic) is an abstraction and alienation of human life; it is a spiritual and "divine" process. The bearer or subject of the process (the metasubject) is spirit or *"God, absolute spirit, the self-knowing and self-manifesting idea."* Man and nature become mere predicates, and Hegel's identical subject-object is "mystical."[123] This is the only possible result if the philosophy of identity is presupposed: "the *absolute subject* as a process of self-alienation and of return from alienation into itself, and at the same time of reabsorption of this alienation, the *subject* as this process; pure *unceasing* revolving within itself."[124] One should remember that this is not an attack on spirit as such, but on spirit as a universal subject.

It is an attack on the fact that Hegel's dialectic (negation of negation) is the abstract form of the real, living act of human negativity; for Hegel, the content of that negativity is only formal. Thus these forms of abstraction must remain neutral to any real content, detached from "*real* spirit" *(wirklichen Geiste)* and "real nature."[125] The new meta-subject appears as the labor of the human species, or what one might term the concrete epistemological-practical subject(-object). Man creates while knowing and knows while creating; he is created in his knowledge and known in his creation. And the critical element of the dialectic of negativity extends to existent reality as well as to consciousness.

What, then, is Hegel's achievement for Marx? It is his demonstration that determinate concepts existing in independence from nature and spirit are results of the alienation *(Entfremdung)* of human thought and human nature, and that in reality they form a whole as moments in the process of abstraction. Marx praises this philosophy of internal relations and dialectical totality. But he recognizes that in Hegel's *Logic,* where this process is traced to the point of "absolute idea," we are forced to move into the realm of nature. The transition from the *Logic* to the *Philosophy of Nature,* where idea externalizes itself, is the movement from abstraction to intuition, and is difficult for the abstract thinker to accomplish. It is at this point that Hegel's dialectic breaks down. We are brought back to nature, and once we encounter it abstractly, we encounter nothing. In Hegel the whole of nature simply reiterates logical abstractions in "sensuous external forms." The philosophy of identity prevents us from going further. In other words, we are driven to admit that the externality of nature is really an "error" or a defect. Since idea is the truth, nature is the form of its "other-being" and as such is deficient being which must be superseded.[126] And thus in Hegel we must "return" to the *Philosophy of Mind,* again revealing the philosophy of identity. For Marx, on the other hand, to sustain the dialectic at this point of the transition to nature is possible only in praxis, the synthesis of man and nature through social labor.

Marx's Legacy

To conclude, we have seen that in Marx the synthesis which overcomes the distinction of subject and object is not based on a philosophy of identity and thus is not an absolute synthesis. To be sure, Marx argues for a unity of man and nature which is primarily the result of a subject. But the subject is a natural being and as such does not produce an absolute unity in which nature disappears into the subject. If nature is indeed determined by man, it still retains an externality, independence, and even a mystery beyond the efforts and reach of man. There is still an "objective" nature.[127] In other words, a dialectical tension between subject and object is maintained so that even if labor synthesizes man and nature, they both retain an objectivity and independence. Marx preserves this dialectical tension which originally and partially appeared in Kant's theory and receded in Hegel's philosophy of identity. There is a *metaxic* quality to dialectical theory; the dialectic is always somewhat ambiguous in character.[128]

However, even if nature has an objective character, it is still only available to us through our labor in history. From an epistemological point of view, nature itself is contingent. It is objectively independent from man only up to a point and insofar as it is not conceived of as the mere alienation or externalization of spirit. The objectivity of nature enters into a cooperative relationship with man once it is mediated by social labor. Nonetheless, that mediation never destroys the dialectical tension which appears with each new historical encounter of man and nature.

Within this framework, the outline of a new dialectical epistemological orientation begins to take shape. The synthesis of subject and object achieved through social labor appears as neither a logical structure nor an absolute unity. Although Marx views the relation quite differently than Kant and Hegel, he retains Kant's theory of the nonidentity of subject and object and Hegel's historicization of that relation; subject and object enter into changing relations with each other through history.[129] The process of labor transforms both nature and man, and at each turn in history, a new subject-object unity must be forged. It is for this reason that Marx never really argues for an "end of history."[130] Indeed, the dialectical union of subject and object becomes truly historical and open, in the sense that it is both contingent on and a product of the efforts of human beings creating and re-creating their social existence from generation to generation.

Thus Marx, like Kant, does not assume the guaranteed identity of subject and object, but he does hope that such a unity or dialectical identity can be achieved historically by human labor in the efforts to overcome alienation. In such efforts, human subjects know themselves through the labor of past subjects; the past becomes a conscious part of the present, a living memory. Above all, the new synthesis is conceived as both historical and relative, two characteristics which seem to be crucial to later developments of a dialectical theory of knowledge.

Perhaps before leaving Marx, mention should be made of an important criticism of the interpretation presented in the previous pages, a criticism which argues that Marx's view of the self-formative process of the human species through labor involves a "reduction" and thereby aids in the positivist atrophy of epistemology. The argument runs as follows: When Marx actually practiced his dialectical mode of inquiry, he conceived of history as being constituted equally by both material activity and the critique of consciousness, or labor and reflection; yet the philosophical self-interpretation of his inquiry seemed to be restricted to the level of labor. Therefore, rather than leading to a radicalized critique of knowledge, Marx's development too readily allowed for the emergence of an instrumentalist positivism.[131] Although such a criticism points to a problem in Marx, there is a question as to whether it is overdrawn.[132]

I prefer to argue for a different emphasis. Marx's critique of Hegel certainly focuses upon establishing the objectivity of nature and man and the sensuousness of human experience and knowledge. And in terms of the rehabilitation of material life and human laboring praxis, it makes sense that for Marx the phenomenological reconstruction of human experience and the history of mankind could not remain at the level of self-consciousness. This is the sense in which *Capital* might be regarded as a concrete *Phenomenology of Mind,* a reconstruction of the historical experience of the human subject in its totality. But the essential question is whether this development, along with the reconceptualization of the meaning of *Aufhebung* and the introduction of a newly interpreted epistemological and practical historical metasubject grounded in the labor of self-creation, is a "reduction" or a "dialectical corrective" to Hegel's critique of Kant. If the latter interpretation is accurate, it may be that Marx went overboard in his obsession for recovering "objectivity" and "labor," to the growing neglect of subjectivity. This is a point, as we shall see, to which the phenomenology of Merleau-Ponty is very sensitive. In any event, if we interpret Marx's project as furnishing a dialectical corrective rather than a reduction, then we are led to a new and crucial point in the evolution of dialectical theory.

Alienation is now isolated as the key to the Hegelian dialectic, and social labor, which includes both knowing and acting, is established as the key to the resolution of that alienation. In this sense, the epistemological synthesis of subject and object, of reason and the senses, is given a practical and radically human dimension. Marx leads us to an orientation which seeks the resolution and reresolution of subject and object in praxis and which therefore recovers what we might call the concrete epistemological-practical human dialectic. It is this point in the evolution of dialectical theory that sets the stage for our departure into certain twentieth-century philosophical developments of the dialectic.

We have spent considerable time with Kant, Hegel, and Marx in this chapter for three reasons. First, the developments of dialectical theory in their thoughts continue to yield important insights in their own right. Second, it seems important to establish firmly the roots of twentieth-century dialectical theory. Third, and perhaps most important of all, if we are without a sound awareness of the language, vocabulary, and way of thinking that emerge from these roots, it becomes inordinately difficult to comprehend the dialectical philosophical developments in our own century; our journey becomes more strenuous. We turn in the following chapters to more contemporary developments of dialectical theory that prove valuable for an enriched view of political inquiry.

3   The Development of Dialectical Marxism

In one of the most recent books published on political theory, John Gunnell argues that during the past decade the debate between behavioralism and revived political theory has subsided in favor of applied social science and public policy analysis.[1] This development is reflected in the emergence of university courses devoted to the rapprochement of political theory and public policy. As one who has taught such courses, I can attest to this new fascination of political theory with public policy issues. After all, one can find there attempts to bring questions of practice and "values" back into political science. Although to an extent this is a laudatory and promising endeavor, it often entails a lack of awareness of the kinds of questions and developments I have briefly suggested in the last two chapters. As we enter the postmodern age, it may be that political theory can become a new kind of enterprise, one that can go beyond any reconciliation of political theory and positivism through the midwifery of public policy analysis.

Therefore, in the next two chapters I focus on the seminal development of two twentieth-century movements which assist in reconceptualizing the epistemological and practical concerns of an enriched and broadened view of political inquiry: dialectical marxism and dialectical phenomenology. I deal with the potential union of the two in chapter 5. It is my belief that these two movements form the core of an epistemological orientation for political inquiry which emphasizes the dialectical ambivalence in our efforts to know and to act. It is an orientation which recognizes the illusion of unconditional objectivity without falling prey to extreme subjectivism, calls forth practically creative and critical engagement in the world without dismissing the importance of reflection, and argues for the historically relative nature of knowledge without surrendering the search for truth. What distinguishes these movements from other forms of twentieth-century "relativism" is that they embrace the dialectic of subject and object and the dialectical unity of theory and practice.[2] Furthermore, although the orientation which emerges from these movements is radically open-ended and contingent, it also entails a sense of political direction and commitment for the future.

Dialectical Marxism as Political Theory

Whether or not one concedes the idea of a more or less continuous tradition of political theory from Plato to Hegel, it is usually believed that the enterprise associated with that idea came to some sort of end with Karl Marx—or at least that political theory was never quite the same after Marx.[3] It is clear that Marx believed he was radicalizing previous political theory by arguing that it become a creatively practical and revolutionary enterprise, although it is not so clear that he wanted to dismiss or negate the numerous insights inherited from that tradition. As is well known, Marx hoped to realize the insights of past philosophy by abolishing philosophy qua isolated, merely contemplative philosophy. Whether this goal entails the abolition of reflection as such is open to debate. But it may be that Marx's intention resembles his view of "abolishing" art. If we live truly artistic lives, so the argument goes, then there may be no need for "art" as a special and isolated sphere of activity. Likewise, if we can live truly philosophical and reflective lives, then there may be no need for "philosophy" as a separate, professional, and specialized activity. Although it would be stretching the point, and although numerous protestations will abound, there seems to be a kinship here with Socrates. In any event, it is possible that Marx's development of dialectical theory calls for a fundamental reconstitution of political theory which avoids the two extremes of abolishing all reflective inquiry as such and of transforming philosophy into positivist science. In this sense, political theory would come to occupy a middle position between philosophy and science.[4]

Although Marx's thought can be interpreted variously as ideology, economics, sociology, history, or revolutionary strategy (and these views certainly have foundation in Marx), it is as political theory and philosophy that it is of interest to us. Regardless of the numerous ways in which Marx breaks from the history of political theory, he consciously inherits and incorporates much from that history: the classical Greek conception of the importance of community; the view of freedom handed down through Rousseau and Hegel; and the conception, also from Rousseau and Hegel, of human nature as "metastatic," or open-ended and constantly changing. As political theory, what has emerged

as most promising and most troublesome is Marx's dialectical attempt
to reconcile philosophy and politics, to realize philosophy politically.
"Marxism," although Marx rejected that term, was to become simultaneously political theory and political practice. Unfortunately, these
two "sides" of marxism have not developed hand-in-hand historically.
The living unity of the two has been aborted by Marx's detractors and
devotees alike. Detractors have argued that Marx's project destroys
philosophy and culminates in the practical enslavement of human beings.
The more generous critics take Marx as just another participant along-
side Hobbes, Rousseau, and Hegel in the great conversation of mankind.[5] Unreflective devotees, on the other hand, have lauded Marx for
having done away with a useless enterprise and for creating the new
ultimate science of man; this is the sense in which marxism has become
reified ideology, and thought has been reduced to an ideological weapon.

Marxism in its more open-ended and dialectical developments has
emerged as one of the most coherent and influential dialectical theories
of politics in our time. As political theory it argues, as we shall see,
that the process of human inquiry should become critical, constructive,
and future oriented, that the alienated dilemmas of philosophy be resolved both theoretically and in human political praxis, and that reality
be conceived of and dealt with in terms of its historical and social
relations. In other words, it argues that the real search for a free, just,
and truly human social existence is at once a philosophical and a political quest. Politics becomes more philosophically self-reflective and
informed, and philosophy becomes more politically grounded and
concerned.

As political practice, however, marxism's development has been
largely dismal. A major reason for this, I believe, is that the marxism
which has become politically powerful and well known has been primarily informed by the positivistic rather than dialectical development
of marxist theory. For Marx, the point of philosophy was to change
the world, but to change it on the basis of a thorough and nondog-
matically open understanding of the world. A politics informed by this
view would involve communal human action which is open, self-critical, and liberating. Instead, most marxist political practice, grounded
in a positivistic self-interpretation, has evolved in a nondialectical direction which construes the relationship between theory and practice
as an instrumental one. As such, the "metasubject" of history has
become the Party rather than free human laboring praxis. The practical
life of the majority of human beings has become the "matter" to be
worked upon and molded; the Party resembles an impoverished version
of Hegel's absolute spirit. If for the most part marxist politics has
transformed theory nondialectically and positivistically into ideological
apology and scientistic analysis, thereby destroying philosophy without

fulfilling it, then the development of authentic dialectical and critical marxist theory has found no political party and practice.[6] This state of affairs does not necessarily indicate the theoretical failure of dialectical marxism so much as it does the inordinate difficulty of the union of philosophy and political practice as a project for mankind.

Some Essential Elements of Dialectical Marxism

Before turning to an examination of selected examples of dialectical marxism, it is helpful to summarize briefly a few of the crucial characteristics of that orientation. An articulation of some philosophical points which distinguishes dialectical marxism from its positivistic interpretation, and which thus can assist an alternative view of political inquiry, focuses on the following issues: ontology, epistemology, the theory-practice relationship, methodology, the nature of history, and alienation. The dialectical view of these issues as grounded in Marx's own thought forms the departure point for twentieth-century dialectical marxism.

We have already observed how Marx inherited Hegel's ontological philosophy of internal relations, which regards all reality as dialectically relational. Reality is conceived as neither a collection of atomistic units nor an indistinguishable whole. Rather, it is conceived as a concrete totality of open-ended and changing relations.[7] Furthermore, all reality is in a sense social reality (or the reality of social relations) since our experience and conception of reality can never be divorced from our existence as radically social beings. Our perception and knowledge of, and our activity in, reality is always grounded in our sociality. This is not to say that all reality can be reduced in Durkheimian fashion to a certain conception or element of the "social," but that reality in all its dimensions can never escape relatedness to social being. Hence ontology is for Marx fundamentally social ontology.

To argue that all reality is social reality, if one is to avoid a sociological solipsism, makes sense only if society is not conceived as an ahistorically reified structure or as a set of logically independent units or factors. For Marx, each "factor" of reality we isolate for examination is a "relation." As such, each factor (be it state, labor, value, religion, class, man, or whatever) is not only related to all other factors (in varying degrees of explicitness) but also contains as its nature a cluster of relations which are the other apparently independent factors as well as its own core meaning. In other words, everything is related, but each "thing" possesses the "whole" within it as relations. Thus each factor exists in relation (connection) to all others and it exists as a Relation (it contains the whole of other factors as internal relations to itself).[8] If each factor of reality is related internally as an ensemble of relations as well as externally to other factors, it is also related historically to itself and other factors. As Bertell Ollman puts it, "each social factor [is] internally related to its own past and future forms as well as to the past and future forms of surrounding factors."[9] Reality, which is Marx's "object" of study, is no object at all; he does not examine "society" but "society-conceived-of-and-experienced-relationally," which is to say, in terms of its historical and internal relations.

Thus the nature of reality commands that Marx never really study "things"; he can only study "things-as-relations," which are forever changing. However, he does not deal with relations between things in terms of such concepts as "causality" or "linear determination," which requires a conception of reality as only externally related, closed, and self-contained units or factors. Rather, he deals with those relations in terms of such concepts as "expression" and "manifestation."[10] For Marx, both in reality and in our consciousness, the "subject" of examination is only given to us through forms of expressions and manifestations of existence.[11] Our conscious awareness of reality is always a conceptualized one. Thus, in rather Kantian fashion, the things of reality that we know are related to us through their expression and manifestation and through our conceptualized categories.

Marx's dialectical-relational conception of reality contains crucial implications for how we understand political inquiry.[12] Perhaps most important, the view that the basic unit of reality is not a thing (nothing) but a concrete, open-ended relation bridges such abstract bifurcations as cause and effect, nature and society, individual and society, fact and value, and so forth. In terms of the recent debate over the fact-value distinction, a distinction Marx rejected, Ollman argues, "if one cannot conceive of anything one chooses to call a fact (because it is an open-ended relation) without bringing in evaluative elements (and vice versa) the very problem orthodox thinkers have set out to answer cannot be posed."[13] As we shall see, the relational ontology of a dialectical marxism can be aided by existential phenomenology. If Marx wants to demonstrate that the abstract dichotomies of nondialectical social science ignore the relational character of reality as a dialectical totality, so Merleau-Ponty wants to demonstrate that those same dichotomies dissolve in the radical conjunction of self, others, nature, and history in the *Lebenswelt*.

We examined Marx's development of a dialectical theory of knowledge in chapter 2; it forms a central element of dialectical marxism. For Marx, knowledge intrinsically involves the concrete dialectical relation of subject and object and of theory and practice. A positivistic marxism ignores this dialectic in knowledge and becomes a "science of the real"; thought and knowledge become a mere reflection of the "laws" of history and society, and practice becomes the technical application of nomological principles in an attempt to predict and manipulate reality. Theoretical concepts become mere reflections of the material world. This kind of marxism forgets that philosophical concepts not only reflect the truth or falsity, the meaning or nonmeaning, of their ontological reference, but also continually and inherently reconstitute and restructure the nature of reality itself. For dialectical marxism, knowledge is not a compendium of systematically related propositions about "the world"; it is the active engagement of consciousness in a reciprocal relation with the world and thus is constantly caught up in a simultaneous knowing and changing of the world.

Marx's concrete dialectical epistemology, which intrinsically unites theory and practice in the process of inquiry, calls for partisanship to become involved in thinking (that is, to become critically reflective and self-reflective) as well as for thought itself to pursue truth not for its own sake, but in the interest of a world in the making. Indeed, seeking truth for its own sake, as investigation devoid of any interest, is ultimately impossible. Partisanship which is critically self-reflective does not abolish contemplation. In the words of Ernst Bloch, "Partisanship which has been 'thought through' proceeds in this manner to the end, with the *vita activa* not supplanting the *vita contemplativa,* but going beyond it."[14] Marx's epistemological orientation as epitomized in Thesis XI on Feuerbach suggests that wisdom's ultimate conclusion cannot be an "inactive idolatry of purely contemplative theory." The result of an artificial alienation of theory and practice in the process of inquiry can be dramatic: "One has only to remember that a disregard of the practical consequences in the age of the atom bomb has involved criminal irresponsibility."[15]

While the concept of "dialectic" forms a general principle and sensitivity underlining and permeating the entirety of Marx's thought, especially his view of the nature of knowledge and reality, it also informs his method and has pertinence for the methodological concerns of political science generally.[16] As a methodological principle, the dialectic serves several purposes for Marx.[17] First, it serves as a way of perceiving reality that remains faithful to our original perception of reality as an endless maze of relations and connections. Reality appears internally related and in constant change. An examination of one aspect of reality (such as a facet of nature) always involves us in an examination of other aspects (such as particular elements of society or history).[18] We begin with a perception of the interconnectedness and flux of reality and proceed to a clarification of the details and nature of those connections and their transformations.

Second, the dialectic is a method of inquiry. Marx's view that the world is relationally contained in each of its parts, and that real concreteness refers not to the particular abstractions selected for analysis but to the totality of relations, leads him to inquire into the internal relations within and between the abstracted units of reality. To be sure, we always begin our study with certain abstractions (such as value, class, or law), but we never lose sight of the need to return with these abstractions to their connections to the concrete relational whole of reality. Thus dialectical inquiry presupposes the concrete relational nature of reality and proceeds through the process of abstraction to analyze a particular subject in the different forms of its development and by tracing out its inner connections, only to return in the end to the "interconnected whole, to show the relationships between the parts."[19]

Third, the dialectic serves as a mode of exposition. The presentation of the material revealed by dialectical inquiry must itself be dialectical; that is to say, a work must appear as an interlocking whole and not as an artificially segmented and compartmentalized presentation of what is unified and connected in reality.[20] In writing about a subject, that subject must be treated in terms of its appearance from different perspectives as well as pursued into and out of the particular forms it assumes at different times.[21] Finally, it means that language and concepts themselves must be flexible, allowing different words to mean one thing, and one word to refer to many things, depending on the perspective and purpose of the moment.[22] In sum, truth for Marx is always ontologically relational and historically relative; it does not stand still for facile examination. The method of dealing with it must be appropriate to it.

For a dialectical marxism, then, the concept of dialectic appears as an important element in shaping our endeavors in ontology, epistemology, methodology, and in construing the theory-practice relationship. If we accept it as somehow an immanent constituting principle of both reality and knowledge, the dialectic tempers our quest and desire for absolute and final knowledge. For Marx, any philosophy which pursues truth as a static and eternal verity results in "irresponsible speculation and the reification of concepts."[23] This holds true as well for any positivism which tries to reify the objective world and our understanding of its "laws." And it especially holds true for a positivistic marxism that tries to objectify the concept of dialectic itself, transforming it into a transcendental principle or natural law, and thereby destroying its openness and vitality. For a dialectical marxism, the dialectic of reality and knowledge remains an open-ended and vitalizing principle incapable of any facile, rigid formulation. The dialectic is like a swift sparrow; we can shoot it down or put it in a cage, but we can truly understand it only while it is in flight, always a little beyond our grasp.

Knowledge is dialectically related to reality and history, which themselves are always in dialectical movement. Truth itself is dialectical, continually changing, and as elusive as it is real. The movements and facts of historical and social existence are not mere reflections of a superior true reality, even though things are always more than they appear to be. Nor are these movements and facts mere gestures and superficialities determined by the more fundamental laws and processes of nature. The "facts" of reality are relational and dialectical movements which simultaneously reflect and creatively redirect the actual development of the real human world. History is not simply the evolution of human wishes and dreams any more than it is the evolution of natural, determined processes. It is neither the unraveling of the *Weltgeist* nor the record of mundane, fleeting, immanent human efforts separated epistemologically and practically from a transcendent, immutable, and eternal truth. Rather, history appears as the synthetic activity of man and nature. It is the prolonged interplay of man and nature existing in a "reciprocally determinate relationship," open-ended in possibility, past and future, and thus it has a certain contingency. Yet it also possesses *logos* or meaning which gives it coherence and makes understanding possible, and thus it has a certain "logic." The former admission calls for man's creative intervention in the world while the latter calls for his careful understanding of it.

Marx's dialectical philosophy calls for reality to be viewed as the reflective and actively redirective existence of human beings in relation to a continually changing and relational world. Man as fundamentally "social man" is viewed dialectically "as a totality of social relationships, changing through history—and, in the last analysis, a being as yet undiscovered and unemancipated."[24] Man is the focal subject-object of history and reality: as subject he participates in the creation of the world; as object he is created by the world. He is the creator-creature of the world. Knowledge is the inseparable joint creation of subjective activity and external reality moving through history. Marx's dialectical-historical ontology and epistemology are again forcefully underlined and driven by the struggle for the unity of theory and practice.

The epistemological-practical quest for a union of theory and practice focuses particularly upon an understanding and changing of one of the most basic facts of our current existence: alienation. The attempt to understand alienation entails the effort to overcome it in the direction of wholeness and freedom. Freedom is understood, not as the absence of boundaries and obstacles to movement (including "mental" movement in speech or text), but as conscious activity ripe with meaning, and as the realization of man's creative and artistic talents and possibilities.[25] In view of our understanding of political inquiry, the concept of alienation plays an important dialectical role. It transcends the orthodox positivist dichotomies of fact and value, description and prescription, is and ought, and "political science" and "philosophical ethics." As a dialectical concept, it can be a powerful and clarifying description of a fundamental fact of human social existence, and at the same time it is a descriptive fact that carries within itself an implicit judgment and prescription concerning the value of human being. A political science concerned with the understanding and abolition of alienation is a political science in the service of concrete freedom and community, one that engages itself in the world.

The foregoing remarks have only indicated generally some of the essential elements of a dialectical marxism. They are rooted in Marx's own dialectical philosophy and need to be recovered and integrated in any dialectical and critical theory derived from Marx. An ignorance or rejection of these points results in an uncritical, scientistic marxism incapable not only of clarifying the world, but also of transforming it humanistically.

We turn next to a few individuals within the marxist tradition who have confronted positivistic marxism from the perspective of dialectical theory. Of primary interest is their criticism of the methodological and metaphysical forms of determinism which dominate positivistic and objectivistic conceptions of marxism, and which militate against the importance of freedom, human subjectivity, and moral responsibility.

Some Expressions of Dialectical Marxism
in Critique of Positivistic Marxism

In this section I have chosen only four thinkers among the many possibilities to represent the evolution of a dialectical marxism in opposition to its positivist variants.[26] Although there is a certain arbitrariness to the selection, it is not without method. Antonio Gramsci represents one of the first and still most promising attempts to counterpose a dialectical to a positivistic marxism. Georg Lukács is one of the earliest and most influential contributors to a dialectical marxism, working from within a more orthodox marxist environment. Maurice Merleau-Ponty's interpretation of marxism, as I shall argue in chapters 4 and 5 as well, is one of the most open of our century, indeed of the past four decades. And Leszek Kolakowski represents one of the more recent attempts to revitalize a dialectical marxism in the face of positivist orthodoxy. The lives of these four thinkers span the majority of our century. Gramsci and Lukács, and to some extent Merleau-Ponty, worked without the availability of Marx's early writings, yet remained remarkably true to them. Kolakowski began his theoretical endeavors within a Communist society. All four stand among the most creative, subtle, and open minds in the marxist tradition.

It is commonplace to associate individuals like Gramsci, Lukács, Merleau-Ponty, and Kolakowski with a "humanist marxism," or some would argue a "soft-hearted (and soft-headed) marxism." Although the former appellation is not totally unhelpful, I believe that their distinction as marxist humanists lies mainly in the common dialectical character and sensitivity which permeates their thoughts. With this introduction in mind, two warnings are in order. First, while it is possible to locate a kind of loose tradition of dialectical marxism, we would go amiss by thinking of it in terms of some sort of self-conscious and unified school or position. Second, what follows is not meant to be a complete and systematic account of the whole of these individuals' complex thought; it is simply a focused and, one hopes, suggestive reading of their contributions to the broad evolution of dialectical theory.

Gramsci

One of the earliest marxist thinkers to challenge positivistic marxism and recover dialectical marxism was Antonio Gramsci.[27] In the face of a marxism understood by Engels in *Anti-Dühring* as a series of scientific laws known as "historical materialism," and by Bukharin as a "scientific sociology," Gramsci's marxism appears so novel as to gain him the title "neo-marxist."[28] All of his theoretical endeavors are permeated by his opposition to positivistic marxism, which he sees as degenerate. Indeed, in his concern to contest the Hegelian ideas of Benedetto Croce (as Marx contested Hegel and Engels contested Dühring), Gramsci conceives of the need for an "Anti-Croce" which would bring together "not only the polemic against speculative philosophy but also that against positivism, mechanicism and degenerate forms of the philosophy of praxis [i.e., marxism] itself."[29]

The most dogmatic form in which positivistic marxism expresses itself is that of determinism: either a vulgar economic determinism for which an ideological superstructure is a mirror reflection of impersonal economic forces, or a metaphysical-historical determinism for which history is a reflection of a supreme, objective principle that preordains the end of history. But it also expresses itself in various forms of reductionism, nondialectical (or metaphysical) materialism, absolute historicism, and in the view that marxism exists primarily as a rigid, scientific "method." All of these forms are interrelated and commonly inspired by a positivistic understanding of human knowledge and reality. Gramsci protests against all forms of marxism submerged in the positivist dogma and spirit.

Essential to the criticism of positivistic marxism is the recognition of the centrality of dialectic. It is not only a principle active in reality and knowledge but one which links the two in the process of inquiry in a mutually reciprocal relationship. The dialectical unity of knowledge and reality, consciousness and existence, and subject(ivity) and object(ivity) forms the basis of the concrete dialectical unity of theory and praxis, which is for Gramsci the "philosophy of praxis." If the dialectic is seen as the core of marxism, then positivistic and deterministic interpretations of marxism are precluded from the beginning by definition. Positivism and determinism are forms of closure; they presuppose marxism as a closed system of propositions and laws. Yet the concept of dialectic requires openness, for it points always to the fundamental centrality of open-ended relations.[30] If reality consists of open-ended relations, then any attempt at a determinism becomes lost in the dust of concrete reality itself. Thus a dialectical marxism in general requires a quality of openness which is negated on principle by positivism and determinism. This openness is crucial for Gramsci.[31]

Gramsci especially rejects deterministic, objectivistic, and positivistic elements in marxism in terms of their consequences for a human revolutionary praxis. Deterministic marxism has a one-sided view of reality: "reality is a product of the application of human will to the society of things [and the dialectical interaction thereof]; therefore if one excludes all voluntarist elements, or if it is only other people's wills whose intervention one reckons as an objective element in the general interplay of forces, one mutilates reality itself."[32] Gramsci strikes at positivism and determinism in one blow:

> Every act of prediction presupposes the determination of laws of regularity similar to those of the natural sciences. But since these laws do not exist in the absolute or mechanical sense that is imagined, no account is taken of the will of others, nor is its application 'predicted.' Consequently everything is built on an arbitrary hypothesis and not on reality.[33]

Gramsci reintroduces human will and subjective elements to marxism in order to salvage the integrity of reality from objectivistic tendencies. This is particularly true in his criticism of mechanical understandings and justifications of a view of "external objectivity" and the objective unity of the world. Such understandings forget the historicity of objectivity itself: "Objective always means 'humanly objective' which can be held to correspond exactly to 'historically subjective': in other words, objective would mean 'universal subjective.' "[34] The kind of objectivity sought by mechanical views of reality is contingent upon the historical efforts of subjective human beings. In other words, the unity of knowledge and being, or subject and object, depends upon the historical achievement of the human subject, understood as the historically united human race.[35] In the face of positivistic marxism, as well as other forms of objectivism, this means nothing less than that knowledge and reality themselves are humanly and historically contingent and relative. The positivistic and objectivistic separation of human subjectivity and "real" objectivity is an illusion:

The idea of 'objective' in metaphysical materialism would appear to mean an objectivity that exists even apart from man; but when one affirms that a reality would exist even if man did not, one is either speaking metaphorically or one is falling into a form of mysticism. We know reality only in relation to man, and since man is historical becoming, knowledge and reality are also a becoming and so is objectivity, etc.[36]

Only if the dialectic of subject and object and the profound historicity of knowledge and reality are understood in this way can dialectical marxism be seen in its proper relation to both idealism and mechanical materialism.[37]

Not only, however, is the integrity of reality violated by an objectivistic marxism, but the consequences of such a deterministic self-understanding entail a distortion and vitiation of the role of human beings in history as well. There emerges a kind of fatalism which expresses itself either in quiescence or in a rigid aversion to compromise and adjustment. For if one combines "the iron conviction that there exist objective laws of historical development similar in kind to natural laws" (positivism) with a notion of "a predetermined teleology like that of a religion" (metaphysical determinism), one is led to the conclusion "that any deliberate [human] initiative tending to predispose and plan these conditions [of history and for revolution] is not only useless but even harmful."[38] Man is extracted from history, if not from life itself, to such a degree that history becomes in fact no longer human history at all; the active dialectical relation between the human subject and the facts of reality dissolves. While circumstances are making human beings, human beings can no longer make the circumstances human; the subjective human response to reality impotently disappears. To surrender the efforts of human will to an already determined History (this is more Hegel than Marx), is to presuppose mistakenly that history is an already constituted whole: "The unity of history . . . is not a presupposition, but a continually developing process."[39] History is an open process contingent upon the intervention of human subjective will if it is to move toward unity and the reconciliation of human beings.

Gramsci reveals what deterministic marxism disguises from itself: mysticism and political weakness. Economic determinism is the expectation that economic forces develop inevitably toward crises which will of themselves produce foreordained historical events. For Gramsci, this view entails nothing but "out and out historical mysticism, the awaiting of a sort of miraculous illumination."[40] Economic forces and crises produce only open possibilities, not mechanical necessities:

It may be ruled out that immediate economic crises of themselves produce fundamental historical events; they can simply create a terrain more favourable to the dissemination of certain modes of thought, and certain ways of posing and resolving questions involving the entire subsequent development of national life.[41]

Deterministic, fatalistic, and mechanistic elements in marxism operate as stupefying drugs for those to whom it speaks.[42] They allow objective "revolutionary Providence" to act in the place of human subjective activity. The futility of mechanical determinism, for Gramsci, must be demonstrated continually: "Indeed one should emphasize how fatalism is nothing other than the clothing worn by real and active will when in a weak position."[43] Dialectical marxism rejects the consequences determinism holds forth for the human subject in history.

Gramsci's criticism of positivistic marxism is directed also at the intrusion of positivistic and scientistic method into the self-understanding of all social and political inquiry. His criticism focuses upon the obsession with scientific prediction, its basis in the fact-value and is-ought distinctions, and the epistemological domination of social science by the natural sciences. The positivistic attempt to study society with the methods of the natural sciences leads to an impoverished conception of politics and political science, which is now subsumed under "sociology."[44] Gramsci's criticism here is twofold. First, it involves the uncritical scientism of positivist marxism as social science. He questions the value of "the so-called exact or physical sciences and the position they have come to acquire within the philosophy of praxis, a position of near-fetishism, in which indeed they are regarded as the only true philosophy or knowledge of the world." For Gramsci, what needs to be "critically destroyed" in positivistic marxism is the concept itself of "science," which "is taken root and branch from the natural sciences, as if they were the only sciences or science *par excellence,* as decreed by positivism."[45] Marxism must free itself from domination by a nondialectical, positivistic self-understanding of inquiry.

Second, Gramsci's criticism argues that positivistic method alienates subject and object and leads to a faulty understanding of politics. Under its direction, the importance of subjective human will and initiative is dismissed in favor of the search for immutable laws and conditions which regulate society. Such an effort violates the understanding of social reality as a totality of social relations involved in a process of continual transformation. Social reality is not amenable to objectivistic, scientistic dissection; nor can it be understood in terms of the separation of fact and value, is and ought. For social inquiry to deal exclusively with pure facts or the "is," results in superficial distortion. It is not a question of whether the fact/is should be studied to the exclusion of the value/ought, or vice versa, but whether the distinction is an accurate one. For Gramsci, the complex of social reality encompasses a necessary unity of is and ought. What is important is the manner in which the "ought" ought to be considered: whether as an object of "concrete will" or as "idle fancy, yearning and daydream." The real union of the "is" as effective reality and the "ought" as concrete will in marxism requires that we operate on the terrain of effective reality, but that we do so in order to transform it: "What 'ought to be' is therefore concrete; indeed it is the only realistic and historicist interpretation of reality, it alone is history in the making, it alone is politics."[46]

Thus Gramsci rejects the movement of positivistic marxism with its reductionist and determinist metaphysics and its uncritical faith in scientific method. He opts to develop a dialectical marxism where reality is conceived as a complex of relations which are open-ended and constantly changing. Positivistic marxism attempts to abstract reduced elements of reality as absolute determinants of the whole while claiming universality and objectivity. Dialectical marxism refuses this attempt. It also refuses to develop the dialectic as a scientific method of proof and prediction. The philosophy of praxis cannot be reduced to a science capable of predicting the future; prediction only has meaning if it is understood as the projection of the limits and goals of a "program."[47]

For Gramsci, marxism is a conception of the world and as such is philosophy. To be sure, it is a philosophy of praxis, but it is still a philosophy and not an uncritical ideology or a baseless pragmatism. It remains open to other conceptions of the world and does not close itself off to dialogue and interaction with them. In response to the positivist arrogance of having "surpassed" the primitive philosophy of the past, Gramsci offers a criticism:

> To judge the whole philosophical past as madness and folly is not only an anti-historical error, since it contains the anachronistic pretence that in the past they should have thought like today, but it is a truly genuine hangover of metaphysics, since it supposes a dogmatic thought valid at all times and in all countries, by whose standard one should judge all the past.[48]

Indeed, in the struggle against positivistic marxism, Gramsci goes so far as to claim that "the most important philosophical combination" to take place has been that between the philosophy of praxis (marxism) and "idealistic tendencies," and not that between marxism and scientistic positivism.[49] It is in the sense of the foregoing that positivistic marxism must be seen to misunderstand not only the meaning and value of marxism, but the nature of social and political reality as well.

Lukács

The primary contribution of Georg Lukács to the critique of positivistic marxism lies in his appearance as one of the first marxists to revitalize the philosophical, Hegelian dimension of marxism and to recover the centrality of the dialectic.[50] One of the major characteristics of positivistic marxism, or of the "vulgar Marxists," is the attempt to eliminate dialectics from a "proletarian science." This leads to a reality understood in terms of "obedience to laws" and vitiates the relation between theory and practice by viewing reality as an immutable, impenetrable objectivity. Thus it leads to a reductionist marxism. A dialectical marxism, on the other hand, insists upon viewing reality as a "concrete unity of the whole," as a totality of relations undergoing continual change, impossible to understand in terms of abstract, absolute laws. It perceives reality as an internally related totality, the various elements of which are incapable of reduction and absolute objectivization. Indeed, the change in any element entails change in relation to the whole, and thus the form of objectivity of the whole itself changes.[51]

In this sense, the empiricist and positivist attempt to understand the "facts" of reality as value-free and ahistorical is inadequate. Such an attempt is grounded in an ignorance of the fact

> that however simple an enumeration of 'facts' may be, however lacking in commentary, it already implies an interpretation. Already at this stage the facts have been comprehended by a theory, a method; they have been wrenched from their living context and fitted into a theory.[52]

If facts are inseparable from value-laden interpretation, they are also inseparable from their historical character. The facts of positivistic investigation are historically conditioned and do not exist as immediately given and ahistorically pure.[53] In order to understand any aspect of reality it is necessary to examine its historical character and its relation to the totality of reality. The pseudoobjective and -scientific method of positivism shatters this unity of phenomenon, history, and totality and results in distorted, abstract understanding. On this basis, a dialectical marxism cannot pretend to discover immutable laws which become traditions for preservation; otherwise it becomes positivistically reified and incapable of changing as reality itself changes; it becomes closed rather than open to the historical and relational character of reality itself. Dialectical marxism "is no guardian of traditions, it is the eternally vigilant prophet proclaiming the relation between the tasks of the immediate present and the totality of the historical process."[54]

A dialectical marxism grounded in an awareness of the relational concrete totality of life rejects such abstract dichotomies as subject and object, thought and existence, form and content, and materialism and idealism. Lukács's argument for the overcoming of these dualisms is evident in his treatment of the problem of the relations between freedom, necessity, and determinism. For Lukács, as for Marx, previous materialism and idealism were incapable of resolving the problem of freedom and necessity because both were caught up in an alienation of subject and object. Materialism dismisses the idea of freedom by subjecting man to the deterministic laws of natural necessity (pure objectivity), while idealism preserves the idea of freedom only to transform it into an ineffectual ghost (pure subjectivity). What is required is an awareness of the contingency of laws of nature, scientific laws, or necessity: "For it is only with the discovery of the 'intelligible contingency' of these laws [the universal calculus of positivism] that there arises the possibility of a 'free' movement within the field of action of such overlapping or not fully comprehended laws."[55] The apparently insoluble dilemma of freedom and necessity, or of voluntarism and fatalism, is a result of "the impossibility of comprehending and 'creating' the union of form and content concretely instead of as the basis for a purely formal calculus."[56] The dilemma arises out of a primarily abstract, one-sided, and contemplative approach to reality, and its resolution lies in the creative unity of theory and practice.

Thus the "solution" to the apparent dilemma of freedom and necessity, and of subject and object, does not lie in a dogmatic declaration for one side or the other. It lies instead, first, in a recognition that the acceptance of such antinomies as freedom and necessity as possessing a self-evident existential basis is based on the mistaken notion that thought enters into an unmediated relationship with reality as it is given. Thought is mediated with reality in a process of mutual creation and interaction, which is to say, in the concrete dialectic of subject and object. Both deterministic materialism, which claims that reality influences us "by virtue of laws alien to us," and abstract idealism, which retains the problem at the level of consciousness, miss the point.[57] And so the solution lies, second, in the recognition that the antinomies of thought cannot be overcome simply in thought but must be resolved in practical life by way of the conscious human creation of unalienated reality.

As we have seen with Gramsci, there are two types of historical determinism into which marxism degenerates. One involves a metaphysical determinism applied to history (the belief in a "grand logic"), for which Hegel is probably more justly criticized than Marx. The other involves an economic determinism applied to history, the theoretical seeds of which it is possible to discover, though imperfectly, in Marx's thought itself. Economic determinism claims that the political, social, and cultural substance of every historical "stage" is a direct function of the economic-material substratum of society. Metaphysical determinism asserts that there is an inevitable and inexorable linear progression of historical stages toward a clearly determined "final goal," the end of history. On the basis of Marx's dialectic, Lukács resists both of these nondialectical, positivistic distortions of Marx's thought. One of Lukács's important contributions to a dialectical marxism is the re-establishment of the contingency of history and the importance of conscious, subjective human action in history. The accomplishment of a social and political revolution is never guaranteed by mysterious forces; it "can only be the fruit of the *conscious* deeds of the proletariat."[58]

Thus Lukács argues against the notion of a metaphysical guarantee of the end of history: "the 'realm of freedom' is not a gift that mankind, groaning under the weight of necessity, receives from Fate as a reward for its steadfast endurance. It is not only the goal, but also the means and the weapon in the struggle." Freedom is possible only if "mankind consciously takes its history into its own hands." But the fact that freedom is contingent upon human efforts does not mean that history is totally fortuitous; it "does not negate the 'necessity' of the objective economic process, but it does confer on it another, new function."[59] Human beings cannot struggle for freedom above and apart from the process of economic forces which are never entirely in their hands; rather, their freedom is tied up with their developing awareness and control of their own socialization and destiny. It can be achieved only by consciously working with, not against or apart from, the forces beyond their immediate control. This is the meaning of the "making of history"; it is not made by fiat but only by a dialectic of subject and object in historically contingent efforts.

If the end of history is not metaphysically guaranteed, neither is the substance or quality of social existence in history absolutely dictated by autonomous economic forces working independently of human beings. For Lukács, the most that can be expected from the "logic" of history and the development of economic forces is the emergence of certain opportunities. Human beings can never ignore the empirical reality of economic conditions which shape their lives and possibilities, but neither must they surrender to absolute domination by any "autonomous" economic forces. A revolution in the system of production may be an "essential precondition" for political revolution, but "the revolution itself can only be accomplished by people; by people who have become intellectually and emotionally emancipated from the existing system."[60] Nothing is guaranteed by the development of economic forces.

Human beings must become aware of the "logic" with which certain economic and social processes have developed throughout history, and they must be able to emancipate themselves from the reified control of such forces in order to begin a transition to the conscious control of their own destiny. But the process is not determined by the economic forces; the emancipation "does not take place mechanically parallel to and simultaneously with economic developments. It both anticipates them and is anticipated by them."[61] This is what positivistic marxism forgets. And perhaps Lukács himself is derelict for occasionally forgetting that "objective economic developments" themselves are ultimately created by human beings. For although we must seriously face the difference between the "immediate capability of men" and the "historically mediated capability of mankind," to overobjectivize economic developments is ultimately to underestimate the potential of human beings.

Thus Lukács reminds a positivistic marxism that history and society are contingent and not determined by inexorable laws. Crises, which are expressions of economic and social conditions, are not resolved by deterministic forces in material life which dictate how we are to react. Thus "the course it [ideological transformation] actually takes does not, however, run parallel in any automatic and 'necessary' way with that taken by the objective crisis itself."[62] A crisis needs to be resolved by the free and conscious activity of human beings. The creation of a humanistic reality is contingent upon conscious human efforts. In this sense, "the realm of freedom" itself cannot be regarded as a "state" guaranteed of being attained apart from the human historical process which can lead to it. One must not "separate the 'realm of freedom' sharply from the process which is destined to call it into being."[63] A dialectical marxism cannot alienate means and ends; the goal becomes part of the process and the process part of the goal.

For all his contributions to the struggle against positivistic marxism, Lukács still in a sense dismisses inquiry into the idea of freedom, which is central for dialectical marxism. The proletariat "must not allow itself to be pinned down on the whole complex issue of freedom." Furthermore, "freedom cannot represent a value in itself. . . . *Freedom must serve the proletariat, not the other way round.*"[64] To be sure, Lukács is justifiably concerned with transcending abstract notions of freedom and making it concrete and practical. But to counter the claims of abstract freedom by making freedom totally subordinate to proletarian dominance does not solve the problem. Rather, by bracketing theoretical inquiry into the substance of freedom and by allowing a reified Praxis to reign over theory, it destroys the vital dialectic of theory and practice.

In other words, to argue that the proletariat use the state, not to serve the interests of freedom, but to hold down its adversaries, as Engels would also have it, is to alienate the "proletarian struggle" from its goal of freedom and human emancipation. By suspending the continual need for theoretical inquiry into the content of freedom, Lukács runs the risk of falling into a nondialectical separation of form and content. In his emphasis on man's conscious creation and control of his own history and destiny, which is the form freedom must take, he forgets that how we go about the struggle is constantly contingent upon how we view the content and goal of freedom. To lose sight of the content of the vision cannot help but distort the form of the struggle. When Lukács argues that "the 'realm of freedom,' the end of the 'prehistory of mankind' means that the power of the objectified, reified relations between men begins to revert to man," he correctly identifies freedom as man's conscious creation and control of his own destiny.[65] But although it is crucial that we create, it is no less crucial what we create.

Merleau-Ponty

Maurice Merleau-Ponty's is one of the most dialectical, open, and exciting interpretations of the problems posed by marxism in our time, and it forms the strongest impetus for the union of marxism and phenomenology in dialectical theory. Of special concern to Merleau-Ponty were the deterministic forms marxism had adopted since its inception, a concern prefigured by his struggle against positivism and determinism in his earlier development of phenomenology.

The argument for determinism requires that man exist as a "thing," an object, in order for him to be completely determined by external factors. The argument for absolute freedom, on the other hand, requires, as Sartre maintains, that man exist as pure consciousness. But for Merleau-Ponty, man is revealed as neither a mere thing nor a bare consciousness; he exists in both ways at once, in a unity of consciousness and body. Thus there is never determinism and there is never absolute choice. Insofar as we are born of a world which is already constituted, we are acted upon; insofar as we are born into a world which is never completely constituted, we are open to possibilities.[66] There is a dialectic of freedom and necessity. In this sense, Merleau-Ponty finds the dilemma over free will and determinism to be unnecessary:

> The rationalist's dilemma: either the free act is possible, or it is not—either the event originates in me or is imposed on me from outside, does not apply to our relations with the world and with our past. Our freedom does not destroy our situation, but gears itself to it: as long as we are alive, our situation is open, which implies both that it calls up specially favoured modes of resolution, and also that it is powerless to bring one into being by itself.[67]

There is always an ambiguity involved in trying to detect in this dialectical interchange the share contributed by our freedom and that contributed by the situation.[68]

The marxism required by economic determinism and mechanistic materialism claims to possess a conception of social reality based on ahistorical lawlike understanding. For Merleau-Ponty, this is a mistake:

> A Marxist conception of human society and of economic society in particular cannot subordinate it to permanent laws like those of classical physics, because it sees society heading towards a new arrangement in which the laws of classical economics will no longer apply.[69]

Economic forces in history are not given as an objective natural order; they are the results of projects which pass through consciousness with both interest and motive. These projects are a result of diversified intentions pursued in different ways within a complex, changing totality of human relations. Class consciousness, for example, is never simply determined by objective economic forces: one never becomes a revolutionary proletarian simply by virtue of the fact of one's objective position in the productive process, any more than one does only when one becomes conscious of one's situation in common with others. Rather, it requires an interchange of both. Neither class consciousness nor objective situation can be simply and directly deduced from the other.

Economic determinism ignores the subjective dimension of class consciousness: "what makes me a proletarian is not the economic system or society considered as systems of impersonal forces, but these institutions as I carry them within me and experience them."[70] To be sure, one does not exist as a proletarian simply by some intellectual operation devoid of concrete motives and concrete relations to society. But it is the case that there is a certain dialectical ambiguity between one's "way of being in the world" within a certain institutional framework and the consciousness one has of his situation. In this sense, a revolution is neither the result of blind economic forces operating apart from the conscious interests and motives of human beings nor the result of totally free and conscious unilateral choices by human beings. It is an ambiguous movement where certain crosssections of human beings (workers, peasants, and so forth) find themselves at a point where they all perceive something in common at stake. They are not brought to this crossroads by any "mysterious force," but neither do they completely choose how and when they will be there. Neither revolutionary nor reactionary class consciousness is a matter simply to be observed or decreed; rather, "before being thought it is lived through as an obsessive presence, as possibility, enigma and myth."[71]

Economic determinists forget that marxism is a nonreductionist philosophy of totality. They forget that "the greatness of Marxism lies not in its having treated economics as the principal or unique cause of history but in its treating cultural history and economic history as two abstract aspects of a single process."[72] The attempt to reduce all social and political existence to the economic order leads to the kind of abstraction from the whole Marx tried to avoid. The concept of dialectical totality militates against the reduction of the whole to one of its elements. Therefore, as Merleau-Ponty maintains, "Economic life is not a separate order to which the other orders may be reduced: it is Marxism's way of representing the inertia of human life; it is here that conceptions are registered and achieve stability."[73] History does not consist simply of impersonal economic forces any more than it does of ideas alone, separated from material existence. Nothing can be isolated in the total context of history. It is only "because of their greater generality" that

> economic phenomena make a greater contribution to historical discourse—not that they explain everything that happens but that no progress can be made in the cultural order, no historical step can be taken unless the economy, which is like its schema and material symbol, is organized in a certain way.[74]

If dialectical marxism rejects economic reductionism and determinism, so it also rejects the metaphysical determinism that results from the Hegelian conception of a rational history combined with the presumption of absolute knowledge concerning the meaning and end of history. Elevating history to the level of an absolute metaphysic leads in practice to the surrendering of human efforts to an unknown god, with the exception of the efforts of a "chosen few" who possess the secret and can "guide" the rest of humanity. Merleau-Ponty tries to salvage dialectical marxism from the consequences of this metaphysical determinism. He tries to salvage the notion of a meaningful history in which man plays a concrete and decisive role without allowing for *a* meaning to dominate human beings in the process. Thus he introduces the idea of a dialectic of meaning and contingency in history: "History has a meaning, but there is no pure development of the idea. Its meaning comes into contact with contingency at the moment when human initiative founds a system of life in taking up again the various givens." Contingency does not destroy the possibility of a meaningful history, but simply reminds us that "history does not work according to a model; it is in fact the very advent of meaning."[75] To dismiss contingency is to dismiss mechanistically the importance of human subjectivity in history. History is not a coherent system which develops in a straight line and simply awaits the gaze of our comprehension. If it contains rationality and meaning, so it also is not protected from irrationality, regressions, and nonmeaning.

A dialectical criticism of positivistic marxism reminds us that as soon as the freedom of human initiative comes into contact with any meaning in history, that meaning runs the risk of being missed, destroyed, or transformed into something else; there is no guarantee that meaning or rationality will survive. Human decisions can, and quite often do, bring unexpected consequences, and human beings respond to these surprises by inventions which often transform the original problem itself. To expect total knowledge of where the diversions of history might lead us is folly. To presume absolute knowledge of a predestined final solution to the problems of human existence in history is a mistake:

> One historical solution of the human problem, one end of history could be conceived only if humanity were a thing to be known—if in it knowledge were able to exhaust being and could come to a state that really contained all that it had been and all that it could ever be.[76]

Such a presumption ignores the dialectical openness and ambiguity of lived experience.

Thus Merleau-Ponty reminds marxism of the dangers of determinism, particularly of unconditionally surrendering to something which cannot possibly be known absolutely. Metaphysical determinism leads to the "adoration of an unknown god" understood as the "end of history" and can only result in the kind of reification and alienation which, for Marx himself, dismisses the importance of man-the-subject in history. To forget that "history does not have a direction like a river but only a meaning, not a truth but only errors to be avoided," is to hypostatize human praxis.[77] To surrender the efforts of human will to a reified "transcendental praxis" is to "eliminate human freedom with its spontaneity and risks."[78] A metaphysical determinism applied to history ignores Marx's poignant reminder: "It is not 'history' which uses men as a means of achieving—as if it were an individual person—*its* own ends. History is *nothing* but the activity of men in pursuit of their ends."[79]

But again, Merleau-Ponty's emphasis on the contingency of history does not lead to a rejection of any meaning or logic in history. The "logic of history" means, first, that "events of any order—and economic events in particular—have a human significance, that in all its aspects history is integral and makes up a single drama"; and it means, second, that "the phases of this drama do not orderlessly follow one another but move toward a completion and conclusion." And the contingency of history means that these events which form the order of a single drama "are nonetheless not rigorously bound together, that there is a certain amount of free play in the system.''[80] Without contingency, history would display no human qualities or flexibility. But without logic or meaning, history would display no structure: "History would never move in any direction, nor would it be possible to say that even over a short period of time events were conspiring to produce any definite outcome.''[81]

Dialectical marxism confronts positivistic marxism by arguing against a closed, deterministic view of history in favor of a view which is open-ended and contingent. But although history is open, it is not totally open. The freedom of our subjectivity takes place only in concrete contact with meaning and objectivity. Nevertheless, meaning in history does not form a monolithic unity but is continually altered by our subjective encounters with it at different times:

> We are not asserting that history from end to end has only one meaning, any more than has an individual life. We mean simply that in any case freedom modifies it only by taking up the meaning which history *was offering* at the moment in question, and by a kind of unobtrusive assimilation.[82]

For Merleau-Ponty, a dialectical marxism rejects the assumption that we can escape the confines of concrete historical conditions through the declaration of our absolute freedom. And it equally rejects the assumption that freedom exists only in the service of a history pre-determined in terms of both its meaning and its end—and in the face of which human beings have no avail. Rather, it calls for concrete engagement in changing the world within a framework of the dialectic of meaning and contingency, and of the ambiguity and uncertainty which accompanies our every act.

A Living Marxism and Leszek Kolakowski: Dialectical Contributions To and Fro

As a form of dialectical theory, marxism involves two relational forms of openness.[83] First, as an epistemological orientation for social and political inquiry, dialectical theory involves openness to the question of the absolute and hence a rejection of self-closure to transcendence. In this sense, it requires openness to the history of philosophy on its own terms, hence to its own history and heritage. But, second, it also demands that any absolute stance be recognizant of its own open-ended status; it requires the relative contingency of any absolutism, the openness of the absolute to the nonabsolute. This may seem a contradictory requirement, one which may never be resolved in dialogue or even approached from the two respective poles. The priest and the jester may never communicate if each insists upon the absoluteness of his resoluteness.[84] But a dialectical orientation to inquiry cannot require an absolute non- or antiabsoluteness, for then it falls prey to its own antiabsolutist critique. Thus in being necessarily self-critical, a dialectical marxist orientation can only be continually non-absolutely nonabsolutist.

The dialectical position creates a tension, but one created by the nature of reality itself. The maintenance of the nonabsolutist position requires a recognition and appreciation of ambiguity, uncertainty, and relativity. In contemporary philosophy, some have been able to maintain an open, nonabsolutist antiabsolutism (such as Merleau-Ponty's existential phenomenology) while others have fallen prey to their own critique by blindly adopting an absolutist antiabsolutism (such as Sartre's).[85] Those who are certain and absolute about uncertainty and nonabsoluteness have come full circle. In recent political thought, this same clash has appeared. While some perspectives have been able to maintain a truly "dialectical dialectic" and an open, relative historical-relativism (such as those of Marx, Gramsci, and Merleau-Ponty), others have fallen into the object of their original critique and have presented us with a "nondialectical dialectic" and a closed, absolute historical-relativism, a position untenable on its own premises (such as those of Engels, Lenin, Bukharin, and Althusser). The tension is related here to the realm of epistemology; but epistemology leads to the realm of ontology, and the relation between the two forms the basis for our understanding of the relation of knowledge and reality, and for an understanding of how we change reality.

Again, this viewpoint involves a tension, a tension ultimately irresolvable because a dialectical position can never require its absolute resolution nor contain the belief that absolute resolution is the necessary solution. Once this position, which is actually dialectical philosophy itself, surrenders to the tension or believes it has conquered it for one side or the other, then it truly surrenders its own nature and loses its grasp on the world. Hence dialectical philosophy, particularly marxism and phenomenology, can only continue to attempt the resolution of the irresolvable, which never means, however, that everything is irresolvable or that there is no practical resolution for what is resolvable.

In the face of dualistic tensions, no dialectical philosophy can choose for one or the other pole alone, for dialectical philosophy sacrifices nothing willingly and always wants "both."[86] We live as well as think this ambiguity, and in terms of a radical praxis, to forget it is to fall into the abyss of illusion and futility. But at the same time, we are called forth to transform and to resolve the various contradictions and tensions—and we have no other choice but to attempt it. We are faced with the apparently simultaneous and paradoxical impossibility and necessity of immanentizing a total eschaton. The jester must always desire to be the priest without actually becoming the priest and while knowing that to be the priest is to be dead.

Marx's epistemological contribution is often misinterpreted either as a form of pragmatism or as a form of positivism.[87] The latter position (found in Engels and Lenin) ultimately reduces knowledge to a rather simplistic and mechanistic mirror reflection of material reality; it is nondialectical both in terms of epistemological subject and object as well as in terms of ontological *en soi* and *pour soi*. Pragmatist theory differs from Marx's epistemology in another way. To put it crudely, for pragmatism something is true because it is useful; for Marx, something is useful and important because it is true, or can be true if it is not "actual." For positivistic marxism, practical activity is primarily the verification of prior theory. It is not simply an epistemological category as it is for pragmatism; it is confirmation of a correct understanding of the *en soi*, or independent reality. For dialectical marxism, to pose the epistemological question of the consciousness-reality relation either in terms of simple practical activity and our organic adaptation to it (pragmatism) or in terms of our attempt to "read" reality correctly and bring man and society into conformity with it (positivistic marxism) is to misconstrue the issue. The question should be posed instead from the perspective of consciousness and reality understood in terms of the reciprocally active creation of each other. Neither biological adaptation nor imitation and mechanical reflection is the proper formulation of the relation between consciousness and reality, or man and nature; it lies rather in the concept of dialectical and mutual creation as mediated through labor and accessible through active humanization. We neither create ex nihilo nor are we simply and completely acted upon by the overwhelming reification of the *en soi*.

The Left, informed by a dialectical marxism, should see itself in terms of the attempt to bring about the union of philosophy and politics.[88] Its task lies in Marx's formulation of the nature of political philosophy, which is to say, the correlative political realization of philosophy and philosophical realization of politics. In this sense, a vision of the good society is an indispensable aspect of the movement of the Left, if it is to have an idea of where it is moving and in the light of what.

Perhaps Kolakowski would be better off to utilize the concept "paradigmatic vision" instead of "utopia" for this idea. This makes sense if by paradigm one means a pattern, a vision by social consciousness of an end and of historical tendencies toward realization of that end. A pattern is just that, a general vision, not an individually constructed model or blueprint in what Kolakowski calls the "narrow" sense of utopia. In any event, utopia or paradigm is indispensable to the Left both as a vision of the future as well as a necessary and integral part of creating the conditions for a particular future. The tasks of traditional philosophy and "humanism" must never be discontinued. Althusser's demand for the replacement of "theoretical humanism" by "real humanism" must be amended by Garaudy and Kolakowski in the sense that the work of "theoretical humanism," or philosophical philanthropy, must be continued.[89] We can never reach the point of the political realization of philosophy, the actualization of the content and discoveries of humanism, and hence reach real humanism or concrete utopia, if we lose sight of that content by claiming that it has become either self-evident or obsolete and futile.

A dialectical marxism must further indict escapism for being based on an internal contradiction.[90] The escapist is indicted for his blindness to our inherence in the process which is the world, as well as to the inextricable connection between thought and existence, theory and practice. The indictment is based on the old truism that no choice is indeed a choice. Hence escapism is capitulation; to refuse to act is to act for those acts and forces which emerge and then to claim, "They had to come about because they had to come about, and I did not and could not have any part of it; my hands are clean." For the dialectical marxism of Kolakowski, Merleau-Ponty, and others, this is the most arid of human moral deserts. The result is the same for both the escapist and the epigone, who claims not to escape but instead surrenders to the "opiate of the demiurge," to Progress, History, *Weltgeist,* or whatever deification allows the attendant illusion of surrender of human moral responsibility. The motivations of the escapist and the epigone may be disparate, but the real effects are not.

Put most simply, Kolakowski attempts to demonstrate the necessity, desirability, and ultimate inescapability of human moral responsibility in the face of "relative determinism," historical necessity, and political choice. His demonstration rests partly upon the claim that determinism as a theoretical formula and ethical individualism as a practical attitude toward reality are not contradictory. To say that moral judgments and choices are not logically deduced from, or dependent upon, historical knowledge and necessity is not to say that we have a hopeless relativity and moral baselessness. It is simply to say that historical necessity does not determine morality. Morality is related to and emerges from social and historical contexts and is set within the limits of ultimately indeterminate necessity. But this is quite different from saying that that necessity is all there is, and that we cannot but choose to follow it. This connection is mechanistic and blind to the facts of human awareness themselves.

Values or moral choices are "unprovable" at base, and one works them out in conjunction with others in social and historical reality. But one cannot appeal to that reality in hopes of escaping or predetermining the nature, direction, and effects of those choices. Kolakowski attempts to make the individual realize his responsibility in any political and social movement. Only by rejecting monist absolutism in history and by rejecting a total appeal to a suprahistorical power—that is, by conceiving history as relativistic and morally contingent—can the burden of responsibility be placed where it actually belongs: squarely on the backs of individual human beings living and laboring socially.

In this sense, Arthur Koestler's dilemma is a mistaken one.[91] To choose to become a "Communist" or not on the basis of historical necessity and the unerring direction of history is, Kolakowski argues, to frame the question in the wrong manner. Historical necessity cannot dictate moral choice to us, unless we hypostatize and deify it. Any logical connection between historical "necessity" and moral judgment is untenable. As for the relation between utopia (or paradigm or "theoretical humanism") and effective reality, again, an either-or formulation is grounded in a faulty perception. Although Althusser is not completely wrong for opposing theoretical humanism to real humanism, he is looking at the relation in a maladjusted manner. The relation exists in terms of a dialectic of utopia and reality. It is only the pursuit of the hopes and demands of utopia in excess of the apparent possibilities of reality that allows for any real progress to be brought about out of the potentials of reality.

Kolakowski maintains that this is a major task for intellectuals: to formulate, criticize, and struggle for the excessive hopes and demands of utopia, and to do so continually and unrelentingly.[92] Like Gramsci, Kolakowski perceives the intellectual, spiritual, and moral bonds of society (Gramsci's notion of "civil hegemony") as possessing a stronger and more lasting bond and power than the relations of political power and force (Gramsci's notion of "political hegemony"). Hence the intellectuals' tasks of creating, interpreting, and formulating those bonds and the theoretical foundations and goals of political praxis are "indispensable conditions" for the existence and movement of concrete humanism. At one level, what is required of intellectuals is rigorous criticism of damaging, dehumanizing, and unexamined relationships between political society and the academic world of philosophy and science, which is to say, criticism of political restrictions on research subject matter, "politically correct" truths, scientific cynicism, "untouchable truths," and so forth.[93] For "Communist" intellectuals, these tasks are crucial for the salvation of marxist humanism at the hands of a politically powerful and dehumanizing positivistic marxism.

Kolakowski's praise of inconsistency is as much a recognition of the dialectical and ambiguous character of reality as it is an approbation.[94] It is a praise of the self-criticism and critical self-awareness that dialectical theory requires in the process of human inquiry. It is a praise of openness to the contradictions and antinomies of the world, tensions that inhere in the world, nature, and history. It is a willingness to accept uncertainty and ambiguity, which is to say, the complexity of human life itself, while struggling without illusions or guarantees to overcome uncertainty, ambiguity, and contradiction. When Kolakowski speaks of the "elementary situations" which defy and limit inconsistency, thus making inconsistency inconsistent (that is, the only "consistent inconsistency" is inconsistent inconsistency) he is really speaking of the core of humanism, including dialectical marxist humanism. That core contains the principles of human dignity, the integrity and intrinsic worth of every individual human person, and the indestructible value of human life. These principles are not open for dispute or suspension; they are not open for inconsistency; they are only open for clarification, concrete realization, and universal fulfillment.

These are some contributions Kolakowski offers to a dialectical marxism which is a living marxism. They are responses to the contributions a living, dialectical marxism offers to the human condition and the human project. A living, dialectical marxism is a marxist humanism; it is a rare philosophy in its willingness and inherent tendency to be wedded to the movement, ambiguity, and inconsistency of human life and historical reality. Hence it is a philosophy which is forced to struggle unendingly within the tensions that life and reality present to us. One thing is certain, and that is, that the project of such a philosophy can never consider itself finally said. For as Kolakowski puts it, the rest must be done.

4 The Development of Dialectical Phenomenology

Phenomenology and Political Inquiry

While it is not too difficult to discern the important role of marxism, as both philosophy and political inquiry, in the evolution of dialectical theory, such is not the case when we encounter phenomenology. As will become evident, phenomenology emerged in the beginning as a philosophical movement concerned primarily with epistemological and methodological questions and appeared to have no interest in political inquiry, prescription, or transformation. Furthermore, phenomenology has been seen to develop as a descriptive and interpretive rather than as a critical and political mode of inquiry. Even today, serious attempts to demonstrate the contributions of phenomenology to political theory often focus on its interpretive role.[1] I suggest that phenomenology, up to its appearance as "existential phenomenology," is not incapable of providing critical social and political understanding and prescription, as well as playing an important role in the evolution of dialectical theory.

It has already been suggested that the development of a positivistic marxism, rooted in the thought of such individuals as Engels, Lenin, and Bukharin, has on the whole suppressed the philosophically critical and methodologically dialectical character of marxist theory. Not only has positivistic marxism led to forms of economic reductionism, determinism, and methodological scientism, but it ignores epistemologically the interior and subjective dimensions of human social life. Although some of the more important exceptions have been noted in chapter 3, in general, marxism has developed positivistically to the point where it has become objectivistic and antiphilosophical. But if

90

this has been the fate of marxism, on the whole, the opposite has been true of phenomenology.

The two movements of contemporary existentialism and phenomenology were born respectively with Kierkegaard and Husserl as endeavors unconcerned with political life. The former surfaced as a subjective concern with man's inner life, while the latter emerged as a transcendental-subjective concern with "essences." The fusion of these two movements in an "existential phenomenology" has too often resulted in a concern for subjective intentionality and as a method of pure description; as such, it has often become subjectivistic and anti-political, or at least unpolitical. Just as we have witnessed attempts at the "rephilosophicalization" of marxism as a dialectical and critical theory of politics, so we can witness attempts at the "politicization" of the concerns of existential phenomenology as a radical theory of method, description, and interpretation.

In the twentieth century, we have been confronted by two major, influential philosophical movements: phenomenology and the linguistic, or ordinary-language, philosophy which grew out of positivistic analytic philosophy.[2] For Continental philosophy, Husserl appears as a major turning point for contemporary thought, whereas for Anglo-American philosophy, it is Wittgenstein who has primarily served that function. These two movements have reached the point where phenomenology appears to Anglo-American philosophers as an exotic trend, "metaphysical poetry," and muddled thought, while ordinary-language philosophy appears to Continental philosophers as "trivial, philistine, and infra-philosophical." This situation has often led to an impasse: "While there exist two major living, vital, expanding movements in philosophy today, both of them interested in communication, and one of them expressly centered on the analysis of language, they cannot understand one another."[3] Although James Edie wrote these words more than twenty years ago, they still seem to hold considerably true today.[4] As we shall see, it is phenomenology that ultimately appears as one of the most important developments of post-Kantian dialectical theory capable of informing contemporary political inquiry.[5]

Phenomenology is a form of "critical philosophy" characterized by its continually self-aware and self-critical efforts to penetrate to radical foundations. One proponent goes so far to argue that it is not simply another philosophical position or view, but that "phenomenology *is* critical philosophy."[6] As an attempt to penetrate simultaneously to the foundations of both consciousness and the "things themselves" of experience, phenomenology unifies the classical interests of rationalism and empiricism. Like dialectical marxism, phenomenology attempts to confront the totality of reality. By attempting to deal with both radical foundations and the totality of experienced reality, phenomenology

seems to compensate for deficiencies in both positivism and ordinary-
language philosophy. The former confines itself to the physically observable world and neglects the subjective, intentional dimensions of
experience. The latter relegates itself to a "second-order" discipline
whose purpose is to clarify the language about experience and reality;
as one critic has it, here the philosopher becomes a "janitor in the hall
of science."[7] Finally, in the face of both positivistic marxism and the
objectivistic behavioralism of recent political science, phenomenology
tries to recover the importance of subjectivity as an indispensable dimension for understanding and acting in the social and political world.

One could argue that it is up to a self-critical and dialectically sensitive political science to lend an ear to a critical philosophical method
capable of penetrating to the foundation of reality and knowledge. But
of course it is not "up to" any hypostatized "political science" to do
anything, any more than it is "up to" phenomenology to become politically oriented and engaged. It is, however, our responsibility as
students of, and participants in, social and political life to engage ourselves in an effort to unite philosophy and politics. In the face of current
forms of political theory and practice, dialectical marxism and existential phenomenology form a possible foundation for such an effort.
Both of these movements provide insights into how we can prevent
political science from alienating the perennial questions of political
theory (philosophical anthropology, philosophy of history, the quest
for the good society) from the historical realities and exigencies of
everyday life. Both can inform a political science which does not encounter the present as an ahistorical "given" to the neglect of the past
and the universal, and which does not seek the abstract universal to
the neglect of the concrete particularity of everyday lived experience.
An examination of the manner in which dialectical marxism and existential phenomenology can converge to provide these kinds of insights
is deferred until the next chapter. For now, our attention is directed
to the development of phenomenology as it bears upon the foregoing
issues.

Phenomenology from Husserl to Merleau-Ponty:
From Transcendental to Existential Philosophy

It is scarcely possible in one chapter to give due treatment to the
complex history of phenomenology.[8] What follows is a brief rendering
of one possible interpretation of that history, centered around a few
of its major figures. Special attention is devoted to those individuals
who have contributed most abundantly and creatively to the emergence
of an existential phenomenology which is both dialectical and relevant
to political inquiry.

Husserl

Phenomenology emerges with Edmund Husserl as a self-conscious movement, a form of transcendental philosophy.[9] As such, it draws inspiration from the Kantian roots of all transcendental philosophy. Phenomenology parts company from Kantian philosophy, however, by removing the restrictions Kant placed on investigating the foundations of transcendental subjectivity as such. In light of the goal set by Husserl, Kant's transcendental philosophy is considered to be "far from accomplishing a truly radical grounding of philosophy, the totality of all sciences."[10] In any event, as a form of transcendental philosophy, Husserl's development of phenomenology is a response to the objectivistic, uncritical self-understanding of science, which takes the natural appearance of the world as given and final.[11] Transcendental philosophy itself, however, attempts to penetrate to the foundations of consciousness and the objects of consciousness and inquires "back into the ultimate source of all the formations of knowledge"; it involves "the knower's reflecting upon himself and his knowing life," in a self-critical, self-reflexive manner.[12] As a mode of penetrating to foundations, phenomenology emerges as a particular self-understanding of philosophy.[13] Indeed, for Husserl, the whole movement of modern philosophy leads in the direction "toward a *final form* of transcendental philosophy— as *phenomenology*."[14]

In order to penetrate to the foundations of knowledge and experience, Husserl developed phenomenology as a pure philosophical method free of all presuppositions. The phenomenological reduction *(epochē)* is developed as a method by which the intentionality of everyday life is suspended in order to "grasp the world" as essential phenomena. Intentionality signifies the relationship between consciousness and an object, through which consciousness in active experience indicates, interprets, and "constitutes" the object of the relation.[15] In other words, it is the way consciousness directs itself toward objects in order to give meaning to and structure experienced reality. But that meaning of intentional experience is neither objective nor subjective; it emerges at the point of contact between consciousness and the world. And it constitutes the "natural attitude" of everyday life and experience.

The "phenomenological reduction" methodically suspends or "brackets" all judgments contained in the dogmatic natural attitude toward the world in order to recover from the beginning the constitution and essence of our cognitive relation to the world of things.[16] The phenomenological reduction is the method of returning without presuppositions to the "things themselves" and to the foundations of our intentionality in the world. The transcendental *epochē*, which is necessary for the phenomenological reduction, is thus a philosophical act of pure reflection. This does not lead to a study of isolated essences, but to a study of essences as they are abstracted from the unity of concrete experience in order to transform them into concepts which rediscover and explain that experience. It is only with such a phenomenological method, Husserl argues, that true science and philosophy can be radically grounded. By clarifying the transcendental origins of the world contained in our intentional experiences, the phenomenological reduction requires that science critically re-examine its foundations:

> Thus I disconnect all sciences relating to this natural world. . . . I make absolutely no use of their standards. I do not adopt a single one of their propositions however evident these propositions may be; I take none of them, no one of these propositions serves me as a foundation.[17]

The phenomenological method calls for a thorough and continual self-examination of all forms of knowledge.

In his struggle against uncritical objectivistic science, then, Husserl emphasizes the importance of radical foundations, critical self-inquiry, and the intentionality of consciousness. The entire enterprise is aimed at a recovery of the "intentional origins" of meaning in the world, that is, of the subjective or "intersubjective" constitution of the world itself as it is and as it is concretely given.[18] But this is no return to a mere relativistic psychological subjectivism. Rather, it is an argument for a "transcendental subjectivity" which constitutes the world and emerges as a kind of radical empiricism.[19] Husserl's transcendental phenomenology appears as a kind of empiricism only insofar, first, as it confronts what is directly experienced in the world and, second, as the "things" of experience form the criteria for knowledge and evidence. But as radical empiricism, it goes beyond the empiricism of the classical tradition from Locke to Russell, and presupposed in positivism, by arguing for a richer and expanded realm of experience than that restricted to particular sense data alone. It thus goes beyond traditional empiricism as well as traditional rationalistic idealism.[20] It is idealism insofar as it returns to consciousness which intends and constitutes the world, but not to the point where the essences of any ultimate reality exist transcendentally and independently of the concrete world of lived experience.

In the face of previous rationalism and empiricism, Husserl's phenomenology serves a purpose similar to that of Marx's *Theses on Feuerbach*. Both Marx and Husserl recognize the uncritically blind and reductionist character of past materialism and empiricism. A primary target of criticism for phenomenology is the uncritical scientific naturalism which becomes the basis for the "positivistic restriction of the idea of science."[21] Phenomenology serves to reveal the philosophical and transcendental subjective foundations of empiricist science in order to ground a truly universal, self-clarified science. Yet at the same time, phenomenology refuses to separate philosophical reflection from its basis in the lived experience of the world. As Thévenaz comments on Husserl, "It is not possible to stop experiencing the world—not even, and especially not, when one reflects on it, for reflexion is still a way of intending the world."[22] The separation of subject and object, and of consciousness and life, which Marx attacked as constitutive of both rationalism and empiricism, is criticized by phenomenology for ignoring the fact that lived intentional experience is the essential root of philosophical reflection itself. Thus the detachment of philosophy from life is misleading. Again, as Thévenaz puts it, "Philosophy is involved in life, and when one imagines that it is detaching itself, it is because it is living the world differently, more intensely."[23]

The radical empiricism of the phenomenological method finally leads us to the centrality of the lived world, or life-world *(Lebenswelt).*[24] The *Lebenswelt* is the prereflective, preconceptual, intersubjective, and immediately experienced world of everyday life. It is this foundational world which is forgotten and ignored by the development of scientific objectivism. For Husserl, scientific objectivism results in the mathematization of nature, which is to say, it results in a mathematical reconstruction of empirically observed processes. In so doing, scientific objectivism selectively idealizes and distills the fuller meaning of the *Lebenswelt,* upon which it is ultimately dependent. Thus scientific work ignores its historical presuppositions and unreflectively takes the lifeworld for granted. In other words, the prescientific presuppositions of science in the everyday life-world are neglected, resulting in a loss of the subjectivity of science and of the need for the self-investigation of the foundation of science itself.[25]

Phenomenology sets out to recover the "standpoint of subjectivity" in the *Lebenswelt* by which the nonscientific presuppositions of science might be illuminated. We are faced here with two "worlds": the "objective-scientific" world of positivistic science, which is a nonperceivable, nonexperienceable, theoretical-logical substruction of the world, and the "subjective" life-world, which is actually experienceable and self-evidently, immediately given and experienced in perception as the "thing itself." Knowledge of the former world is grounded in the self-evidence of the latter world.[26] Despite appearances, however, the establishment of this important relationship does not lead us to the recovery of the world as "ours" in an existential and historical sense; the concept of the *Lebenswelt* is a philosophical not a historical one. Once we reach the *Lebenswelt,* it is bracketed by the transcendental

epoché in order to grasp the transcendental-phenomenological constitution of the life-world in its essential and ahistorical structure.

In other words, the recovery of the *Lebenswelt* in trancendental
phenomenology ends by leading us not toward but away from the world
of concrete historical existence. We are led to the "absolute" transcendental subjectivity which constitutes the world. We find that the
totality of the *Lebenswelt* itself is structurally dependent upon the
intentional object-constituting consciousness, understood as absolute
transcendental ego. Thus, in a rather Hegelian manner, we are led to
recognize that the *Lebenswelt* and mankind itself exist "as a self-ob-
jectification of transcendental subjectivity which is always functioning
ultimately," and thus functions absolutely.[27] Husserl wants to return
to the subjectivity which ultimately "aims" and constitutes the world
in order to recover the relationship between science and the natural
human life interests.[28] Naturalism, positivism, and scientific objectivism have ignored this need and thus have resulted in an alienation of
science and life. Therefore, although Husserl's desire hints of the unity
of theory and practice, it falters by demanding an absolute and objective
basis in transcendental subjectivity.

In *The Crisis of the European Sciences,* Husserl is motivated by a
perceived link between theory and practice. He believes that the "radical life-crisis of European humanity" is linked to a theoretical crisis
brought on by the positivization of science, resulting in a life-alienated
objectivism. One witnesses here another similarity between Husserl
and Marx. Not only are both motivated by a profound radicalism in
method and conception of philosophy and a shared antipathy toward
both rationalism and empiricism, but Husserl in the *Crisis* appears to
recognize the importance of the link between philosophy and political
praxis. However, for Husserl the solution to the problems of social
and political praxis lies in pure theory itself. The problem here is twofold. On the one hand, transcendental phenomenology as the pursuit
of pure description offers no basis for critical evaluation and judgment
of social and political life. Despite his intentions, Husserl exhibits his
own form of objectivism and detachment by arguing that the phenomenologist qua phenomenologist leads only a theoretical life, a life of
pure *theoria,* and thus is incapable of evolving in the process of inquiry
itself practical criticism of political life. The goals of a transcendental
or "pure" phenomenology must perforce require abstinence from direct critical evaluation of social and political life.

On the other hand, given Husserl's concern in the *Crisis* for the practical political state of Europe in the 1930s, his response to conditions
of real historical life remains an abstract, impotent one and retreats into
the realm of traditional theory. The crisis of the sciences, Husserl argues, can be solved only by a philosophy and science reconstituted

by transcendental phenomenology. But the solution to the social and political crisis for Husserl is the same! He sees only two escapes from the crisis of European existence. One is the downfall of Europe into barbarity, which is what actually happened, and the other is the rebirth of Europe through a "heroism of reason that overcomes naturalism once and for all."[29] In other words, the resolution of both the philosophical and the political crises lies in the domain of pure philosophy itself. Husserl seems accurate in his assessment that the objectivistic, positivistic development of the sciences has resulted in the impossibility for theory to provide a rational basis for life. But he errs in believing that the alienation of theory and practice can be overcome by transcendentally, phenomenologically grounded theory itself.[30] Transcendental phenomenology leaves us powerless in the face of social and political reality. This is where Husserl forgets Marx's reminder that the problems of philosophy must *also* be solved in practical life, and that philosophy can only realize and fulfill itself by abolishing itself as pure, isolated theory.

Various points of congruence emerge between Marx and Husserl. They share the view that philosophy must be critical, especially of various forms of objectivism and absolutism which disguise the nature of lived, concrete reality. They share an intense radicalism which desires to go to foundations, especially in returning us to the world as it is lived and experienced apart from philosophical and scientific mystifications and abstractions. They both recognize that philosophy is grounded in the experiences of everyday life. They both desire to confront the totality and interrelatedness of reality. Husserl's discovery of the radical intersubjectivity of the *Lebenswelt* leads us to a recollection of the radical social character of human life so crucial to Marx's thought. And they both, Husserl particularly at the end of his life, recognize the need for theory to confront and inform praxis, and for philosophy to be realized in life. Yet despite these congruences, which seem to facilitate the development of a critical phenomenology of political society, the founding of phenomenology with Husserl, as transcendental philosophy, points primarily in a nonpolitical direction.

Heidegger

The largely nonpolitical beginnings of phenomenological philosophy in Husserl's thought were maintained and continued in the thought of his most important student, Martin Heidegger.[31] Although Heidegger contributes very little to the evolution of dialectical theory, his thought is worthy of brief mention because of his importance in the development of phenomenology. With Heidegger, phenomenology begins to move away from Husserl's late idealism and toward an interest in the realm of existence; transcendental phenomenology becomes existential phenomenology. Heidegger's goal is to uncover the structure and meaning of the *Dasein* ("Being-there"), which is understood as the "Being-which-we-are," or human-being-in-the-world.[32] The phenomenological reduction so important to Husserl is discarded as something that can lead only to the realm of transcendental subjectivity and "ideal essences." For Heidegger, the point of phenomenology is to get at man's concrete "ek-sistence," which is possible only by analyzing the *Dasein* without the encumbrance of the transcendental ego, or the concept of transcendental subjectivity. Phenomenology now searches for the ontological meanings of concrete existence. Thus Heidegger's phenomenology becomes a *Fundamentalontologie* which seeks to uncover the categories of existence and show the relation between the *Dasein* and the "world." In this way, Heidegger begins to transform phenomenology from transcendental to existential philosophy.

However, as we inquire more deeply into Heidegger's project, we discover a number of problems with his development of an existential phenomenology, especially in light of the evolution of dialectical theory. First of all, his work often reveals a more fundamental concern with ontology than it does with concrete human existence. Although he argues, for example, in favor of the importance of the historicity of existence, there is something ghostly and fleshless about the existence of which he speaks. It lacks a serious reference and sensitivity to what seems to be truly human, in the sense of concrete individuals. Furthermore, Heidegger's conception of historicity is nondialectical. Unlike that of Hegel and Marx, Heidegger's historicism possesses no sense of *Aufhebung* which would allow for the reintegration of past and present. Rather, his approach is often characterized by a desire to abolish or destroy absolutely the lived meaning of the past. To an extent, he shares with Nietzsche a nondialectical historicist conception of knowledge and reality.[33]

In a sense, Heidegger's phenomenology becomes not so much an "existential" as a "hermeneutic phenomenology."[34] There is a sense in which it is always a preparatory enterprise concerned with "meaning" and becomes ever more removed from a serious interest in concrete human existence. Phenomenological inquiry into human existence is transformed into an interpretive preliminary to ontological inquiry into Being. The analysis of the *Dasein* goes beyond an interest in the things themselves to an analysis of the Being of all beings. Heidegger further radicalizes Husserl by making explicit the ontology implied in phenomenology's search for the foundations of knowledge and experience, a search which points in a transcendental direction. Phenomenology as *Fundamentalontologie* now asks, according to Heidegger, the only real question: "What is the meaning of Being?" Unlike Husserl, Heidegger is no longer concerned simply with the foundations of knowledge, but with the ultimate foundation of Being, which makes possible the meaning of all Being, including human being. It is clear how the original existential themes of Heidegger's hermeneutic phenomenology become ontological themes.

The search for the foundation of all foundations ultimately leads us to a dead end in Heidegger, unless one considers the arrival at nihilism and obscure mysticism to be a "live end." This is evident in Heidegger's notion that the most fundamental character of human existence is the projecion of death. Although this is a complex issue in his thought, and although Heidegger does allow that "authentic existence" involves our willingness to "choose" the world that is given to us, there still seems to be a strong emphasis placed on human existence as Being-toward-death. On the ontological level, the search for the foundation of foundations leads to the conclusion that the foundation of Being is Nothingness.[35] The going beyond of all foundations leads to the radical Nothingness of all foundations, to the "void without ground" *(Abgrund)*. Thus Heidegger's *Fundamentalontologie* leads us to a beyond-ontological Nothingness and results in a *méontologie,* which is to say an "ontology of non-being."[36]

From his early concern with the structure of the concrete existence of man in the world, or with the *Dasein* as the place of all places where Being manifests itself, Heidegger is led to an obsession with the ultimate foundation and revelatory character of Being. Although he contributes the important notion that meaning is not simply "given" to the world, but is "received" from the world in our encounter with it, we discover in the end that Being actually reveals man rather than the other way around. There seems to be no authentically existential phenomenology here, but instead a concern with Being revealing itself. Thus human existence becomes a manifestation of Being, the ultimate foundation of which is Nothing. In the same sense, the fact that man can participate in the "revealing of what is" does not indicate that he possesses freedom in the face of the world; rather, freedom "possesses" man.

Regardless of these problems in Heidegger's thought, at least in terms of a dialectical theory of knowledge, we should not minimize his influence on the further evolution of phenomenology. Nor should we ignore the different ways in which Heidegger shares the concerns of other dialectical theorists. His critique of the oppressive power of modern technology to subvert the very nature of critical thinking with a form of instrumental rationality stands as a monumental contribution to later dialectical and critical theorists. His influence on Lukács and especially Marcuse, for example, should not go unmentioned. Indeed, there is much in Heidegger's thought that adds to our understanding of the philosophical shortcomings of all forms of objectivism and scientism. There is still probably much to be gleaned from his critique that might aid in our understanding of human inquiry.

In any event, with Heidegger phenomenology has moved to a sort of metaphysics, and ultimately to a transmetaphysics which ends up in a mystical nothingness. This attempt to move beyond Being shares somewhat in the spirit of Hegel's endeavors, especially insofar as "thought" *(Denken)* is seen as capable of comprehending all things. More important, Heidegger's development of phenomenology is iron-ically close to Husserl's later search for "essences," especially when compared to the developments of Sartre and Merleau-Ponty. Ulti-mately, Heidegger's neglect of concrete human existence pushes the concerns of social and political life to the periphery of phenomenology. Indeed, the fact that existential phenomenology was developed in its early stages as philosophy without any inherent connection to a dia-lectical and critical theory of political life is evident in the ease with which Heidegger overtly supported a political movement which could hardly be called self-critical or dialectically open, much less humanist. Regardless of the importance of some of his insights into the social and political problems of our time, especially his critique of technological modes of thinking and living, I would argue that Heidegger seriously hinders the evolution of a dialectical theory that can inform contem-porary political inquiry.[37]

Sartre

As is well known, phenomenology is developed in a thoroughly ex-istentialist direction by Jean-Paul Sartre and Maurice Merleau-Ponty. One of the earliest expressions of existential phenomenology is found in Sartre's *Being and Nothingness,* which stands as probably the most famous of the two men's efforts.[38] Like Heidegger, Sartre returns to the work of Husserl in order to radicalize transcendental phenome-nology, and like Heidegger, he returns to Husserl in order to demon-strate the superfluity of the concept of transcendental ego.[39] Unlike Heidegger, however, Sartre's rejection of Husserl's transcendental ide-alism and the transcendental ego is not aimed at uncovering the priority of revealed Being, but at evoking the importance of real creative ex-istence. His radicalization of Husserl's phenomenology is an attempt to humanize it, not by focusing upon transcendental subjectivity or the *Dasein,* but by centering analysis on the existential, individual person.

Sartre's endeavor to "existentialize" phenomenology is grounded in his understanding of human existence as consciousness. His "phenom-enological ontology" is based upon an analysis of human consciousness rather than of the Heideggerian *Dasein.*[40] But in contrast to Husserl, Sartre is interested in the more clearly existential aspects of conscious-ness. Thus he abandons the quasi-Kantian purpose of Husserl's inquiry and examines consciousness not in terms of a constituting transcen-dental subjectivity, but in terms of concrete individuals confronting the everyday world with projects and choices. Sartre's phenomenological analysis of consciousness in *Being and Nothingness* produces what is probably his most notorious concept: the nothingness of consciousness. Consciousness, which is understood as the essence of human existence, emerges as a radical nothingness, completely transparent and with no "content." This is to say that the self-as-consciousness is a total "lack of being." This notion becomes clearer if we examine Sartre's central distinction of the for-itself *(pour soi)* and the in-itself *(en soi)*.

Sartre performs a complete ontological dissection of subject and object when he posits the absolute separation of *pour soi* and *en soi* as two "modes of being." The *en soi* denotes reality in its fullness; it is the nonconscious and opaque world of reality "out there," rich with meaning and content. It is everything; it is, in a word, Being. The *pour soi* is nothing less than human consciousness itself; it is the conscious and transparent spontaneity which confronts the inertness of the world. The *pour soi* is the empty, lucid, and transparent nothingness of consciousness; it is, in a word, Nothingness. For Sartre, the separation of the *pour soi* of consciousness and the *en soi* of reality is a fundamental one. The abyss between the two is unbridgeable. As it has been insightfully said of the separation of *en soi* and *pour soi:* "The result is a picture of the Cartesian Mind-Matter dichotomy cast in the form of an Hegelian dialectic that is eternally fated to have no synthesis."[41]

This radical detachment of empty and transparent consciousness from the fullness and opacity of the world is not only possible but necessary, especially if we consider the obsessive centrality of absolute freedom in Sartre's thought. For Sartre, man is free, but in order to be free he must be absolutely free from any determination. Anything less, any partial or relative freedom, is self-contradictory and nonsensical. Therefore, consciousness must "possess" nothing, and must be filled with no determining content. If consciousness is not nothing, then it is determined, and man is not free. For this reason, the fundamental basis of human freedom must entail the "necessary atheism" of consciousness. In other words, human freedom is ultimately dependent upon the possibility of consciousness positing ex nihilo in the world; anything short of this results in determinism. Everything, then, is exterior to consciousness, which is "emptied out" from the very beginning. This nothingness which is consciousness is what forms the ground of freedom. It is in this sense that Sartre is led to a "philosophy of doing," where "to be is to act."[42] Thus whereas for Husserl phenomenology recovers through the phenomenological reduction "what is," for Sartre phenomenology leads us to the creation by consciousness of "what is for us."

On the basis of the definition of human being as absolutely free and detached *pour soi,* it is clear how Sartre is led to an extreme individualism. His view of social reality is grounded in an individualism conditioned by an understanding of man as pure and free consciousness. When one consciousness confronts another, it inexorably tries to objectify it, thereby leading to the projected annihilation of the consciousness of the Other.[43] This dismal state of affairs is necessary, according to Sartre, because consciousness as transparent, pure subjectivity cannot allow itself to become the object of another pure subjectivity, which is unavoidable unless that other subject is in turn objectified. The very condition which allows us to be free, the nothingness of our subjectivity, is threatened when we are caught in the objectifying gaze of another subject. We run the risk of becoming a "somethingness," which means that we become determined by the Other. This notion in Sartre vitiates the possibility of real community and leads to a view of society as continual and inherent conflict, where the *pour soi* is embodied in individual persons involved in continual flight from, and the struggle and combat against, one another.[44]

In this light, Sartre's rather unusual alliance with marxism can be understood. Because of his emphasis on action and the engagement of the individual in history, Sartre was led through the French Resistance movement to find a home in marxism.[45] But it was largely nondialectical marxism, understood as an alliance against a common enemy rather than as an affirmation of radical and dialectical intersubjectivity and community. As will become evident in chapter 5, this is one reason Sartre's efforts to unify existential phenomenology and marxism more often than not hinder the evolution of dialectical theory.

Merleau-Ponty

If Sartre develops phenomenology in the direction of analyzing the detachment of existential consciousness from the world, his one-time friend and collaborator, Maurice Merleau-Ponty, emphasizes the inextricable, necessary attachment of consciousness to the world, a development fraught with dialectical relations. With Merleau-Ponty, we discover the first and most coherent expression of a dialectical existential phenomenology. Unlike Heidegger and Sartre, Merleau-Ponty focuses the phenomenological project on an understanding of the *Lebenswelt*, the intersubjective life-world. And unlike Sartre's focus on the phenomenology of pure, individual-personal consciousness, Merleau-Ponty directs phenomenology to the phenomena of perception as they are securely anchored in the subject as lived-body. He develops a phenomenology of our radical attachment to and presence in the world. Opposed both to an idealistic phenomenology which focuses simply upon consciousness and to an empiricist-realist phenomenology which focuses upon "the world," Merleau-Ponty proposed a dialectical phenomenology in which consciousness and the world are dialectically and reciprocally related. Thus his phenomenology develops as a mode of uncovering the inherent involvement of human existence in the world, particularly as it is grounded most fundamentally in our perception of the world.

Phenomenology is still, as it was with Husserl, a search for essences, but with two differences. First, essence is found and replaced in existence. Second, therefore, phenomenology is not concerned with pure essences, since a complete reduction is impossible. Thus the phenomenological reduction does not lead us to pure essences any more than it does to Heidegger's disembodied *Dasein;* rather it leads us to being-in-the-world which is grounded in a corporeal subject. The radical reduction leads neither to transcendental subjectivity nor to the pure nothingness of consciousness, but to the consciousness of our indestructible relation to the world. We are "full" of being, and we are "through and through compounded of relationships with the world," so that we are a subject which is embedded in the world or, in a sense, which *is* the world. The world is not something apart from us which we "posit" or which we possess; it is something we "live through." This phenomenological view of our attachment to the world opposes the view that freedom is grounded in the lucid nothingness of consciousness. Freedom is not, as for Sartre, the absolute and unconditional positing of the *en soi;* it is the situated and conditioned interaction of the subject-as-lived-body with the world.[46] Freedom is rooted in the world in a dialectic of consciousness and reality. Man is the dialectical junction of the *pour soi* and the *en soi*.

If Merleau-Ponty's phenomenological road to the *Lebenswelt* leads to our fundamental attachment to the world as a dialectical union of *pour soi* and *en soi,* it also leads to our fundamental intersubjectivity. His recovery of the intersubjectivity of the *Lebenswelt* reveals the essential social nature of man. Not only are we in the world, but we are in the world with others. Our primordial, intentional way of being in the world lies in the intersubjectivity of a common world; it forms the shared element and commonality of our experiences and meanings. The primordial sociality of the *Lebenswelt* is experienced not as Sartre's alienated conflict of consciousnesses but as the reciprocity of subjects. If we are relational "through and through," so we are also social "through and through." This social dimension of phenomenology is crucial for Merleau-Ponty, as we shall shall see in the next chapter.

Merleau-Ponty's phenomenological attempt to discover our most original way of being in the world leads him to the primacy of perception. For if phenomenology is to go "to the things themselves," it must return to the prereflective *Lebenswelt,* which is to say, to primordial perception. It is neither consciousness nor Being which is primary; it is the world-and-our-relation-to-it-in-perception. The world revealed in perception is the "cradle of meanings, the direction of all directions, and ground of all thinking" beyond which we cannot push.[47] For Merleau-Ponty, our primordial perception of the world presupposes meaning or pre-existent logos in the world.[48] Meaning is the "ambiguous but fundamental Logos, already present in our original relation to the world."[49] The "primacy of perception" means "that the experience of perception is our presence at the moment when things, truths, values are constituted for us; that perception is a nascent *logos*."[50] Thus it means that in perception we cannot escape meaning. Instead of Sartre's claim that we are "condemned to freedom," we find that because we are perceptually rooted in the world "we are condemned to meaning."[51]

That meaning is inescapably present in our original relation to the world does not mean that meaning resides in the world independent of us, any more than it means that we can create meaning ex nihilo. Rather, it emerges at the point of contact with the world and is a dialectical product of consciousness and reality, given expression by our every word and act in the world. Hence Merleau-Ponty's phenomenology introduces a dialectic of meaning and nonmeaning grounded in perception and expressed in action on the concrete level of historical-political existence as a dialectic of logic and contingency. The presupposition of meaning and logic in the world and history is already found in both Hegel and Marx. But together with Marx, Merleau-Ponty dialectically introduces the element of contingency and nonmeaning. Without meaning and logic there is neither history nor philosophy, and without nonmeaning and contingency history would become nonhuman:

> There would be no history if everything made sense and if the world's development was nothing but the visible realization of a rational plan; but neither would there be any history—or action, or humanity—if everything was absurd or if the course of events was dominated by a few massive and unalterable facts.[52]

Like Marx, Merleau-Ponty insists upon meaning in history without succumbing to Hegel's postulation of *a* meaning in history. A dialectic of rationality and irrationality, and of logic and contingency, in history calls forth the efforts of men to make history consciously. If there is no guarantee that any end of history will not be chaotic and absurd, then men and philosophy must become engaged in praxis. We must "join" history rather than contemplate it as if it were an object removed from the consciousness-body of our everyday lives.

Merleau-Ponty develops existential phenomenology in a dialectical direction. In the first place, although phenomenology's project remains essentially descriptive, it is also concerned with the nature of itself. Thus, like all dialectical theory, it becomes self-reflexive and self-critical and never presupposes itself; this is what Merleau-Ponty means by the need to pursue a "phenomenology of phenomenology." Furthermore, the principles uncovered by phenomenological inquiry are related to praxis. The experience of perception itself "summons us to the tasks of knowledge and action":

> If we admit that our life is inherent to the perceived world and the human world, even while it re-creates it and contributes to its making, then morality cannot consist in the private adherence to a system of values. Principles are mystifications unless they are put into practice; it is necessary that they animate our relations with others.[53]

Indeed, this connection between theory and practice emerges with the phenomenological discovery that the body-subject is more fundamental than the transcendental epistemological subject. Our being-in-the-world is initially a practical relation and leads to the necessity of action and praxis.

In the *Lebenswelt,* Merleau-Ponty discovers a radical union of subject and object. Our most original way of being involves a dialectical union of self, others, nature, and history. The nondialectical separation of subject and object dissolves in the perceived dialectical unity of the perceived world. The "chief gain from phenomenology is to have united extreme subjectivism and extreme objectivism in its notion of the world" as neither subjectivity nor objectivity, but intersubjectivity.[54] In this same sense, the radicalness of the lived world calls forth the overcoming of the nondialectical *pour soi-en soi* distinction: "Unless I learn within myself to recognize the junction of the *for itself* and the *in itself,* none of those mechanisms called other bodies will ever be able to come to life; unless I have an exterior others have no interior."[55] Finally, in the social-political and historical dimensions of the *Lebenswelt,* we discover a dialectic of logic and contingency which calls for our engagement in the world to create history so that meaning "wins out" over nonmeaning. As with Marx, the synthesis of subject and object is dynamic and historical and remains to be achieved. It is never guaranteed nor given a priori as something complete.

Just as Marx provided a dialectical corrective to Hegel by recovering "objectivity," so Merleau-Ponty provides a dialectical corrective to Husserl's transcendental phenomenology and Sartre's nondialectical existentialism.[56] In the face of Husserl, he recovers the "body" and replaces it in the subject. The body becomes the dialectical mediator of consciousness and the world. In the face of Sartre, he recovers the primacy of concrete intersubjectivity and sociality and points to the dialectical unity of the *pour soi* and *en soi.* In the face of both of them, he demonstrates the intrinsic social nature of the lived world in such a way that it illustrates the necessary and concrete ties between phe-

nomenological insight and the real process of political existence and
history, which is praxis. Phenomenological efforts must take place in
the face of the indestructible coherence of action and history, consciousness and existence, and theory and practice. Beyond Husserl,
Heidegger, and even Sartre, dialectical social relations become central
to a self-critically politicized phenomenology. It is this dialectical existential phenomenology of Merleau-Ponty that provides the basis for
a real union of dialectical marxism and phenomenology—one which
overcomes both transcendental and nondialectically existential phenomenology, as well as the dominance of positivistic marxism.

Some Dialectical Directions in Phenomenology

Through the eyes of its core thinkers, we have seen some of the
dominant themes in phenomenology from its origins in transcendental
philosophy to its formulation as dialectical existential philosophy. With
this in mind, it is possible to summarize some of the essential elements
of that development which point in the direction of dialectical and
critical theory and are relevant to our conception of political science.

Phenomenology can be seen as self-critically radical philosophy. Its
radicalism springs from Husserl's concern for the crisis of positivistic
science brought about by its "unclarified" status. For Husserl, this
means that the objective-scientific world of positivism is an abstraction
far removed from the primary world of lived experience, in which
science itself is grounded. The reason for this abstraction lies in science's blindness to its own philosophical and experiential foundations.
The result is science's profound "unclarity" about itself:

> An unclarified science is a science unaware of its own ontological
> and epistemic foundations, of its *meaning*. If phenomenology has
> appeared to many to be antiscientific, it is because they have con-
> fused the metaphysics of naturalism with science. What phenom-
> enology does is to 'situate' science (as it does any other derived
> construction of human thought) and to go beyond it in the direc-
> tion of its experiential roots, its foundations which are to be found
> in a more original noetic contact with the real.[57]

This does not mean, however, that a hypostatized phenomenology has
achieved an Archimedean standpoint, a perspective apart from the
world from which it can criticize and describe everything unequivo-
cally. For phenomenology, like dialectical marxism, is in principle self-
critical; it is constantly involved in self-critical clarification of its own
foundations. As Richard Zaner has it:

Phenomenology, thus, must be at one and the same time a criticism of all human engagements as well as of consciousness, and a criticism of itself.

A theory of criticism is necessary to criticism; phenomenology must also include a critical theory of phenomenology.[58]

If phenomenology is involved in a critical theory of the world, it is also involved in a critical theory of itself, or again, in what Merleau-Ponty calls the "phenomenology of phenomenology."

In its attempt to go beyond the abstractions of thought and knowledge to the concrete reality of lived experience, phenomenology has developed as an intensely radical method of description, which necessarily implies change. It penetrates to the presupposed roots of what it is describing, thus making explicit what is implicit. By doing so, it does not leave us untouched; rather, it becomes a method "for changing our relation to the world, for becoming more acutely aware of it." Phenomenology "combines the most radical break with our ordinary and natural attitude *vis-à-vis* the world (in this sense, it is an ascesis of the mind) with the deepening or the consecration of this original attitude (in this sense, it is respect for the real and engagement in the world)."[59] As a method of the most fundamental description of lived experience and thus as a philosophy of lived experience, phenomenology returns us to where the abstract dichotomies of subject and object, and theory and practice, do not exist. It pushes at the same time toward the "roots of subjectivity" as well as toward the "foundations of the objective world." Hence "phenomenology is neither a science of objects nor a science of the subject; it is a science of *experience*."[60] Rather than focus simply upon the objectivity of the world or lapse into a groundless subjectivistic focus upon consciousness, phenomenology concentrates on intentionality as the point of contact between consciousness and reality. When its original concern for the unity of noetic-noematic structures in intentional consciousness finds a dialectical existential corrective in the embodied character of perception, phenomenology strives for the dialectical union of subject and object, which is also the goal of the marxian synthesis.

Existential phenomenology encounters certain similarities with dialectical marxism. Insofar as phenomenology attempts to describe rigorously "the meaning of man's concrete experience, political or otherwise, in his everyday life," it reiterates the task Marx sets for himself.[61] One might say it reiterates half the task, since Marx does not conceive of understanding apart from changing, but then again, neither does a dialectical existential phenomenology. Thus existential phenomenology, like a dialectical marxism, returns to a critique of the origin of philosophy in Plato himself in order to rectify the philosophical "hands-off" attitude toward the concrete existence of the Cave. In this sense, it joins Marx's critique of the abstraction of previous philosophy. Furthermore, both existential phenomenology and dialectical marxism share a common existential reference point, the concrete totality of the world understood relationally.

The *Lebenswelt,* the basic matrix of all human endeavors, includes the historical, cultural, and social worlds. As Merleau-Ponty has it, the *Lebenswelt,* which is our most fundamental ground of existence and experience, is the radical dialectical unity of self, others, nature, and history. Marx's concrete point of reference is the "real individual" understood as a totality of historical, social, and natural relations. Neither Merleau-Ponty nor Marx allows an ontological truncation of reality. Both insist upon confronting the totality of reality, not as a mystical whole, but as a set of relations. If for Merleau-Ponty we are "relational through and through," for Marx we are nothing but "relations." If for Merleau-Ponty we are situated in the world and indeed *are* the world by a sort of exchange, for Marx we are not abstract beings "squatting outside the world," we are the human world and indeed we are as much the whole as we are the individual.[62]

The *Lebenswelt* of existential phenomenology and Marx's "ontology" converge on a number of levels. Phenomenology discovers that the life-world is indestructibly social; it is active, social, and historical in a dialectical unity.[63] And for Marx the meaningful ground of human life is also this radical conjunction of activity, sociality, and history. Man's nature lies in his activity (praxis) and in his intersubjectivity (sociality). For existential phenomenology, man is also an open-ended process of becoming, a network of open possibilities, and thus there is an essential historicity to his nature. For dialectical marxism too, of course, human nature is historically metastatic. It is perhaps at the level of the preconceptual dimension of the *Lebenswelt* that Marx's own ontology is at its weakest, although not in principle antithetical to its investigation. It is here that even more work is required to unite a critical theory of politics with the phenomenological discovery of our prereflective inherence in the world.

In a sense, existential phenomenology might be labeled "radical empiricism." It is a form of empiricism insofar as it insists on confronting the things themselves in experience. It does not, however, restrict knowledge to the realm of atomistic "things" revealed by sensory perception alone. It defines experience in a much broader sense than does vulgar empiricism.[64] In its return to the things themselves, it also returns to the intentional constitution by consciousness of the things themselves and thus recovers the importance of subjectivity. Thus existential phenomenology refuses, as does a dialectical marxism, to succumb to the illusion of the subject-object distinction: "subjectivity and objectivity are only two moments of the same phenomenon."[65] It conceives the starting point of knowledge as residing neither in the object alone as sense experience (empiricism) nor in the subject alone as cognitive experience (rationalism), but in total experience located as a unified subject-object, for it seems to be true that "man is not just a thinking subject, he is active and affective as well as intellectual." And thus "existential phenomenology makes a serious attempt to achieve the unity of theory and practice," or the concretely active union of consciousness and existence.[66] Its goals point in the direction of continuing what Marx sets out to do with the knowledge and praxis of social and political reality.

Perhaps it is useful at this juncture to point out a misguided criticism of phenomenology: that it is confined to interiority. Such a criticism can be found, for example, in the work of Edo Pivcevic.[67] Now it is often true that phenomenology begins with the realm of human interiority, whether it is understood in terms of transcendental or existential subjectivity. In its dialectical formulation with Merleau-Ponty, however, phenomenology begins with the dialectical contact and union of interior and exterior. It is not imprisoned in the realm of interiority and has no problem dealing with "other people" and "the objective world." It is unsurprising that Pivcevic ignores this dialectical phenomenology when in his summary of the limitations of "all phenomenologists," he totally neglects Merleau-Ponty.[68]

To conclude, phenomenology, in essence, is description. But it is no ordinary or bland, reductionist or pseudoobjective description; it is a form of description which is a "radical searching for foundations" and thus contains an element of transcendentalism.[69] Phenomenology offers a mode of describing reality, including political reality, which can transcend the mode of a "subject" describing an "object" and indeed tries to overcome the dualism itself. It uncovers and lays bare the principles so often presupposed and hidden in the scientific pretense of contemporary behavioralist and positivist political science. At the same time, it forces traditional political theory to come into contact with the experience of our everyday lives. As a form of critical theory, dialectical existential phenomenology possesses the capability of recovering the perennial questions of previous political philosophy (which positivism and empiricism so quickly cast aside), and of situating and integrating them in the ongoing process of concrete existence.[70] The fact that as self-critical theory it can do so without transforming itself into a scholastic traditionalism, an unreflective ideology, or a scientistic pragmatism, makes it a crucial participant in the evolution of a dialectical theory that can enrich our view of political science.

Merleau-Ponty's Recovery of Interiority and Prereflectivity:
Prologue to the Convergence of Marxism and Phenomenology

By way of transition to the next chapter, it is instructive to note
Merleau-Ponty's contribution to the theme evoked earlier in chapter
2. Our concern in that chapter was the careful excavation of the foundations of contemporary dialectical theory, which uncovered the attempts of Kant, Hegel, and Marx to elucidate a synthesis of subject
and object. At the end of chapter 2, I suggested that Marx's effort to
recover objectivity in the face of Hegel may have led to the point where
the importance of subjectivity threatened to be neglected altogether.
And indeed, the ignorance and destruction of subjectivity has generally
characterized marxism in our century. Merleau-Ponty's work can be
seen in the light of this problem.

As with Marx's theory, the dialectical existential phenomenology
of Merleau-Ponty is expressed as a dually oriented critique of both
rationalist and empiricist understandings of human inquiry. One of the
reasons for this connection is the fact that Hegel's thought appears as
the source of both marxism and phenomenology: "All the great philosophical ideas of the past century—the philosophies of Marx and
Nietzsche, phenomenology, German existentialism, and psychoanalysis—had their beginnings in Hegel."[71] This is especially true of phenomenology since Hegel is the first philosopher to characterize his
philosophical approach as such.[72] If the ultimate source of phenomenology lies in Hegel, its self-conscious appropriation as a movement
is located, as we have seen, in Husserl, the "fountainhead" of phenomenology.[73] We have also seen how phenomenology developed from
Husserlian transcendental phenomenology to the existential phenomenology of Sartre and Merleau-Ponty.

What I am suggesting here is that Merleau-Ponty's elaboration of a
dialectical existential phenomenology is inspired in the same direction
as the development of dialectical theory from Kant to Marx. We find
in Merleau-Ponty's thought an explicit refusal to succumb to the abstract epistemological duality of subject and object, which thus continues in the tradition of Marx's search for a concrete epistemological
dialectic. Furthermore, it is the strongly dialectical character of Merleau-
Ponty's thought that separates him both from most phenomenology
(including that of Hegel, Husserl, and Heidegger) and from most existentialism (including its Christian development by Kierkegaard, Mar-
cel, and Ricoeur and its radical humanist development by Sartre).

Merleau-Ponty's dialectical critique of the distinction of subject and
object, found in the rationalism of traditional philosophy and in the
empiricism of modern positivism, originates with a different emphasis
than it does in Marx, however. It focuses upon the prereflective and

prerational dimension involved in our living of the world, a dimension of our experience and existence which reveals our primary inherence in the world before reflection itself. Our primordial perception of the world forms our original relationship to the world, a relationship which is prerational and preconscious.[74] Thus our way of being in the world and of knowing the world involves a radical dimension which is a form of unreason.

The recognition that we are first of all "in the world"—"we are born into reason as into language"—entails that the experience of unreason and the prereflective become part of a broader form of reason itself, and that we incorporate our embodied primordial relation to reality in our process of inquiry and knowing: "The experience of unreason cannot simply be forgotten: we must form a new idea of reason."[75] In this sense, the rational meaning after which knowledge seeks is caught up in the embodied existence of prerational inherence, which is itself related to unreason. Therefore, for example, the "meaning of a work of art or of a theory is as inseparable from its embodiment as the meaning of a tangible thing—which is why meaning can never be fully expressed. The highest form of reason borders on unreason."[76]

Merleau-Ponty argues against reflective detachment or abstraction from our situation or "situatedness" in the world. He argues for philosophy's cognizance of its radical existential inherence in the world. Philosophical inquiry cannot pretend to abstract itself from the world: "consciousness always exists in a situation."[77] In the spirit and direction of Marx, the philosopher is reminded that he too inheres in the world and history. It is thus that Hegel's masterful account of the dialectical totality fails at the level of comprehending Hegel's existence: "He has taken everything into account except his own existence, and the synthesis he offers is no true synthesis precisely because it pretends ignorance of being the product of a certain individual and a certain time."[78] Therefore, like Marx's, Merleau-Ponty's dialectical critique of traditional philosophy focuses upon its incomplete and deficient concept of knowledge and reason. Like Marx, he insists upon a new self-understanding of philosophy and reason. For Marx, reason is concretely active as a human predicate and is grounded in historical praxis. For Merleau-Ponty this is also true, but reason is further grounded in the concrete prerational dimension of the *Lebenswelt*. Thus praxis itself involves the experience of unreason and prereflectivity. The dialectical totality of reality not only involves the realm of praxis but also the no less meaningful realm of our primordial, prereflective living of the world. Traditional philosophy forgets that it too is involved and situated in the totality of experience and meaning as defined by Merleau-Ponty.

Dialectical existential phenomenology revitalizes Marx's dialectic of consciousness and being, or subject and object. Man-as-subject does not stand detached from or transcendent of reality-as-object. The relation between subject and object is not merely an epistemological one as it is in Kant. As with Marx, the relation is one of being, although not one which presupposes the philosophy of identity as it does in Hegel. In other words, the only way to approach the world, know the world, and do something in the world lies in man's involvement in nature and history:

> The relationship between subject and object is no longer that *relationship of knowing* postulated by classical idealism, wherein the object always seems the construction of the subject, but a *relationship of being* in which, paradoxically, the subject *is* his body, his world and his situation, by a sort of exchange.[79]

Here we recover the objectivity of the human subject emphasized in Marx. Man is defined as "a relation to instruments and objects—a relation which is not simply one of thought but which involves him in the world in such a way as to give him an external aspect, an outside, to make him 'objective' at the same time he is 'subjective.' "[80]

However, Merleau-Ponty provides a dialectical corrective to Marx's overemphasis of objectivity, which itself was a dialectical corrective to Hegel, by recovering the subjective interiority of man. But the corrective applies more strongly to "Marxism" than it does to Marx. Marx, after all, is critical of Hegel's forgetfulness of his own existential subjectivity, and his criticism of previous materialism is that it ignores the subjective character of concrete, objective human activity and praxis. Merleau-Ponty reminds those who "shudder at the very word 'subjectivity' " of Marx's first thesis on Feuerbach.[81] Yet there is a marxism which denigrates this dialectic in Marx, develops into an objectivistic, metaphysical materialism, and lends credence to an empiricist and positivist outlook. This is a marxism "which absolutely denies interiority, which treats consciousness as a part of the world, a reflection of the object, a by-product of being, and finally, to use a language which has never been Marxist, as an epiphenomenon."[82] This marxism loses the character of a dialectical philosophy and becomes another form of metaphysical philosophy.

For Merleau-Ponty, marxism is justified in its focus upon the object and history. However, it is justified not in the sense that the subject ceases to be important or real, but in the sense that previous philosophy's focus upon the subject has resulted in and confirmed the philosopher's existential refusal "to work at transforming the world"; it has revealed "his anxiety before the real humanity which *creates* itself through work and through praxis rather than seeking to define itself once and for all."[83] Marx's emphasis upon history and objectivity rests upon

the idea that we have no choice, that we are through and through
the product of history, thrown without reservation into the world.
For Marxism, whatever subjective justifications may be brought
forth, exclusive reference to the interior is objectively an absten-
tion and a way of avoiding the concrete tasks imposed on us from
the outside. In a word, we are involved.[84]

The emphatic marxist focus on objectivity is an attempt to save the
subject, not to destroy it.

Merleau-Ponty aims at recovering the subjectivity and interiority of
man in order to preserve the dialectic of subject and object in Marx
from its degeneration into objectivistic, positivistic, and nondialectical
marxism. Man is not simply the objective result of nature, one natural
object among many, as is the case with simple naturalism and epistemological empiricism. Nor is he simply spirit or self-consciousness,
which constitutes the consciousness of the world, as is the case with
Hegel. Rather, man has a special way of being in the world for which
the various contradictions of consciousness and nature, subject and
object, are neither illusory nor reducible one to the other; their relation
is a living, communicative bond.[85] Man is again a concrete subject-
object; he is incarnate being-in-the-world. Marxism "is not a philosophy of the subject, but it is just as far from a philosophy of the object:
it is a philosophy of history" in which men "daily create their lives
anew" and for which man is the subject-object, the product-producer.[86]

Thus the synthesis of subject and object, of consciousness and reality, is not a de jure one as in Hegel, which results in political quietism,
but a de facto one, which results in a continual unrest. It is a synthesis,
as we have seen, which has to be made continually in praxis over time,
and cooperatively by concrete individuals.[87] The synthesis, first, lies
in the future and always "remains to be done" and, second, relies upon
coexistence among men.[88] The arrival of unalienated "total man" is
always historically and communally contingent. The dialectical force
which is the vehicle of history is neither objectified social nature, nor
world spirit, nor collective consciousness. It is

man involved in a certain way of appropriating nature in which the
mode of his relationship with others takes shape; it is concrete human *intersubjectivity,* the successive and simultaneous community
of existences in the process of self-realization in a type of owner-
ship which they both submit to and transform, each created by
and creating the other.[89]

Dialectical existential phenomenology's recovery of human interiority is thus also a recovery of the radical intersubjectivity crucial to
any phenomenology of the social world. It suggests that in order to
preserve Marx's concrete dialectic of the human subject, we must also

develop theoretically our understanding of human consciousness, although we do so neither apart from its relation to praxis nor apart from its prereflective dimensions. If Marx argues that consciousness is an aspect of social life, he also argues that social life is an aspect of consciousness. Therefore,

> the Marxist discovery of social existence as the most 'interior' dimension of our life . . . not only admits but demands a new conception of consciousness on the theoretical plane, which would establish a basis for both its autonomy and its dependence by describing it as a nothingness which comes into the world and which could not keep its liberty without engaging itself at every moment.[90]

It is, for Merleau-Ponty, this view of consciousness which marxism has "*practiced* in its most powerful concrete analyses, if not formulated in theory." In terms of maintaining the dialectic of subject and object, which involves the relations of inner and outer, a "living Marxism should 'save' and integrate existentialist research instead of stifling it."[91] In other words, the concrete dialectical totality, which is the object of marxist inquiry and transformation, must have all its dimensions taken into account, including the interiority and prereflectivity of man's inherence in the world.

These reflections indicate how Merleau-Ponty specifically contributes to the evolution of dialectical theory. For Merleau-Ponty, again, all forms of both rationalism and empiricism maintain a faulty and alienated duality of subject and object. The former entails an abstraction from lived existence, while the latter entails an abstraction within the whole of reality and is thus reductionist in character. In this sense, the competition between traditional philosophy's reliance upon detached and abstracted subjectivity, and positivism's reliance upon a reductionist objectivity, is an illusory rivalry. In its most general formulation, Merleau-Ponty states it as follows:

> There can be no rivalry between scientific knowledge and the metaphysical knowing which continually confronts the former with its task. A science without philosophy would literally not know what it was talking about. A philosophy without methodical exploration of phenomena would end up with nothing but formal truths, which is to say, errors.[92]

The empiricist self-understanding of human inquiry remains incomplete and one-sided by dismissing subjectivity and blinding itself to its own subjectivity. Whether one speaks of traditional positivism or of scientistic "marxism," it errs as long as it fails to confront the real subjectivity of human consciousness and action. As long as traditional philosophy imprisons itself in concepts and beings of abstract reason it, too, is incomplete and one-sided. This is true insofar as traditional philosophy removes subjectivity from concrete existence and "shatters our inherence in the world."[93] From the perspective of the meaning of the relation of reason and the senses, of subject and object, a dialectical theory of knowledge requires a self-awareness of the fact that we exist before we reflect.[94] And that inherence in the world is historically "situated," or relative.

Thus the development of a dialectical theory of knowledge requires that the process of human inquiry be grounded in and oriented to the total concrete world. For both Marx and Merleau-Ponty, meaning or logos in the world presupposes the concrete unity of subject and object in praxis and social life. With this dialectical turn, we are again brought around to the realization that philosophy can only fulfill itself by "overcoming" itself as isolated philosophy and as a process of abstract reason.[95] Marx calls the new self-understanding of human inquiry by the name "critique"; Merleau-Ponty suggests that this same conception of philosophy as "concrete thinking" also goes under the name "existential philosophy."[96] The self-understanding of the process of human inquiry must return, then, to the dialectical totality of the concrete world, a world which is dialectically and historically relative. Only now, with dialectical existential phenomenology, that totality includes our primordial, prereflective perception of, and way of being in, the world, and must be taken into account by a dialectical theory of knowledge. The totality of reality—the matrix within which we know and change the world—has a new dimension and a fuller and richer meaning and dialectic than it does in Marx.

5 Contemporary Dialectical Theory

The Confluence of Marxism and Phenomenology

During the past few decades, the evolution of dialectical theory appears to have taken two important forms relevant to the pursuit of political inquiry. One of these involves recent developments in "critical theory," to which we turn in the next chapter. The other involves various attempts to unify or reconcile the traditions of phenomenology and marxism. Both of these forms of contemporary dialectical theory hold forth important and promising insights for a reoriented view of the future of political science.

The confluence of marxism and phenomenology has found a number of expressions. In a rather loose sense, one could even return to Marx's encounter with Hegel to find the earliest. In a more realistic sense, however, we can locate early expressions of the "meeting" of dialectical marxism and phenomenology, in varying degrees of implicity and explicity, in the following cases: certain aspects of Gramsci's work; Lukács's encounters with Husserl's work; Marcuse's early encounters with Heidegger; and especially the efforts of Sartre and Merleau-Ponty.[1] More recently, we find proponents of such a union in individuals such as Enzo Paci, Fred Dallmayr, and Richard Bernstein, just to name a few.[2]

The purpose of this chapter, however, is not to recount all of these various expressions in detail. Rather, it is to introduce what I believe is one of the most fruitful attempts to express the confluence of marxism and phenomenology, an attempt which we find in the work of Merleau-Ponty. Toward the end of the chapter, I examine some more recent developments along these lines. What I hope to suggest is that the developments of marxism and phenomenology, as forms of dialectical theory, have internal connections with each other, and that there is no

116

need to view them as totally separate movements which require an artificial or contrived "synthesis."[3] Finally, I want to suggest that a greater awareness of these kinds of developments can considerably enrich our view of political inquiry.

One Attempt at the Marriage of Marxism and Phenomenology: Sartre and Merleau-Ponty

The Historical and Cultural Context

It is important to note that the attempted marriage of marxism and phenomenology by Sartre and Merleau-Ponty took place within the context of the Second World War, the Nazi Occupation, and the French Resistance.[4] The war brought a tragic climax to the general breakdown of old French society from 1917 onward, a breakdown characterized by a growth of meaninglessness, alienation, and a crisis of confidence. It had at least two major effects on French intellectuals like Sartre and Merleau-Ponty. It made them realize the theoretical need for philosophy and thought to become engaged in history and politics, and it brought to light the practical need for cooperation, community, and commitment.[5] The Resistance movement provided a way to fulfill these needs, particularly in the role played by the French Communist Party. The Party provided an organized basis for commitment, responsibility, cooperation, and confidence. In the face of ethical ambiguity and impotence, it offered a framework for certainty and action. In this light, Sartre and Merleau-Ponty were surrounded by an atmosphere of marxism.

The cultural context of Merleau-Ponty's and Sartre's efforts was at least twofold. On the one hand, as we have seen, they both emerged from the German phenomenological tradition of Husserl and Heidegger, which also involved a renaissance of interest in Kierkegaard and the problems of "existence." On the other hand, the development of their thought took place at a time of serious questioning of the entire Cartesian heritage of French philosophy and culture. Three centuries of Cartesian influence suffused the intellectual climate of France, resulting in a penchant among intellectuals for abstraction and rationalism. These qualities were seen by Sartre and Merleau-Ponty not only as philosophically inadequate, but as obstacles to the kind of philosophy their time demanded. Thus they rebelled against various forms of abstraction dominant in their own national philosophical culture. Sartre and Merleau-Ponty searched for a philosophy of concrete existence and a philosophy of engagement and commitment. From their beginnings in phenomenology, they were thus led to a rediscovery of marxism as providing the political content and direction of such a philosophy.

Philosophy and Ontology

It would seem that any attempt to unite phenomenology and marxism requires that they share a basic conception of the nature of reality. Without such an understanding, the union of the two appears doomed to failure from the beginning. It is at this level that the early phenomenological inquiries of Sartre and Merleau-Ponty into the nature of reality emerge with quite different conclusions. We find that the phenomenological ontology of Merleau-Ponty is compatible, while that of Sartre is incompatible, with a dialectical marxism.

In a sense, Merleau-Ponty's *Phenomenology of Perception* is a response to the phenomenological ontology of Sartre's *Being and Nothingness*. Earlier, in *The Structure of Behavior,* Merleau-Ponty had already rejected a dualism of *en soi* and *pour soi* as being an inadequate hangover of Cartesian thought. He argues instead for a fundamental ontological unity of mind and body, or subject and object, and for the inseparability of all being from its status as "perceived being."[6] In the *Phenomenology,* the argument against both Cartesian rationalism and vulgar empiricism is continued in terms of the concrete perceptual rootedness of all reality. What emerges from a phenomenology of perception is a conception of a radical inseparability of mind and body. Mind and body do not exist as two distinct realms of being, but form a primary unity as the lived body-subject.[7] Philosophical reflection therefore is never detached from, but already inherent in the matter or object at hand.[8] Consciousness is never a transparent subject and the body is never an opaque object, as they are for Sartre. Rather, the body-subject is an incarnation of experience, and man is an indivisible subject-object.

For Merleau-Ponty, reality, human reality in particular, cannot be understood simply from the perspective of matter. This does not mean, however, that man is pure consciousness. To argue thus is to adopt a Cartesian dualism. It is this kind of dualism which emerges from *Being and Nothingness.* As previously noted, Sartre's phenomenological ontology is grounded in the dichotomy of the *pour soi* and the *en soi,* which exist in direct opposition to each other.[9] The *en soi* is the independent, self-contained world of unconscious reality; the *pour soi* is, in a word, man, understood as pure, lucid consciousness grounded in completely free nothingness and possessing no "content."[10] Sartre's "emptying" of consciousness and his replacement of the Cartesian *cogito* with the notion of "there is thought," leads to an impersonalization of consciousness disembodied from the world (*en soi*). In Merleau-Ponty's view, to perceive human reality as impersonal and empty consciousness results in the fact that man "becomes cut off from all things, from his body and his effective existence."[11] In this sense, Sartre returns in spite of his intentions to a form of the rationalistic Cartesian dualism of subject and object.[12]

Sartre's phenomenological ontology of *en soi* and *pour soi* has important implications for an understanding of social reality.[13] This is particularly the case when one considers his phenomenological ontology of the "Other" and the problem of human community. In *Being and Nothingness*, the argument for the impersonality of consciousness entails a nothingness of consciousness, the lack of all content in consciousness.[14] Sartre attempts to abolish all external and internal limits on consciousness in order for the kind of freedom which posits ex nihilo to exist for man. The only remaining barrier to absolute freedom lies with the Other, another radically free and transparent consciousness. For the self to be radically free, it is necessary that it exist in complete isolation. When it encounters the freedom of others it can only pit itself against them in conflict. When another consciousness casts its gaze upon me it transforms me into an object, and thus robs me of my freedom and subjectivity. An encounter with the Other necessarily involves an attempt to "nihilate" the consciousness of the Other through its objectification.[15]

On the basis of such an ontology of Others, experience of community can only be mediated and indirect. Human beings qua pure, free consciousnesses can exist together in only two fundamental ways: either as an "us-object," in which case we are objectified by a Third while we ourselves are in conflict; or as a "we-subject," in which case we stand side-by-side *à deux* against a common enemy, pursuing a common "project."[16] This latter case involves temporary "truces" and "understandings" between conflicting consciousnesses, and it forms the basis for Sartre's marxism. At the most basic ontological level, then, we can never finally escape the objectification of our radical subjectivity and the restriction of our radical freedom inherent in our relationship with the Other. The "Look" of the Other is always there, and the shame and enslavement we feel by it can only be overcome through a nihilation of the freedom and subjectivity of the Other. This fundamental human conflict is inescapable.

Merleau-Ponty rejects Sartre's phenomenological ontology and its implications for community. Since Sartre's ontology stops at the state of the pure nothingness of consciousness, with the negation of the opacity and meaningful content of the human subject, it stops at the point of man's existence *at* the world and neglects man's inherence *in* the world. The relationship between the *en soi* and *pour soi,* and between the self and others, is too exclusively and rigidly antithetical: "The antithesis of my view of myself and another's view of me and the antithesis of the *for itself* and the *in itself* often seem to be alternatives instead of being described as the living bond and communication between one term and the other."[17] The conflict between human beings is more thoroughly grounded in the intersubjectivity of human community. If "Hell is other people" (a theme of Sartre's play *No Exit*), this does not mean that "heaven is me": "If other people are the instruments of our torture, it is first and foremost because they are indispensable to our salvation. We are so intermingled with them that we must make what order we can out of this chaos."[18]

The Sartrean notion of the inherent conflict involved in the objectification of the Look does not go far enough. Our very awareness of that conflict is contingent upon the awareness of "our reciprocal relationship and our common humanity." We cannot deny each other without a prior mutual recognition of our consciousnesses: "my consciousness of another as an enemy comprises an affirmation of him as an equal"; and furthermore, "I discover myself in the other."[19] For Merleau-Ponty, the freedom for which Sartre searches can only be found in community, in the dialectical relationships among human beings, not in the isolation of individual consciousness. For Sartre, there is no remedy for the contradictions of the for-itself and the for-others, "with the result that his dialectic is truncated." Merleau-Ponty's ontology of Others is grounded not in nihilation and conflict but in affirmation and community: "I live not for death but forever, and likewise, not for myself alone but with other people."[20]

If one were boldly to summarize in a word the essence of Merleau-Ponty's phenomenological ontology, it would have to be "radical intersubjectivity." "We are inextricably and confusedly bound up with the world and others."[21] Merleau-Ponty's fear of existentialism in the hands of French writers is that it will fall into an "isolating" analysis of consciousness rather than focusing upon our sociality in terms of "intersubjectivity, a living relationship and tension among individuals."[22] Merleau-Ponty's phenomenological ontology leads to an understanding of marxism for which the vehicle of history is neither matter nor consciousness, but "the successive and simultaneous community of existences in the process of self-realization." When Sartre therefore questions how materialism can be dialectical, Merleau-Ponty replies that in marxism "matter"—and, indeed, "consciousness"—is never considered separately: "It is inserted in the system of human coexistence where it forms the basis of a common situation of contemporary and successive individuals."[23]

From his beginnings in phenomenology, Merleau-Ponty is led to a union of existential phenomenology and marxism because both "movements" are concerned with the ontological centrality of intersubjectivity. Phenomenological inquiry into the *Lebenswelt* leads him to an ontology of dialectical totality compatible with dialectical marxism. It leads him away from an ontology characterized by Cartesian-like dichotomies such as that of *en soi* and *pour soi,* which involve a complete alienation of subject and object. One might generally characterize Sartre's ontological inquiry into the structure of consciousness with such notions as conflict, separation, detachment, fear of face-to-face relationships, and the impossibility of concrete intersubjectivity. Merleau-Ponty's inquiries lead in the opposite direction, and one is reminded of the simple words: "We die alone, but we live with other people; we are the image which they have of us; where they are, we are too."[24]

Marxism

Before the war, neither Sartre nor Merleau-Ponty exhibited much interest in politics. Sartre's prewar concerns were not only nonpolitical, they were in a sense nonsocial; his developing phenomenology was concerned with individual consciousness. Although Merleau-Ponty's prewar concerns were not directly political, his developing phenomenology was already forming the groundwork for his postwar social philosophy.[25] Nonetheless, with the leisure to think of others as totally separate lives, and not feeling the need to be involved, they were unaware of the peculiarity and contingency of their historical time and situation: "Plato was as close to us as Heidegger, the Chinese as close as the French—and in reality one was as far away as the other. We did not know that this was what it was to live in peace, in France, and in a certain world situation."[26]

War, occupation, and resistance changed all of that for the two French philosophers. It led them to involvement through marxism, although their approaches to marxist thought differ markedly. The war brought for Sartre the awareness of a need for concrete responsibility and commitment. In spite of the implications of his phenomenological philosophy, he was drawn to marxism primarily through his emotions and a temper of mind, and only in a negative way. His resolve to turn from "Being" to "Doing" involved an attempt to throw himself into ideological commitment as a way of escaping bad faith and ethical ambiguity.[27] Marxism became an engagement of the heart. There is no clear and necessary connection between his philosophy and his politics, something Sartre himself admitted.[28]

With Merleau-Ponty, on the other hand, the attraction to marxism was mediated by philosophy. His understanding of Marx and marxism was grounded in an understanding of Hegelian philosophy, first made available to him through Kojève's famous lectures on Hegel in 1936. In Hegel, he found an approach to the dynamic idea of intersubjectivity. In Marx he found this same idea combined with the notion that men participate in making their own history and meaning in a laboring praxis that can be liberating. Much like Gramsci, Merleau-Ponty interpreted

Marx's response to Hegel, not in terms of materialism confronting idealism, but in terms of a concrete dialectical philosophy of human action confronting an abstract dialectical philosophy of spirit. Thus marxism does not replace Hegelianism with a new absolute, metaphysical philosophy of history; rather, it becomes an open way of understanding man's historical possibilities and of understanding the "flesh of history."[29] In contrast to Sartre, Merleau-Ponty's entrance into marxism is characterized by a much clearer and nonarbitrary connection between his philosophy and his politics.

From these beginnings, the two men's understandings of marxism continued to develop in different directions. Sartre's became increasingly abstract, rationalistic, and dogmatic, while Merleau-Ponty's became increasingly concrete, dialectical, and open. The abstract quality of Sartre's marxism is evident not only, for example, in the view that class and race antagonisms are collective enactments of the Sartrean drama of the Look, but also in his approach to the politics of his time: his growing political manicheanism and his absolute commitment to the Communist Party. It was particularly this absolute ideological commitment and loyalty to the Party that disturbed Merleau-Ponty, for it relied upon rationalistic dogma and acceptance of a political vocabulary of the nineteenth century which was not only abstract but inadequate for the changes and forces confronting the middle of the twentieth century.[30]

Perhaps the divergent approaches of Sartre and Merleau-Ponty to politics and marxism are most clearly revealed in the character of the rupture of their relationship. Even in their early postwar collaboration on *Les Temps Modernes,* Merleau-Ponty's suspicions of the possible effects of Sartre's abstraction and absolutism are revealed by his preference to remain anonymous, writing for the journal under pseudonyms. But the real storm came in 1950 with the outbreak of the Korean War. This was a period of deep division in the French Left and of continuing revelations about Stalinist terror and the Siberian camps. For Merleau-Ponty, this was the year of the unmasking of Stalinism, which revealed in the place of a marxist humanism an inhuman authoritarianism. It was asking too much for him to believe that the Korean War was an unequivocal case of aggression by the United States and South Korea. The orthodox Communist view of the events of this period could be accepted only by ignoring the facts and by living in abstractions, something from which Merleau-Ponty had tried from the start to free himself.[31] Commitment does not involve a denial of reason but an attempt to go beyond abstract reason; thus commitment can never be absolute.

While Merleau-Ponty's commitment was suspended in 1950, Sartre's became even more absolute. He was converted to a trenchant pro-

Soviet communism. After Duclos was arrested, he had sworn: "An anti-Communist is a rat. I couldn't see any way out of that one, and I never will." Of his alienation from Merleau-Ponty he wrote:

> In the language of the Church, this was my conversion. In 1950, Merleau too, was converted. Each of us were conditioned, but in opposite directions. Our slowly accumulated disgust made the one discover, in an instant, the horror of Stalinism, and the other, that of his own class.

And his conclusion: "I swore to the bourgeoisie a hatred which would only die with me."[32] The result of this conversion was the publication of *The Communists and Peace* and the realization that "the USSR wants peace. It has to have peace. The only threat of war comes from the West."[33] His loyalty and commitment were proclaimed, and they were absolute.

By 1952 the break between Merleau-Ponty and Sartre was complete, and they saw nothing of each other for the next four years. The rupture reveals the difference in their understandings of marxism, in terms of both style and content. As Sartre recalls, "We were each recruited according to our aptitudes: Merleau when it was time for subtleties, and I, when the time of assassins had come."[34] During this period, Merleau-Ponty attacked at length *The Communists and Peace* as an abandonment of dialectical marxian method and as an acceptance of marxism on pure faith.[35] His understanding of marxism had become ever more relativistic and skeptical, whereas Sartre's had become ever more absolute, dualistic, and abstract. And it is clear these different approaches to marxism were rooted in their earlier phenomenological inquiries.

One might simply recall some of the notions that recur often in their respective philosophies. One finds in Sartre these themes: conflict, nothingness, detachment, "Hell is other people," separation, transparency, lucidity, clarity, uncompromising commitment, absoluteness, certitude, and so forth. We have seen how they intertwine in Sartre's thought. One finds in Merleau-Ponty other emphases: intersubjectivity, coexistence, inherence, fullness, attachment, opacity, ambiguity, compromise, relativity, contingency, and so forth. Only by looking at Merleau-Ponty's development in his later thought of the self-understanding of marxism can the impact of his understanding of phenomenology on the union of phenomenology and marxism be gauged—especially in terms of its divergence from the efforts contained in Sartre's "phenomenological marxism."[36]

Merleau-Ponty's Adventures

We have seen how Merleau-Ponty's development of a marxian social theory is rooted in and prefigured by his early phenomenological inquiries. For Merleau-Ponty, phenomenology emerges, like dialectical marxism, as an enemy of both rationalism and empiricism, and of idealism and materialism. Also like dialectical marxism, his phenomenology is oriented toward a view of the dialectical historicity of knowledge and reality and is based on a refusal of any Archimedean standpoint which tries to understand the world. Merleau-Ponty's early connections with Hegelian philosophy, phenomenology, and dialectical marxism led him to bypass the positivism underlying much of the historically prevalent marxism. From the beginning, his understanding of marxism distanced him from traditional "Russian communism." His is never a mechanistic, materialistic or scientistic marxism, but one which is subtle, open, and dialectical.[37]

Thus Merleau-Ponty sees in marxism an open and concrete philosophy which tries to understand the flesh of history, the incarnation of ideas and consciousness, and which orients itself to concrete intersubjectivity and the historical possibilities of human liberation through praxis. He sees in Marx a thinker who, in the spirit of the efforts of phenomenology, struggles against the two "fronts" of idealism and positivism, and who understands the "coherence of body, mind, and external world in a totality of experience."[38] Above all, marxism, like phenomenology, is a philosophy which refuses to be seduced by the illusion of form over content and conceptual abstraction over lived concreteness. In social and political understanding this means that

> to understand and judge a society, one has to penetrate its basic structure to the human bond upon which it is built; this undoubtedly depends upon legal relations, but also upon forms of labor, ways of loving, living, and dying. . . . A regime which is nominally liberal can be oppressive in reality. A regime which acknowledges its violence *might* have in it more genuine humanity.[39]

With his phenomenologically conditioned understanding, it was not difficult for Merleau-Ponty to perceive quickly the inhuman historical consequences of a positivistic and dogmatic marxism. Such a marxism too easily degenerates into a tyranny of objectively determined historical forces over the concrete human subject. In the face of the consequences of this marxism, Merleau-Ponty began to see it not as a positive truth immanent in the logic of history apart from human subjectivity, but as a theory of the relationship between theory and practice, or between consciousness and reality. This antipositivistic relativization of marxism is already apparent in *Humanism and Terror,* although it takes place within the context of a "classical" marxism:

Our task is to clarify the ideological situation, to underline, beyond the paradoxes and contingencies of contemporary history, the true terms of the human problem, to recall Marxists to their humanist inspiration, to remind the democracies of their fundamental hypocrisy, and to keep intact against propaganda the chances that might still be left for history to become enlightened once again.[40]

The relativization of marxism becomes more central and forceful in his last explicit work on political theory, and especially in the last complete work he ever published.[41] Here we find the argument that "classical" or "orthodox" marxism must be superseded, that marxism has become a "secondary truth" capable of orienting analyses but no longer capable of representing itself as *the* immutable truth of human affairs.[42]

For Merleau-Ponty, then, marxism still retains its heuristic value and stands alone as an authentic attempt to unite theory and practice and to strive for human universality over alienation and particularism. But the reification and canonization of Marx and marxism, viewed as capable of possessing a truth applicable to all times and places, has transformed a living truth into a collection of ruins, a "classic," open to the archaeology of anyone.[43] Part of the value and truth of Marx's insights was the discovery that reality is a continual process incapable of being understood by theory that refuses to change itself. If the liberal conception of politics as a series of encounters between human morality and particular events is inadequate, so is the marxist conception in which politics is the scientific application of correct theory to the already determined process of human affairs. This is the kind of marxist politics which results from making Marx a "classic." It misunderstands the nature of politics:

Politics is never the encounter between conscience and individual happenings, nor is it ever the simple application of a philosophy of history. Politics is never able to see the whole directly. It is always aiming at the incomplete synthesis, a given cycle of time, or a group of problems. It is not pure morality nor is it a chapter in a universal history which has already been written. Rather it is an action in the process of self-invention.[44]

This puts into perspective a marxist politics guided by a philosophical understanding that has become absolute, un-self-critical, incapable of and unwilling to change. It leads to the view that history can be purified and that a regime may exist on a scientific basis without chance or risk. In a remark presumably directed at Sartre, Merleau-Ponty sees this idea as nothing less than "the inverse reflection of our own anxiety and solitude."

With the consequences of a positivistic marxism in mind, Merleau-Ponty calls for a revolutionary spirit which avoids abstract rationalist inversions of concrete, ambiguous lived experience. He warns against a revolutionary spirit whereby one disguises the state of his own soul, and he warns against an allegiance to a universal history wherein one masquerades his personal dreams and inclinations. These avenues embody the worst kind of bad faith (in the Sartrean sense of lying to oneself): "The important revolutionaries, and first of all Marx, are not revolutionaries in that sense. They lived their time rather than look to it in the hope of forgetting their own obsessions."[45] Such revolutionaries realize that history is not to be merely contemplated but "made," and what they put of themselves into revolution is not "a vague strain of millenarianism" but an acute understanding of events.

This understanding acquires a less leisurely and a more powerful meaning and role than that of previous contemplation, and it requires ever greater moral and political responsibility from theorists and practioners alike. Marxian theory and practice is relativized in the realm of everyday life: "Marx did not speak of an end of history but of an end to pre-history. This means that after, just as before, the revolution the true revolutionary, each day confronting each new problem, rediscovers what is to be done." He can neither sit back and merely contemplate the objective course of events nor assume that his every action is guaranteed to further the cause of truth, philosophy, and history. He is thrown into a sea of ambiguity: "He navigates without a map and with a limited view of the present."[46] For Merleau-Ponty, the dialectic guarantees nothing and expects everything.

After Merleau-Ponty critically traces the "adventures of the dialectic" from Weber through Lukács, Lenin, Trotsky, and Sartre, he concludes that these adventures have resulted in errors, primarily of the naturalistic and positivistic brand.[47] But these are errors through which the dialectic must pass, "since it is in principle a thought with several centers and several points of entry, and because it needs time to explore them all."[48] Indeed, although marxist politics is as undemonstrable as any other politics (in the sense that the synthesis at which it aims is unprovable), it differs in one crucial sense. Politics oscillates "between the world of reality and that of values, between individual judgment and common action, between the present and the future." Whether these poles are capable of union in history cannot be proven, but "Marxist politics understands this and . . . it has, more than any other politics, explored the labyrinth."[49]

The greatest error into which the adventures of the dialectic have lapsed is the facile acceptance of a metaphysical guarantee of the end of history. This error in particular involves a nondialectical understanding and employment of the dialectic itself. The reliance upon "the dialectic'' has led to its reification and to the lack of any phenomenological inquiry into the foundations of dialectical thought and reality. But these erroneous adventures have not eliminated once and for all the importance of the dialectic:

> What then is obsolete is not the dialectic but the pretension of terminating it in an end of history, in a permanent revolution, or in a regime which, being the contestation of itself, would no longer need to be contested from the outside and, in fact, would no longer have anything outside it.[50]

The errors of the adventures of Lenin, Lukács, Trotsky, and Sartre are thus revealed and epitomized.

Merleau-Ponty calls for the end of classical and orthodox marxist adventures of the dialectic. He calls for the emergence of a non-Communist Left as a politics and a political theory which will expose the failure of the historical reality of communism and continue to confront the defects of liberalism. Furthermore, he believes that it is disingenuous to argue that marxism is correct in what it negates and critiques, and incorrect in what it asserts and affirms: "The Marxist critique must therefore be taken up again, re-exposed completely, and generalized, and we were speaking abstractly when we said that Marxism 'remains true as negation.' "[51]

Merleau-Ponty's conclusion is modest: "We would be happy if we could inspire a few—or many—to bear their freedom, not to exchange it at a loss; for it is not only their own thing, their secret, their pleasure, their salvation—it involves everyone else."[52] But his own importance for the adventures of the dialectic is much less modest. Although his review of the adventures is characterized by a sense of resignation and weariness, the fact that he, too, is a part of them inspires hope. What for Merleau-Ponty results in a dejected examination of his past may result for us in an aspiration for the future. His inquiry itself into the errors of the adventures of the dialectic provides a corrective which might guide and inspire different adventures in the future.

Conclusions

Neither Sartre nor Merleau-Ponty ever explicitly completes a union of phenomenology and marxism. Perhaps to do so explicitly would be either artificial or impossible. Such a union may only be possible in terms of a complete reconstitution of the self-understanding of philosophy and political theory, which is not accomplished by a mere manipulation of positions. The particular value of Merleau-Ponty's efforts is found in the impact of his phenomenological inquiry into the nature of reality and knowledge upon his understanding of marxism and politics. He offers us one of the most critically self-aware accounts of marxism of his time. The union of marxism and phenomenology in Merleau-Ponty does not reside in the contrived combination of two separate bodies of doctrines, propositions, and interests. It lies rather in the intrinsic interaction between a critical philosophical movement and a critical theory of politics. It lies in the fact that phenomenology is less a technical body of knowledge than it is a mode of thinking, a way of philosophy which involves radical thinking, an understanding of the philosophical enterprise itself which is founded in critical and self-critical reflection and inquiry.[53] It is this that Merleau-Ponty brings to marxism, helping to awaken it from its dogmatic, uncritical, and positivistic slumbers, and to recover its dialectical and open spirit and content. This is a major value of his "phenomenological marxism" or "marxist phenomenology."

For these reasons, Merleau-Ponty's lessons seem the most important for us to learn from the early attempts to marry marxism and phenomenology. Sartre's destiny in this attempt has too often been absolute ideological acceptance of marxism in dogma. In the conflicts between marxism and existential phenomenology, the openness of the latter usually becomes subsumed in the historical exigencies of the former. Whereas Merleau-Ponty argues that marxism is entering a stage where it is no longer true in its original sense, but where it can still "orient analyses and retain a real heuristic value," Sartre continues to hold onto the "absolute."

In all fairness to Sartre, we must keep in mind that his relation to marxism is made doubly complex by the length of his career and by the many changes in his thought from the appearance of *Being and Nothingness* to the *Critique of Dialectical Reason*.[54] In this latter work, where we find no acknowledgment of his obvious indebtedness to Merleau-Ponty, Sartre tries to move away from the problems inherent in his earlier attempts to unify marxism and phenomenology. I do not believe, however, in light of these later attempts to be both more dialectical and more concrete, that Sartre succeeds on either count. One finds his central concepts of "Praxis" and the "Practico-Inert" taking on an almost mystical significance. The fact that Sartre becomes less dogmatic and more critical of positivistic marxism in his endeavor "to restore the dialectic to its critical foundations," is beyond doubt.[55] Nonetheless, he seems not to have freed himself completely from the confines of rationalism, dualism, and absolutism, which were so evident in his early work. It is for these reasons that I chose to focus our attention on Merleau-Ponty, whose thought is less well known than Sartre's but appears to be much more dialectical and important.

Furthermore, one can detect how Sartre's early phenomenology still conditions his later understanding of the ontology of human relations. Merleau-Ponty's criticism of *The Communists and Peace* might well be applied to the *Critique of Dialectical Reason,* which was completed after his death: "In Sartre there is a plurality of subjects but no inter-subjectivity."[56] But more important, it is Sartre's apparent inability to emancipate himself from the absolute character of his thought that undermines the vitality of his marxian-phenomenological union. In accord with Merleau-Ponty's efforts, it would seem that any union of marxism and phenomenology must fundamentally accept the dialectical contingency and ambiguity of human thought and existence. Ambiguity is not a problem to be overcome; it is a fundamental condition of existence itself.

Some Recent Arguments Concerning the Confluence of Marxism and Phenomenology

The attempt to develop and express a union of marxism and phenomenology neither begins nor ends with Sartre and Merleau-Ponty. Although no dominant "school" has emerged which deals systematically with such a union (and one hopes that none will, for schools have a tendency to become dogmatic), there have been instances of encounters between the two.[57] Furthermore, such encounters never take on the same shape and coloring in every case. They not only are conditioned by the time and thought of each thinker, as we saw with Sartre and Merleau-Ponty, but their differences reflect the openness, richness, and ambiguous tendencies of the movements from which they flow. The illustration of this point is a major concern of this volume.

In recent years, there have been a few attempts to elaborate the promise and importance of a meeting of phenomenology and political science, and especially of existential phenomenology and a critical science of politics. One example of an individual within the field of political science who has exhibited great concern for the contributions existential phenomenology can make to the foundations of political theory is Hwa Yol Jung.[58] I shall enter into a brief dialogue with Jung's introductory but important remarks on this relationship and then indicate some further attempts to reconcile phenomenology and marxism for the purpose of reorienting or reconstituting both philosophy and political theory. I hope that we can then see more clearly some of the possible fruits such an encounter may bear.

The General Relation of Existential Phenomenology to Political Science

It has been said of existential phenomenology that it "makes the transition between transcendental phenomenology, born of the reduction of everything to its appearing to me, and ontology, which restores the question of the sense of being for all that is said to 'exist.' "[59]

Transcendental phenomenology is concerned with the constitution by transcendental subjectivity of forms of experience. Existential phenomenology is concerned less with transcendental subjectivity and more with describing all realms of human existence. It is existential phenomenology which speaks most directly to political science.

Existential phenomenology, as we have frequently noted, is concerned with a penetration of the preconceptual foundation of all thought and existence, which is the *Lebenswelt*. Since the *Lebenswelt* refers to the total world of lived relations among human beings, cultural objects, and nature, including social, historical, and political dimensions, a phenomenology of the *Lebenswelt* has important implications for political inquiry. Its relevance lies in the fact that the life-world is the "basic matrix" for all theoretical activity, and that it is also a social, historical, and cultural world which is the foundation for all social and political activity.[60] More specifically, "the contribution of phenomenological investigation to the theory of politics, society and culture lies especially in its focusing on the meaning of human action."[61] The life-world is the basis of all human action conceived as historical action and open possibility. A phenomenology of the life-world reveals our inextricable relation to the world, grounded in prereflective, primordial lived experience and activity. It also reveals our indestructible intersubjectivity or sociality. Thus it indicates that a separation of theory from practice, or reflection from life, contradicts the unity of mind and body in our original way of being in the world. It indicates also that theory and reflection are rooted in the *Lebenswelt* as social and historical enterprises. The *Lebenswelt* is lived and active, but it is also social and historical.[62] Thus the process of political inquiry itself is rooted in preconceptual social life. For the political theorist this means that "preconceptual political reality serves as the background of his political theorizing, for he is first and foremost a member of that political society which he objectifies."[63]

As philosophy, phenomenology is a form of "radical empiricism." But it is a form of empiricism only if that term is broadened to include the whole of lived experience. More important is its radicalism, which lies in its self-examination and self-clarification as theoretical activity.[64] It is involved in a fundamental questioning of its own presuppositions— in the "phenomenology of phenomenology." It is in this sense that phenomenology is critical of scientistic political science and behavioralism for resting upon unclarified and unquestioned presuppositions as well as for being ignorant of their concrete origins in social existence.

Part of phenomenology's criticism is directed against the abstract dichotomy of subject and object presupposed by the empiricist self-understanding of political inquiry. Behavioralist political science is guilty of focusing on the "external" to the neglect of the "internal," thereby losing sight of the whole reality of the existing human person and the totality of the social and political act. Phenomenology, on the other hand, focuses on the "intentionality" of human thought and action which overcomes the dichotomy of internal and external. The concrete act of thinking itself springs from the inseparable union of *ego-cogito-cogitatum*. Reflection is grounded in lived experience, and the relation between subject and object is an intrinsic one. In this sense, positions of exclusive subjectivity or objectivity are misguided. The notion of intentionality reveals that "subjectivity and objectivity are only two moments of the same phenomenon."[65] This attempt to overcome the dichotomy of internal and external, of subject and object, through the concept of intentionality rooted in lived experience shares somewhat in Marx's attempt to do so through the notion of theoretical reflection rooted in sensuous praxis.

The denial of the separation of subject and object and the view of man as an active, social, and historical being open the way for a dialogue between existential phenomenology and marxist humanism. For Jung, the possibility of this dialogue lies in the fact that both movements are a philosophy of praxis, and that both have a central concern for humanism and thus for the problem of alienation.[66] For the dialogue to be effective, however, requires the elimination of a "deterministic theory of man, society, and history," and its replacement by a "philosophy of human freedom and responsibility," a theme which runs throughout my arguments above.

Phenomenology can contribute to the philosophical self-understanding of political science.[67] For Jung this means overcoming the "cold war" between philosophy and the social sciences. It means overcoming the currently dominant attitude which views political philosophy as concerned with the "normative" and political science as concerned with the "empirical," and with "factual knowledge."[68] Such a division is based upon a rejection of the notion that philosophy is always concerned with and grounded in the real, "factual," lived world, and, as Merleau-Ponty noted, that social science can never escape normative presuppositions and interpretations of the world.[69] A phenomenology of political science is especially helpful in clarifying the sources and meaning of human action or "behavior," which is the central focus of recent behavioral social science. What lacks most in the behavioralist examination of human action is the importance of the meaning of action, which is revealed in the intentional dimension of human action as a nexus of the internal and the external, of subject and object.[70] What is required in order to avoid an incomplete and inadequate understanding of social reality is an examination of the phenomenologically revealed intentional structure of consciousness and action.

For Jung, it is in explaining the meaning of human action that phenomenology's contribution to political science is greatest.[71] Central to
the nature of human action is its multidimensionality. Action is historical, intentional, motivational, and bodily. To say that action is
intentional is not to say that it is merely a matter of subjective inter-
nality. To say that it is bodily is not to say that action is merely a
matter of objective externality or behavior. Rather, it is to say that
action involves a unity of ego and body. The body is our access to
others; it is the necessary mediator and medium of all human thought
and activity. Thinking involves the body and acting involves the intentionality of consciousness: "Thinking is no more the function of
mind alone, as the rationalist has it, than acting is merely a physical
event, as the behaviorist has it."[72] The body is the "crucial locus" for
self- and social interpretation of lived experience and social action.
(How could one even write a sentence without giving evidence of the
concrete unity of mind and body? Such evidence is given also in human
speech, in dialogue itself.) The need to recover the intrinsic connection
between mind and body, or subject and object, was of central concern
to Marx as well. His recovery of "sensuous activity" and the "object"
as a corrective to the rationalism and idealism of Hegel reveals this.
And his attempt to unify theory and practice is partially rooted in this
basic perception.

Phenomenology also reveals the meaning and importance of sociality
for political inquiry. To be a human actor is to be a social being: "Thus
all social philosophy must begin with a clarification of this elemental
problem of sociality as the relationship between the self and the other."[73]
As we have already noted, and as Jung points out, in their beginnings
existentialism and phenomenology were negligent in exploring the social and political dimensions of human existence that our most radical
ontological status entails. That early focus on the "individual," or on
asocial transcendental subjectivity, shifted to a focus on intersubjectivity and sociality. This especially occurred, although Jung does not
dwell on it, with the encounters of phenomenology and marxism. Thus
Merleau-Ponty writes, echoing the spirit of Marx's philosophy of internal relations: "In man's co-existence with man, . . . morals, doctrines, thoughts and customs, laws, works and words all express each
other; everything signifies everything. And outside this unique fulgur-
ation of existence there is nothing."[74] Human existence is social
existence.

A phenomenology of sociality reveals the *Lebenswelt* as "an intersubjective world commonly given to all men."[75] It is important that
our essential sociality be understood in terms of "intersubjectivity"
and not in terms of "collectivism": "The extreme views of both atomistic individualism and totalitarian collectivism, in the final analysis,

vastly misunderstand the nature of sociality.''[76] This is the sense in which Marx, starting from a view of the concrete individual as a social being, criticized both liberal individualism and mystical collectivism. Liberal individualism posits the individual as a self-sufficient subject; in the context of social life, this can only result in a plurality of independent subjects and thus in a form of "interobjectivity." Totalitarian collectivism destroys intersubjectivity by transforming it into a hypostatized Society in which the individual is lost in a mystical collective (this was Marx's criticism of Proudhon). Our sociality must be seen in terms of mutuality and reciprocity.

The phenomenology of sociality illuminates for political theory the dialectic of freedom and responsibility. The exclusive emphasis on freedom in liberal individualism often results in the neglect of social responsibility. (This is something, by the way, that has become of great concern to current public policy analysis.) The exclusive emphasis on social responsibility and "duty to the whole" in collectivism, however, often results in the submersion of freedom. For Jung, real responsibility is impossible without freedom, but freedom is insufficient for the fulfillment of man as a social being. The phenomenological description of sociality as mutuality is not description for its own sake; it contains critical political implications: "In the end the authenticity of being human must be sought in responsibility—moral, social, and political—which lies at the root of genuine reciprocity."[77] As with Marx, the perception of man's essential sociality and his current alienation in and from social existence and concrete intersubjectivity both describes and prescribes. It illuminates the human condition and indicates the task which lies ahead. And as we have seen, the dialectic of freedom and responsibility is a central concern for the development of dialectical marxism and critical theory.

In the face of the "decline of political theory"—brought on by non-dialectical historicism, value-free positivism, the preoccupation with methodology, and philosophical developments unconcerned with political life—existential phenomenology contributes to the reconstitution of the philosophy of politics. For Jung, it offers "a clarification of the meaning of theory for human existence" and "a descriptive disclosure of the intentional meaning of human action and sociality."[78] As repeatedly emphasized, phenomenological description is description of the most radical sort. It penetrates to the foundations of thought and existence and returns us to the world of lived experience, which precedes dichotomies such as subject and object and the abstract formulations by which we claim to understand social and political reality. It critically describes the preconscious concrete unity of what Marx strives to see unified in conscious life through the synthesis of laboring praxis. Jung admits, again without dwelling on Marx, that phenomenology "is concerned with the meaning of theoretical inquiry into human existence and thus with the union of theory and practice, a problem of great importance to the theory of politics."[79]

The phenomenological insights into human intentionality and social relationality offer a firm basis for inquiry into the nature of man and society. There seems to be a unity in the following ideas: the notion that man is neither subject nor object but a concrete, intrinsic relation ("man is relational through and through"); the notion that man is "historical through and through"; Marx's philosophy of internal relations; and the concrete epistemological dialectic. If one accepts this unity, then one catches a glimpse of the distilled essence, foundations, and directions of dialectical theory. On the one hand, we are led to the need for a practical concretization of the insights of previous humanist philosophers of community, such as Plato, Aristotle, Rousseau, and Hegel. The task is one that Marx himself hoped to pursue. On the other hand, we are led to the need for a politicization of the beginnings of phenomenology in Husserl. In spite of the nonpolitical character of Husserl's search for a method by which to understand the *Lebenswelt* and the *Welterfahrendesleben* (life-experiencing-the-world), he nonetheless opened the way to an explication of the historicity and inter-subjectivity of the human life-world. His insights are compatible *in potentia* with those of Marx; the union is not in principle impossible. The insights revealed by Merleau-Ponty's endeavors to express this union are still seedlings. To harvest more completely the possible fruits of such a union is a task that lies ahead.

Some Further Adventures

Jung's essay is only one indication, but a very central one, of emergent endeavors to reconstitute social science at its foundations with the aid of phenomenological philosophy. The success of such efforts is contingent upon the development of more open dialogue between the rich varieties of existential phenomenology and dialectical marxism or critical theory. The connections already exist, even if often implicitly, in Jung's work. One of the most obvious examples is his discussion of the "multiple realities" of the *Lebenswelt,* where he focuses upon "working"—a form of action— as the paramount reality of everyday existence. Working is "most vital for the constitution of the reality of everyday existence," and is the radical ground for all political actions and interactions.[80] Although in need of elaboration, the connection with Marx's laboring praxis is evident.

At first glance, however, there seems to be a problem with Jung's argument in this regard. He draws an overly facile distinction between the "political actor" and the "political theorist."[81] The claim that the theorist as theorist does not participate in the life-world as an actor is perhaps overstated. This is a distinction that would appear dubious to

Aristotle as well as to Marx. It is the kind of distinction Marx struggled to overcome; he considered his own theoretical labor as a form of political activity and praxis. However, upon closer scrutiny of Jung's work, and especially of his latest undertaking in *The Crisis of Political Understanding,* we discover the problem not to be so evident. Jung is not interested in suggesting a fundamental separation of theory from practice; he is speaking more in terms of a working dialectical distinction between two special but not totally distinct ways of existing in the world. Such a working distinction does not seem to undermine the unity of theory and practice as the goal of both dialectical phenomenology and dialectical marxism.

There are today only a handful of scholars who are self-consciously arguing for a union of dialectical marxism and phenomenology, a union which can point the way to an alternative understanding of the process of political inquiry.[82] Their efforts are grounded in at least two basic concerns. First, they arise from the need to provide a critical and evaluative basis for political science. Second, they are guided by the concern for a reformulation of the connection between theory and practice, a concern as old as Aristotle. Although even among these few scholars who are searching for and confronting this alternative orientation there are as many differences as there are in the rich and complex histories of phenomenology and marxism themselves, there are also a number of important commonalities central to a consideration of the reconstitution of social and political theory.

First and foremost is the argument that all social and political theory must be critical. For theory to be critical, however, it must do more than challenge existing reality and theory; it must also be critical of its own premises. A critical posture, such as that inherent in a dialectical phenomenological marxism, must therefore be not only "other-directed" but expressed in continual self-scrutiny and self-reflection as well.[83] A self-critical posture must be combined with a critical attitude toward the world and with an interest in human emancipation. Such an attitude is incipient in both the later Husserl and Marx, who shared a fundamental interest in "emancipating humanity from mythological concepts and fetishized reality, disguised as purely 'objective,' 'natural,' or 'absolute.' "[84] It is for this reason that Husserl was skeptical of the claim to "absolute validity" of the un-self-critical natural sciences, and that Marx was critical of the disguised ideological position of the science of political economy.

Thus the character of the critical theory which emerges from phenomenology and dialectical marxism has a double significance: it is both self- and other-directed. Such theory entails openness to its own foundations and to the world of being. It can never assume that its

foundations are secured in a closed set of presuppositions and propositions. As Enzo Paci puts it, philosophy itself is conceived as

> the human activity in which life resumes the journey toward truth
> by continuously returning to its own origin and by becoming trans-
> formed in the horizon of truth, i.e., by always reconstituting being
> into intentional meaning.[85]

Truth itself is never grasped in its totality once and for all. Truth,
meaning, being, and reality all exist as the horizon of the world. And
although this "horizon" is always present in us, "it is never fully
conquered."[86] There is a fundamental openness and ambiguity in the
relationship between the meaning of truth and human inquiry and activity. Thus, "since truth as the meaningful direction of being can never
be possessed, intentionality is infinite and its goal is unreachable."
This goal, which is always present as a demand, "is the meaning of
truth that is inexhaustible in the world."[87] It is as self-critical reflection,
as criticism of reality for the sake of emancipation, and as complete
openness toward the foundation of theory and the meaning of truth
that the self-understanding of inquiry which emerges from the confluent
development of phenomenology and dialectical marxism is one of critical theory.[88]

Another commonality is evident in the rejection of all forms of objectivism and subjectivism, particularly in terms of the epistemological
relation of subject and object. This central concern forms a major theme
of our inquiry, and it appears in different forms among those who are
currently arguing for a fusion of marxism and phenomenology. Put
most simply, phenomenology emerged with Husserl from a concern
with the inadequacy of scientific objectivity. Thus it was born of a need
to "return to subjectivity," to return to the importance of the subjective
constitution of objectivity itself.[89] Marxism emerged with Marx from
a concern with the reification of absolute subjectivity. Thus it was born
of a need to recover the sensuous objectivity of the human subject.
Although there are phenomenologists since Husserl who have developed phenomenology as a "science of the subject," and marxists since
Marx who have developed marxism as a "science of the object," such
a conception of the importance of both movements misses the point.[90]
The point is that what unites the two movements is the development
within each of a view of the dialectical unity of subject and object.

To be sure, Husserl himself is guilty in his struggle against objectivism of replacing objectivity with transcendental subjectivity, which
becomes another mystical form of objectivity. He never accepted the
possibility of a reconciliation or union of subject and object, or of
thought and reality. The development within phenomenology of an
explicit dialectic of subject and object had to wait until the efforts of

Merleau-Ponty, for whom the dialectic is rooted in the primary experience of perception itself.[91] Such a dialectic already exists in Marx, but it is truncated and destroyed by the development of objectivistic, positivistic marxism, only to be salvaged by a counterdevelopment of critical, dialectical marxism. To conceive the value of a union of phenomenology and marxism simply in terms of the union of a science of the subject with a science of the object is inaccurate; it forgets the importance of the dialectic. To be sure, phenomenology has always emphasized subjectivity, while marxism has emphasized objectivity. But the real value of their union lies in the fact that both have moved in dialectical directions, which has resulted in the attempt by both to overcome dialectically the abstract dichotomy of subject and object.

The recognition of a dialectic of subject and object emerges at different levels among those who argue for the union of marxism and phenomenology. Perhaps most fundamental is the recognition of a concrete unity of mind and body, or of consciousness and existence. A basic discovery of phenomenology is the "*Leib-Seele* unity" and the fact that "the 'mind' and the 'body' are not contraposed, since they are two different ways of experiencing the same subjectivity"; it even becomes impossible "to think of a parallelism of 'mind' and 'body.' "[92] A similar discovery emerges from the view that the purpose of marxist "materialism" is to "vindicate the whole man," and not to "reduce him naturalistically" to a merely sensuous, objective body or thing.[93] Phenomenology and marxism agree that there "is no spirit or consciousness separate from the body, nature, society, and the world that man experiences and contains."[94] This is certainly not to say that spirit or consciousness does not exist or is illusory, but that it only exists in dialectical relation to the body, or object.

The recovery of the dialectic of subject and object is the recovery of the nexus of knowledge and experience, and of analysis and human purpose.[95] In a word, it is the retrieval of the crucial connection of man and the world. It militates against the alienation of man and the world implicit in a subject-object dichotomy. It militates against the view of the subject as a detached thought-substance and of the object as an opaque world of environment. In arguing for a dialectical unity of subject and object, one must be careful not to fall into the trap of the philosophy of identity which argues for an absolute identity of subject and object, thus dismissing the dialectical tension necessary to their relation.[96] To argue for a dialectic of subject and object, whereby no "objective being" can be thought independently of the thinking subject, is not to argue for a nondialectical conflation of subject and object. It is to argue that all objectivity is relative to cognitive subjectivity.[97] Thus all objectivity is as contingent upon subjectivity as the latter is upon the former; absolute certitude, necessity, or fixity resides on neither side of the relation.

The rejection of all forms of objectivism and subjectivism entails, finally, a rejection of both rationalism and empiricism and of the illusory opposition of the two. The debate between rationalism and empiricism often resolves into a debate between reason and experience. Despite the broader limits of knowledge set by the concerns of reason over those of narrow empirical experience, both orientations demand some form of objective correspondence between the knower and the known.[98] This demand ignores the dialectically mutual determination of knower and known which informs us that no objective correspondence can be presupposed. Indeed, the mutually exclusive character of the debate between rationalism and empiricism is an illusion recognized early by Marx.[99] The dialectical theory that emerges from phenomenology as well as from marxism entails, not a choice between reason and experience, but a concrete synthesis of the two in unalienated human inquiry and life.

> In phenomenology, it becomes increasingly more difficult to separate a well-understood empiricism from a well-understood rationalism. Essentially, phenomenology does not allow this separation and appears not as the sum of the two moments, or as their ambiguity, but as their concrete synthesis.[100]

Marx argues that the antinomies of subject and object, or reason and experience, are grounded in and express real, practical human life, and that their synthetic resolution is not a problem of knowledge alone but one of real life.[101] In the same way, the argument of phenomenology tells us that "this synthesis is historical life oriented toward the truth, and it exposes *the dualism between experience and reason* for what it is: the symptom of a crisis."[102]

The struggle against objectivism among those involved in a marxian-phenomenological union expresses itself also in a shared conception of the nature of man. First and foremost in this conception is the idea that man is not confined to a fixed nature. He is open possibilities. His full nature is a synthesis which always remains to be made. The realization of man's nature lies transcendentally in the future. Thus man is a fundamentally open and historical creature. He is not confined to fixed internal dispositions, nor is he merely an objective reactive mechanism.[103] But neither is he a mere combination of the internal and the external. Rather, man's nature is characterized by "intentionality," which militates against a view of him as either an object or a mere constituting consciousness. Intentionality is the nexus of experience and the experienced (in the broadest sense of the term) wherein the meaning of human action and being lies.[104] The radical intentionality of human being-in-the-world eludes a facile identification of man as merely subject or object and requires an open-endedness to our conception of "human nature." Man is never all that he can be. Man is never finished "intending the world," and that involves a restless pursuit of what is not yet fully human in man; our nature, indeed our humanity, is contingent upon the historically open development of our intentionality.

Finally, what appears in common among those working toward a marxian-phenomenological union is the central concern for the relation between theory and practice. This, of course, takes many forms. At one level it involves the need to re-establish the connection between ethics and political life.[105] The current severance of that connection is grounded in the positivist fact-value and is-ought dichotomies which dictate, in Dallmayr's words, "a devaluation of normative-practical considerations in favor of empirical knowledge."[106] The reconnection of ethics and political life in the process of political inquiry requires a reconstitution of the current self-understanding of political science, of which an essential tenet is the fact-value distinction. Critical marxism argues against the distinction on the basis that it disguises ideological and practical positions. Phenomenology criticizes it on the grounds it is an abstraction from the concrete lived experience of the *Lebenswelt*. Together marxism and phenomenology argue that the union of theory and practice requires a recognition of the dialectic of subject and object, the concrete unity of thought and experience, and of fact and value.

Furthermore, essential for a union of marxism and phenomenology is the need for theory to confront social and political life critically. This is to argue that philosophy must actively intervene in reality with a view toward the radical transformation of human life. For Marx this meant nothing less than the "realization of philosophy," the concretization of the unity of subject and object historically through the synthesis of laboring praxis, the purpose of which is the supersession of alienated, irrational human life. Even Husserl, as a philosophical critic of reality, "intended to raise and intensify the acute awareness of his readers of the 'crisis' in order to transform society and its institutions by a more 'rational' way of life, capable of producing a new 'transcendental man.' "[107]

Perhaps most essential to the argument for a unity of theory and practice is the idea that it cannot be achieved artificially. It is not an argument for a third party to take the insights of pure theory discovered through disinterested and detached contemplation or observation and to "apply" those insights to an independently proceeding social reality. Rather, it is a demand for the practical interest in emancipating and transforming an alienated human world to become an intrinsic and inseparable component of the theoretical enterprise itself. It asks that concrete practical interest become the radical foundation for the theoretical process of political inquiry. This interest must constitute and guide the process of inquiry. Thus the humanistic unity of theory and practice, of consciousness and life, in unalienated, whole existence is possible only if the unity is presupposed by, and understood as the essential constituent of, the very nature of all philosophical inquiry.

Despite these many points of agreement, all is not harmonious among those who are working theoretically within the confluent movements of existential phenomenology and dialectical marxism. Even among these few thinkers, there are disagreements over the theoretical substance of such a union as well as over how the union is to be effected. Furthermore, each thinker himself falls prey to various problems and inconsistencies.

With Paci, for example, the union of marxism and phenomenology does not involve a deviation from either movement, but a "demystification" of both.[108] Such a demystification requires criticism of any marxism which understands itself in naturalistic scientific terms as an objective, transhistorical science. According to Paci, an objectivistic, scientistic marxism "demystified" becomes a critical marxism.[109] It is in this sense that, for Paci, marxism is not an ideology but a critique of ideology; a critical marxism must be grounded in a philosophy which is not an ideology.[110] At the same time, a demystification of Husserlian phenomenology requires making explicit the fact that Husserl's critique of the "crisis of the sciences" implicitly entails a critique of bourgeois ideology. For Paci, the crisis of the sciences involves an "occluded use of the sciences that negate the subject." What Husserl's critique reveals is that the crisis of the sciences is a crisis of the capitalist use of the sciences, and therefore a crisis of human existence in capitalist society. Phenomenology demystified becomes "the revelation of the capitalist occlusion of the subject and truth, and the disocclusion of every ideology based on such an occlusion."[111]

For Paci, then, the demystification of marxism and phenomenology reveals the union of the two. It suggests how marxist problems arise within phenomenology and how the phenomenological problematic is already implicit in marxism.[112] It is worth citing his conclusion here:

> The discovery of philosophy is the discovery of the phenomenological analysis necessary for praxis to achieve its desired successes. It is the critique of the past departing from the present. It is rehabilitation and reparation. It is the continual analysis of the situation and the negation of already rendered judgments. It is the inherence in determined and localized presence of the unitary efforts to maintain, in the many parts, the unitary movement and its teleological horizon of truth in the precise evaluation of the various types of alienation and in the recognition of the unitary func-

tion of science and culture. *It is the discovery of phenomenology within Marxism.* The discovery that the sciences are at the service of capital is *the discovery of Marxism within phenomenology.* The struggle against the categorical, and the return to the subject for the foundation of science and philosophy, is the struggle against capitalism.[113]

The movements of phenomenology and marxism are discovered within each other, and ultimately, both are movements which center on the alienation of subject and object. Their union is not artificial but intrinsic, once it is viewed from a dialectical and critical perspective.

But there are problems in Paci, not the least of which is his often uncritical certainty. The apodictic thrust of much of his argument is revealed especially in his insistence on the complete reliability of intuitive evidence.[114] There is too much talk in Paci of phenomenology as the "universal science," of "certain truth," and there are too many tendencies toward viewing phenomenology as a "first philosophy." Paci appears to ignore the necessary openness and ambiguity of the dialectic that is essential for any critical stance. Indeed, his rejection of ambiguity in favor of certainty is the basis of his criticism of Merleau-Ponty.[115] He does not accept Merleau-Ponty's insistence on a phenomenology of phenomenology, on the need for phenomenology to be radically self-reflexive, and thus he seems to fall into the trap of questing after nondialectical, uncritical "first principles."

One could continue to find differences between Paci's attempt and those, for example, of Dallmayr and Bernstein. Dallmayr argues for a critical theory of politics that draws its inspiration from existential phenomenology and critical marxism, particularly that developed by the "Frankfurt School" of Horkheimer, Adorno, Marcuse, Apel, and Habermas.[116] This perspective in political science, according to Dallmayr, can lead us beyond the despair over the possibility of a humanistic political order, to which the "revival of political theory" is a symptomatic response. It can also lead us beyond the dogma of positivistic political science which disguises, and methodologically prevents the treatment of, the object and source of that despair.

Bernstein, on the other hand, argues that social and political theory is undergoing a restructuring movement, from which phenomenology and critical theory have emerged as two of the most important sources of an alternative approach to understanding social and political reality. Although it does not appear to be his intent, there is a certain artificiality to Bernstein's "union" of critical theory, phenomenology, ordinary-language philosophy, and empirical theory. Phenomenology appears on the scene, along with ordinary-language philosophy or conceptual analysis, as providing the interpretive element of a social and political theory concerned with understanding the meaning of human action and being, while critical theory provides the critical element of a re-structuring which particularly unites theory and practice.

Bernstein concludes that social and political theory must be empir-ical, interpretive, and critical.[117] This is an important conclusion, to be sure. He argues that such a convergence is the result of a subtle dialectic and not of a straightforward "combination" of various understandings. Nonetheless, the argument that phenomenology is an "interpretive" enterprise while critical theory provides the "critical" element, sepa-rates too distinctly the insights and contributions of the two move-ments; it also seems to underestimate the historically developed relationship between them. An indication of the inadequacy of this view is revealed by the fact that Bernstein's treatment of recent phe-nomenology focuses on the work of Alfred Schutz, with only scant attention paid to Merleau-Ponty. And his treatment of what I have called dialectical marxism focuses on the critical theory of Habermas, who emerges, as we shall see in the next chapter, from a specific tradition not altogether friendly toward phenomenology. It should be noted, however, that Bernstein's criterion for the selection of Schutz to represent "the phenomenological alternative" is the highly "sys-tematic" character of Schutz's thought, whereas my criterion for fo-cusing on Merleau-Ponty has been the highly dialectical character of his thought.[118]

These explorations of the confluence of dialectical marxism and ex-istential phenomenology provide us with a new way of looking at the process of political inquiry, or at least reveal new dimensions that broaden our view. The dialectical theory that we have thus far seen evolve from its roots in Kant and Hegel through the developments of marxism and phenomenology, is not, and should not be, the result of a contrived manipulation of "positions." An alternative view of polit-ical inquiry should not be conceived of as the product of an intellectual combination of Husserl and Marx, or of Schutz and Habermas, or of some ideal form of transcendental phenomenology and some ideal form of marxism. Although I cannot be totally absolved of culpability in this regard, it has been my hope to suggest otherwise, that is, that there has been an immanent development of an alternative that awaits our recognition and clarification. The movements of phenomenology and marxism are historically relative human expressions and symboliza-tions of a concern with the problems of alienated and irrational social existence, and with the theoretical and practical deficiencies of non-dialectical philosophical inquiry into the human condition. If these movements are simply combined and reified in a new "position," then the dialectic of subject and object, and of philosophical consciousness and historical praxis, will recede and become closed and transformed into a nondialectical principle itself. This is always the danger from which we must protect the openness of dialectical theory.

Therefore, the meaning and insights revealed by the developments traced in the preceding chapters must continue to be reconstructed and developed in light of our own time and situation, which includes the reincorporation of the past and the concrete projection of the future. The adventures traced here cannot be seen as final solutions either to the dialectical reconstitution of political theory or to the real transcendence of unfree and alienated human life. They can only be seen as important prefigurations of what is yet to come, or at least of what still promises to transpire. The various adventures of the marxian-phenomenological confluence in dialectical theory merely illuminate the shape and direction of a possible future for political inquiry, or at least one dimension of that future. But our vision is never completely clear. It is doubtful that we can ever penetrate all the shadows of obscurity; not all the dark corners of these adventures are illuminated. Thus these various adventures serve a double purpose. They help to signify both the tasks and the dangers that lie ahead, in the face of which nothing is guaranteed but our efforts.

6 Contemporary Dialectical Theory

The Voice of Critical Theory

I would be remiss if this study concluded without an examination of another important voice in the evolution of a dialectical theory relevant to political inquiry: the voice of Critical Theory.[1] Although there is a sense in which all of the preceding chapters have entailed a reconstruction of the development of a dialectical and critical theory of politics, I believe that the "Frankfurt School of Critical Theory" deserves specific mention for at least two reasons. First, although the Frankfurt School founded by Max Horkheimer and Theodor Adorno emerged from the same Kantian, Hegelian, and Marxian roots as dialectical marxism and existential phenomenology, it developed in its own distinctive direction. Particularly, it developed toward an analysis of philosophy and culture and away from an analysis of political economy, and it also developed in conscious opposition to the movement of Husserlian phenomenology. Second, as a movement which self-consciously called itself "the critical theory of society," the Frankfurt School enjoyed an institutional base and continuity as the *Institut für Sozialforschung* for almost half a century. Thus as a movement in the development of dialectical theory, it possessed a particularly strong sense of identity in a field of many other similar movements and developments.[2]

For these reasons, as well as for its substantive contributions to the evolution of dialectical theory, a discussion of Critical Theory merits special attention. However, it is important not to infer from this separate treatment that Critical Theory has no connections with the developments traced in past chapters; it should be kept in mind that in earlier discussions I have many times touched base with Critical Theory, especially with Jürgen Habermas, its foremost exponent today.

Unfortunately, it is impossible in one chapter to deal adequately with the many diverse thinkers and complex ideas that make up the history of the Frankfurt School. Hence our attention will be focused on the general origins of Critical Theory, its foundations in the thought of Max Horkheimer, its journey from a position closely related to traditional marxism to one quite distantly removed from it, and finally, on some core dialectical concepts in the thought of its most important heir, Habermas.

The General Origins of Critical Theory as the Recovery of Dialectical Marxism

Political Origins

As with the attempts to unite phenomenology and marxism, the origins of Critical Theory were both political and philosophical. First of all, the Frankfurt School came into being as a response within the marxist tradition to particular important political and historical transformations taking place in the early part of the twentieth century. After the First World War and the Russian Revolution, there was a general eastward shift of the center of gravity of socialist thought, and the concomitant development of a "socialist orthodoxy."[3] Certain important structural changes began to occur in the social and political world which seemed to defy the comprehension of a reified, dogmatic marxist theory. One such development was the emergence of an antidemocratic political system in the country of the first socialist revolution. The political development of a bureaucratic and oppressive Communist orthodoxy presented substantial problems for the self-understanding of marxism as a movement of emancipation and critical enlightenment.

Just as important, however, were developments in the historical structure of liberal capitalism itself, especially in the 1930s. Capitalism appeared to be entering a postliberal stage with the increase of monopoly structures and growing government intervention in the economy ("state capitalism").[4] The proponents of the Frankfurt School felt they had to respond to these kinds of economic and political transformations for which the categories and formulas of orthodox and dogmatic marxist theory seemed inadequate.[5] Furthermore, they had to face the fact of a perceived "withering away of the revolutionary working class," and the general decline of revolutionary class consciousness.[6] Related to this, of course, was the development of a powerful and viable alternative to revolution in the form of social democracy (beginning at least as early as the 1920s). The assumption of an inevitably progressing revolutionary working class became problematical. Again, their perception of these major changes forced the Frankfurt School to develop new categories for analyzing the structure of social and political life as well as to re-examine the nature of marxism itself.

Perhaps most important for the social and political inspirations of Critical Theory was the perceived need to deal with the historical structure and importance of the emergence of advanced industrial-technological society. The rapid development of science and technology, and their role in the integration of the political and social systems, summoned a new and major transformation in the structure of capitalism. The various contradictions and problems involved with the rise of technological-industrial society were seen by the original Critical Theorists to transcend those of classical liberal capitalism. Marx's original starting point in the critique of political economy had to be broadened to the more comprehensive framework of the critique of technical civilization. In this light, the major problem to be confronted by a critical theory of society was the rise of technical rationality and "instrumental reason."[7] From a political point of view, the development of capitalism to a technological-industrial stage involved not only a qualitative transformation of capitalist economy and society, but also a growing integration of, and intimacy between, positivist and technological modes of thought and the ideological defense and maintenance of the "neocapitalist" status quo.[8]

These major historical and political developments in the structure of capitalist society, as well as the emergence of a bureaucratic Communist orthodoxy, engendered for the founders of Critical Theory two basic needs: first, the need to develop a new dialectical and critical theory of society (still within the framework of marxist theory) which could deal with the changes in industrial-technological, postliberal capitalist society; and second, the need to recover the philosophical dimension of marxism which had suffered an economistic-materialistic reduction at the hands of a new marxist orthodoxy. In a sense, the return to a philosophical critique was as much a reaction to the political establishment of a Communist orthodoxy as it was to an interest in pure theory. The mechanistic materialism of the Second International, which formed the theoretical position and center of marxist orthodoxy, was in need of serious re-examination and critique, a critique which had already found seminal expression in Lukács, Gramsci, and Karl Korsch.[9] For all of its political inspiration, however, the development of Critical Theory eventually moved ever further away from the concerns of political economy and praxis, and ever nearer the concerns of culture and philosophy. I shall return to this issue later.

Philosophical Origins

Critical Theory emerged as an attempt to salvage marxism from a degeneration into mechanical materialism. It directed its efforts against the determinism and objectivism of a marxism in danger of destroying the vitality of the dialectic. Thus the Frankfurt School theory was an endeavor to recover a dialectical marxism, and as such it stands in common with the movements discussed earlier in chapter 3. The attempt to restore the critically reflective and dialectical dimension of marxism, understood as a critical theory of society, was predicated explicitly on Marx's epistemology and methodology. The fundamental importance of marxism was seen to lie in its development of a dialectical theory of knowledge and a critical method for analyzing and changing society, not in its development of a deterministic and metaphysical cosmology. Therefore, the recovery of a dialectical-critical epistemology and method was not perceived by the Critical Theorists as a radical "revision" of marxism; rather, it was understood as the recovery and development of the dialectical, core elements of marxism, which had become "residual" through its positivization.

The philosophical origins of Critical Theory, then, are in the return to the centrality of the dialectic in Marx, and hence to the Kantian and Hegelian roots of dialectical theory. Essential to Critical Theory is the reflective reconstruction and re-establishment of the Kantian and, especially, Hegelian epistemological origins of marxism.[10] Through such a reconstruction, a critically self-reflective marxism can refound itself philosophically and dialectically.[11] In a sense, in returning to the Hegelian origins of marxist thought, the founders of Critical Theory found themselves in a position similar to that of the Left Hegelians (including Marx) in the 1840s, with many of the same concerns of developing the Hegelian dialectical method and directing it "materialistically" toward a practical critique and transformation of society.[12]

Apart from confronting important historical transformations, there was, of course, a major difference between the position of the original Left Hegelians and the position at which the Frankfurt School members found themselves: the latter were separated philosophically from Kant and Hegel by the work of such figures as Nietzsche, Bergson, Dilthey, Weber, and Husserl, and they had to confront the reality of a systematized, positivistic marxism. Hence their response was twofold: first, they attempted to deal with and integrate the work of Nietzschean and Bergsonian *Lebensphilosophie* (philosophy of life), Dilthey's hermeneutical historicism, Weberian sociology, Husserlian phenomenology, and especially Freudian psychoanalysis; and second, they attempted to overcome the positivism and objectivism which had invaded marxist theory itself.

These philosophical origins reflect two major characteristics of Critical Theory. On the one hand, from its beginnings it has been opposed to all closed systems of thought which develop a hermetic and inflexible metaphysics. Thus Critical Theory is opposed to any marxism grounded in nondialectical metaphysical materialism and dogmatic solipsism. For the Critical Theorists, the dogmatic reification of marxism has two major sources. It is rooted in an eschatological determinism which posits the metaphysical and logical necessity of an ever-progressing revolutionary working class heading toward ultimate destiny. And it is grounded in the latent positivism of Marx's objectivistic concept of labor which has permitted (unintentionally) the development of an economistic scientism and determinism.[13] The rejection of a reductionist, materialist marxism engendered for Critical Theory a concern for the nondialectical dismissal of the power and importance of the "cultural superstructure." The recovery of a dialectical marxism thus involves a recovery of the cultural dimension of marxism, especially its relation to the critique of ideology.[14]

On the other hand, the Critical Theorists conceived the importance of developing their theory dialectically in critical contact both with changing social reality and with other developing philosophical traditions. Again, therefore, Critical Theory from its beginnings involved an attempt to criticize and incorporate a number of traditions which combined to constitute its rich and diverse philosophical foundation. These sources may be summarized as follows: German idealism (Kant and especially the early Hegel) and its relations to Marx's philosophical basis for a dialectical theory of society; phenomenology (especially in terms of the critique of positivist science and the focus on the life-world); historical hermeneutics (the question of the historical interpretation of meaning); Weberian sociology (particularly in terms of Weber's theory of "rationalization"); and Freudian psychoanalytic theory.[15] Going beyond the inadequate and underdeveloped regions of traditional marxist theory, Critical Theory is sharply attentive to the epistemological, phenomenological, and hermeneutical dimensions of a dialectical theory of society and of the need to develop more fully the concept of "rationality" and the neglected psychological dimensions of marxism.

There are two further important components of the philosophical origins of Critical Theory which need mention: the reinvestigation of the theory-practice relationship and the response to a perceived crisis in the role of science. Because of the degeneration of marxism as a critical theory with the development of Communist orthodoxy, and because of the vitiation of the theoretical and practical impact of critical theory due to the rise and dominance of positivism, the founders of the Frankfurt School were faced with the need to re-establish the link between theory and practice. Indeed, the genesis of Critical Theory is grounded in a concern for praxis, understood not as an external determinism or the instrumental-technical application of theory, but as self-creating and self-generating free human action.[16] The desire for a union of theory and praxis revitalized inquiry into the nature of their dialectic in terms of "critique," or dialectical thought, and into the relationship between the liberation of critical consciousness and the real emancipation of human beings from various forms and forces of domination. In its concern for praxis, the dominant focus of Critical Theory at its beginning was the dissolution of class domination in industrial-technological society, a dissolution for which it was to provide essential enlightenment, and thus actually become part of the new praxis itself.[17]

The interest in political praxis and its re-established connection with the critical theory of society is related to the emergent crisis in the role of science. Horkheimer's concern with the role of science and the inability of positivistically developed theory to liberate man from irrational, alienated, and dominated forms of life, was similar to Husserl's.[18] For the Critical Theorists, however, Husserl's response to the crisis by way of phenomenology and pure *theoria* left the gap between theory and practice untouched and hence did nothing to overcome the impotence of theory in the face of countervailing practice.[19] What was needed was a critical theory in which the theorist was not confined to the realm of pure theory and political detachment. What was needed to combat the crisis in the role of science, and the real social and political crisis it reflected, was a critical theory of society with a practical intent. The development of an advanced industrial system of domination was supported by the positivist self-image of political and value-free neutrality. The knowledge produced within such a system was capable of mediating and controlling "objective" conflict. The naturalistic and objectivistic illusion in positivism's conception of the historical process and of knowledge was capable of representing relationships of dependence and contingency as fixed relationships of necessity and objectivity.

The response of Critical Theory, therefore, had to be seen as a battle against positivistic objectivism which had become ideology. The critique of positivism, and hence of ideology, was viewed by the Critical Theorists as a form of the unity of theory and praxis, which could only be validated by more fundamental revolutionary praxis.[20] The nature and importance of these various origins of Critical Theory for its development as dialectical theory become clearer if we examine in more detail the theoretical foundations of the Frankfurt School in the thought of Max Horkheimer.

Foundations with Horkheimer: "Traditional and Critical Theory"

At the time of the publication of Husserl's *Crisis,* which involved the attempt of phenomenology to deal with the "radical life-crisis of European humanity" and the theoretical crisis grounded in the positivization and objectivization of science, Horkheimer published his famous essay "Traditionelle und Kritische Theorie."[21] It might be noted parenthetically that at the time Husserl and Horkheimer were making phenomenology and critical theory turning points for Continental philosophy, Wittgenstein was paving the way for the development of conceptual-analysis philosophy, or "ordinary-language philosophy," which was to dominate Anglo-American philosophy. Horkheimer's essay (whose opening line is "What is 'theory'?") attempted to confront the same crisis in the role of scientific theory which was the object of Husserl's concern in the *Crisis*. The essay became a sort of manifesto for the Frankfurt School, and it spelled out the central concerns and tenets which constitute the focus of Critical Theory even today with Habermas. Before a brief examination of the theoretical foundations of Critical Theory contained in "Traditional and Critical Theory," however, mention must be made of the influences on the nature of Horkheimer's theoretical concerns in general.

Horkheimer's thought was conditioned early by two elements in Kantian philosophy. First, Horkheimer was influenced by the importance Kant placed on individuality, and hence he was opposed from the beginning to any notion of "totality" into which individuality might be submerged and lost.[22] Second, he was influenced by the Kantian notion of "cognitive activity," which is developed by Marx, and he hence was critical of any "copy theory of knowledge" (especially of the materialist sort) which became a basis for positivistic marxism. Instead, Horkheimer turned to a dialectical theory of knowledge. However, taking his cue from Marx's critique, he rejected the Hegelian phenomenological dialectic insofar as it presupposed the philosophy of identity and absolute knowledge.[23] We find Horkheimer embracing a dialectical theory of knowledge and arguing for a dialectical social science, which is opposed to the pursuit of absolutes in classical idealism and "identity theory," as well as to the empiricist-positivist position, which entails a rejection of everything beyond observable experience.

A further influence on Horkheimer's thought was *Lebensphilosophie*.[24] The "philosophy of life" tradition, rooted in the thought of Nietzsche, Dilthey, and Bergson and later developed (for Horkheimer, degenerated) in various forms of irrationalism and existentialism, was important for two primary reasons.[25] First, *Lebensphilosophie* protested the degeneration of reason into a rigid, abstract rationalism and therefore attempted to recover the spiritual and vital dimension of human thought and life. Second, the *Lebensphilosophen* of the 1930s were engaged in an effort to rescue the individual from various forms of conformism and the irrationality of existing society.[26] However, Horkheimer perceived at least three major problems with the *Lebens-*

philosophie in its extreme. First of all, it embraced too strong an emphasis on subjectivity and inwardness, thus neglecting the historical dimension of thought and life. Second, concomitant with this neglect was an underestimation of the material dimension of reality. And third, the rejection of narrow rationalism evolved into a rejection of reason per se.[27] These three problems prevented *Lebensphilosophie* from developing any connection with political praxis and hence undermined its importance for the development of a critical theory of society.

For Horkheimer, then, what was required in the face of both "idealistic" *Lebensphilosophie* and scientistic marxist materialism was the rescue of materialism from its reduction to a mere antonym of "spiritualism."[28] For Critical Theory, the rescue of materialism from reductionism takes the form of an attack on economic determinism, a critique of "materialist theory of knowledge," and a recovery of the sense of social reality as a dialectical, mediated totality. For Horkheimer, an economic determinism which conceives political activity as a mirror reflection of, and reaction to, blind, determined productive forces is ill-conceived. Indeed, the experiences of both Leninism and fascism have demonstrated the important directive effect that politics has on economic relations and forces, and the fact that politics is capable of a certain autonomy in the face of economic reality.[29] The classical "superstructure-base" relationship is one of continuous interaction.

Furthermore, Horkheimer rejected a materialist theory of knowledge which reduces to an objectivistic scientism or to an absolute metaphysics. Such a theory ignores the dialectical interaction of subject and object, which is a problem of positivism in general, and tends to transform the "dialectic" into an absolute, ontological first principle.[30] This truncates the reciprocal relationship of the totality of reality and its various "moments" and reduces all moments to a particular moment. Hence the materialist theory of knowledge conceives the so-called cultural-superstructure relations as epiphenomenal and derived unilinearly from "material-base relations or forces."[31] But culture can never be seen as epiphenomenal (and hence as less important than productive forces) if one focuses on the totality of dialectical mediations, which is the proper domain of a dialectical and critical theory of society. A dialectical theory of knowledge must recover the importance of culture and its mediated relations to the whole of human reality.

Horkheimer, therefore, argues for a dialectical theory of knowledge which is opposed equally to Hegelian philosophy of identity, to economistic marxist materialism, and to the rejection of reason contained in the devleopment of *Lebensphilosophie*. Critical Theory, grounded in a dialectical theory of knowledge and presupposing a concept of mediated totality, must rehabilitate reason from its process of deterioration. This requires the recovery of a broader and deeper concept of reason *(Vernunft)* which is noninstrumental and uninterested in domination, especially in the domination of nature. A major goal of Critical Theory is the "emancipation of reason" from its "disease" and "derangement" as an "instrument for domination of human and extra-human nature by man."[32] In this sense, in the face of instrumental reason, the "denunciation of what is currently called reason is the greatest service reason can render."[33]

Thus we find that Horkheimer is fighting on two fronts. On the one hand, he is struggling against the rejection of reason as such in *Lebensphilosophie,* which is actually perceived as a new, concealed form of idealism. On the other hand, he is attacking the positivist, scientistic conception of reason and knowledge. He is particularly critical of the fetishism of "facts," which leads to an absolutizing and hypostatizing of facts whereby the current social order is reified. Its reliance upon formal logic and its scientism reveal positivism as a reductionist metaphysics at the same time that it claims to overcome metaphysics. The consequences of the fetishism of facts and scientistic faith are expressed in the fact-value split and the claim to "value freedom" *(Wertfreiheit).*[34] This position results in a justification and preservation of the status quo through the alienation of theory and practice; "value freedom" prohibits criticism of what may be "insane" facts, and thus prevents the possibility of developing a radical praxis.

In the light of this two-front battle, it becomes clearer what for Horkheimer form the two poles of a critical theory of society: radical praxis based on the unity of theory and practice, and the rehabilitation of critical reason. Against the *Lebensphilosophen,* the response to the instrumental, positivistic degeneration of reason must be the revitalization of critical, emancipatory reason. Against positivism, theory must regain a practical interest in transforming the world through collective human action toward human emancipation. It is this conception of the relation between reason and praxis that for Horkheimer and Critical Theory escapes the efforts and understandings of *Lebensphilosophie,* positivism, and even of Husserl.[35] With this discussion in mind, then, we can turn briefly to Horkheimer's formulation of the central tenets of Critical Theory.

In "Traditional and Critical Theory," Horkheimer sets forth the distinction between the two understandings of theory and presents the central points and concepts which define a critical theory of society. "Traditional theory" is the positivistic conception of theory which serves as the regulative ideal for the natural sciences.[36] It is grounded in an objectivistic conception of the world and of knowledge, and it presupposes an objective correspondence between the two if theory is to be "valid." Thus theory operates in terms of the formulation of general, internally consistent and logical principles which objectively and accurately describe the world—and the fewer the primary principles the better.[37] The goal of such a positivist conception of theory

> is a universal systematic science, not limited to any particular subject matter but embracing all possible objects. The division of sciences is being broken down by deriving the principles for special areas from the same basic premises. The same conceptual apparatus which was elaborated for the analysis of inanimate nature is serving to classify animate nature as well, and anyone who has once mastered the use of it, that is, the rules for derivation, the symbols, the process of comparing derived propositions with observable fact, can use it at any time.[38]

This for Horkheimer is the widely accepted, traditional conception of theory. And it seems to be the one accepted in most political science today.

The goal of traditional theory, then, is universal, objective knowledge, and more emphatically, "pure knowledge" insofar as the goal of theory is not "action." Indeed, if there is any interest of theory in action or practice, or any connection between the two, it is understood in terms of technological mastery of the world, or the manipulation of physical nature as well as economic and social "mechanisms."[39] Hence traditional theory is predicated on an extreme separation of thought and action, or theory and praxis. The alienation of theory and praxis is not only reflected methodologically in the fact-value distinction, but is also apparent in the alienation within the individual of "theorist" and "citizen," or theoretical knower and political actor. The "scholarly specialist" qua scientist perceives social reality as extrinsic to his theoretical interests, and qua citizen pursues his political interests in a manner and through avenues separate from theoretical interest and knowledge. The two roles of theorist and citizen are never unified.[40] It is this concept of "traditional theory" which has been uncritically appropriated by the "sciences of man and society."[41]

"Critical theory" is grounded in very different presuppositions. First of all, it does not make a fetish of "pure knowledge" as distinct from and superior to action. Neither does critical theory conceive the relation between theory and practice as an instrumental one in which theory is technically "applied" to practice, particularly in order to regulate a given and accepted social structure. Furthermore, a critical theory of society refuses to accept unconditionally the political-evaluative categories which evolve in a particular society. Horkheimer introduces and defines a critical theory of society in the following way:

> We must go on now to add that there is a human activity which has society itself for its object. The aim of this activity is not sim-

ply to eliminate one or other abuse, for it regards such abuses as
necessarily connected with the way in which the social structure is
organized. Although it itself emerges from the social structure, its
purpose is not, either in its conscious intention or in its objective
significance, the better functioning of any element in the structure.
On the contrary, it is suspicious of the very categories of better,
useful, appropriate, productive, and valuable, as these are understood in the present order, and refuses to take them as nonscientific presuppositions about which one can do nothing.[42]

In a footnote to this passage, Horkheimer calls this activity "critical"
activity and places it within the framework of marxist critique. He
distinguishes the meaning of the term "critical" from its use in the
"idealist critique of pure reason," and relates it instead to the sense
it has in the "dialectical critique of political economy." Hence theory
understood as "critical activity" forms a crucial component of the
"dialectical theory of society."

Horkheimer's conception of critical theory becomes clearer if we
note his definition of "criticism," which appears in another of his
essays:

By criticism, we mean that intellectual, and eventually practical,
effort which is not satisfied to accept the prevailing ideas, actions,
and social conditions unthinkingly and from mere habit; effort
which aims to coordinate the individual sides of social life with
each other and with the general ideas and aims of the epoch, to
deduce them genetically, to distinguish the appearance from the
essence, to examine the foundations of things, in short, really to
know them.[43]

Using this definition, we can detect at least five central aspects of
critical theory. First, critical theory is theory which has practical intent.
Theory has an interest in the practical transformation of the world, an
interest in the improvement of the human condition, which does not
take place apart from the development and liberation of the self-consciousness of individuals actively concerned with and determining their
own destiny.[44] It is in this sense that critical theory must focus on the
"critique of ideology" and the assault on "false consciousness" in
order to assist in the growth of a critical self-awareness in the subjects
of radical change.[45] Although the idea is not developed until later, the
critique of false consciousness seems to be directed at the structure as
well as the content of reified thought, with an interest in recovering
self-recognition as a creating subject in the world, rather than as an
object.[46] Hence it involves not so much the notion of putting "correct
ideas" into thought as it does that of recovering an authentic, dialectical
mode of thought, which overcomes the inversion of subject and object.

In any event, without such an emergent self-awareness, so that the unity of theory and praxis and the transformation of society can be generated not only "from above," the relation of theory and praxis threatens to degenerate into the technical application of theory or simply remains an "academic" problem.

Second, therefore, critical theory maintains an opposition to the notion of "disinterested or neutral research." Not only does such a view of research presuppose the separation of fact and value, which is politically expressed in the service of the status quo, but it is also impossible in a society of nonautonomous men. In other words, since the researcher is part of the society he studies, and that society is not the product of free, autonomous men, the researcher himself cannot avoid being involved in the ensuing "heteronomy."[47] It is thus not only "methodological categories" but also "social categories" that condition and mediate the interest and theoretical insights of the researcher. Third, as is apparent from the earlier definition of criticism, critical theory is concerned with the totality of all aspects of social life. Fourth, it attempts to relate the totality to its historicity, which is to say, to its particular historically relative forms and aims.

Finally, critical theory is radical and foundational. It attempts to penetrate to the foundations of the various aspects of the social totality. In its attempt to distinguish the apparent from the essential through its inquiry into the nature of reality, critical theory returns to the classical origins of *theoria*. In this sense, for Critical Theory the very notion of *critical* theory is somewhat redundant, since criticism is essential to *theoria*. Thus critical theory involves an attempt to recover the "negative function" of theory which has been suppressed by traditional theory. The result of this suppression is the inability of traditional theory to offer a rational basis for the criticism of accepted, given reality.[48]

Perhaps the essential complaint that critical theory, which does not perceive theory to be disinterested, neutral, or divorced from action, lodges against traditional theory is its acceptance and promulgation of the distinction between theory and praxis. For critical theory, this distinction, which is justified by positivism on methodological grounds, is in itself an ideological force; it is an ideological reflection of a society in which theory can only serve to maintain and preserve the existing state of affairs. The goal of critical theory, in contrast, is to seek the unity of theory and praxis, and the only real mark of its success or validity lies in the case when the social contradictions it discovers theoretically are grasped by, and constitute the activity of, those exploited and alienated members of society whose task it is to move society in the direction of social justice.[49] This criterion of success and validity is no less true even if there is no one clearly defined "social class" by whose acceptance of the critical theory one can be guided.

The focus on emancipatory praxis as a criterion of validity for a critical theory of society does not reduce critical theory to pragmatism, however. For Horkheimer, pragmatism (like positivism) identifies philosophy too closely with scientism. Hence the comprehension by pragmatism of the relation of truth to practical activity is too simplistic, instrumental, and nondialectical. As long as pragmatism divorces the connection of knowledge and action from a broader theory of society, it results in formalism and abstraction. Therefore, especially since practical activity is seen as adaptive behavior, the implications of pragmatism are not "critical" but conformist.

Critical theory, then, sees itself as providing the enlightenment for revolutionary praxis. However, Horkheimer is cautious about the danger of theory's degenerating into mere ideological reflection of the momentary empirical desires of the "proletariat" or into mere technical-tactical formulations. In other words, there has to be a certain tension between theory and praxis, or between the theorist and the object of his concern. The theorist must, for example, be as critical of conformist tendencies "within his own household" as he is of the forces of the status quo. Part of this concern for the necessary tension between the theorist and the "class which his thinking is to serve" is grounded in the suspicion that the role of the proletariat in history is not automatically guaranteed. Hence there is the possibility of conflict between the critical theorist and the "classical" material forces of emancipation. If the theorist cannot be seen in the liberal sense as absolutely detached and "above the fray," neither can he be seen as "deeply rooted" in a class. In this latter case theory reduces to nothing less than "totalitarian propaganda." The tension must be maintained, although it is "the task of the critical theoretician to reduce the tension between his own insight and oppressed humanity in whose service he thinks."[50]

Because of the increasingly problematical position of the working class as a revolutionary force, and because, for Horkheimer and the Critical Theorists, the classical concepts of a radical critique of political economy seemed increasingly inadequate, the Frankfurt School began to turn their attention to an analysis of the vanishing of negative and critical forces in society. Thus, rather than developing and revising the classical marxist concepts in the critique of political economy, they began to focus more and more on the cultural and ideological "superstructure" of society neglected by marxism.[51] The Critical Theorists became concerned with the cultural and ideological forces which were instrumental in the "deradicalizing" of potentially revolutionary forces in society and in the further development of a system of domination. Thus they turned their attention to such problems as the nature of authority and mass culture, and to the attempt to reconnect the two poles of cultural superstructure and material structure involved in the "two-sided character of the social totality" with the aid of Freudian psychology.[52]

The Transformation of the Frankfurt School: Toward a "Depoliticized" Critical Theory?

The Critical Theory associated with the *Institut für Sozialforschung* began to undergo major changes in the 1940s.[53] There appeared to be a growing problem with Horkheimer's original goal of uniting political praxis with philosophical inquiry and empirical research. Not only did this task appear ever more difficult, but the world had begun to change drastically. The postwar and postfascist world witnessed the blossoming of a technological-industrial social reality which seemed to require a new theoretical response from a critical theory of society which saw itself in need of changing as history itself changes.[54]

Perhaps most central to the transformation and reorientation of Critical Theory was its movement away from the problems and focus of "orthodox" marxism toward the more general question of the relationship between man and nature. This involved a shift away from a specific focus on the problems of praxis; indeed, as the Critical Theorists saw the need for their theory to become more radical (hence to return to the "root" question of man-nature relations) the attempt to re-establish the relationship between critical theory and revolutionary praxis became more difficult and doubtful. But the move away from an explicit focus on theory-praxis relations and unity had at least three specific historical and social impetuses as well. First, the Stalinist developments in the USSR engendered a sense of distress and depression over the emergence of an antidemocratic system of domination. Second, the classical proletariat in the Western capitalist countries had developed to a point which inspired little basis for a facile faith in revolution. Finally, the growing reflexive power of mass culture as a force capable of integrating various kinds of conflict and contradictions, which could thus no longer be guaranteed of developing in traditionally understood ways, seemed to invalidate any exclusive focus on a critique of political economy to elicit a unity of theory and praxis.

Thus we find Critical Theory taking a direction which rejected the emphasis of its own origins.[55] We find that the centrality of class conflict in the philosophy of history of traditional marxism is replaced by the centrality of the conflict between man and nature. More important, this conflict is perceived and formulated within the framework of the phenomenon of *domination* (which is seen to assume noneconomic as well as economic forms). Hence Critical Theory returns to Renaissance views of science and technology to find the roots of political domination and the connection between instrumental rationality and the mastery of nature. The degeneration of reason into a narrow and technical rationality has from the beginning of modern history been related to the domination of nature, and reason has been understood as a tool for the control of nature and, ultimately, for the domination of man.[56] It is for this reason that the Critical Theorists looked to Vico as a uniquely important figure of the Renaissance, since he refused to succumb to the equation of human praxis and the subjugation of nature and hence prefigured the critique of the Enlightenment.[57]

In other words, for Critical Theory the key to understanding the existence and prevalence of forms of domination lay in the emergence of a scientific and technical conception of rationality, a conception which reached an apogee in the Enlightenment. According to the Critical Theorists, the view of nature as something to be subjugated and controlled for the purposes of human "emancipation," and the concomitant view that this would take place through a process of the "rationalization" of the world contained at least two major faults. First, it involved a nondialectical separation of man and nature. Second, since it superficially equated the technical and formalistic rationalization of the world with any broader and deeper view of reason and rationality, it allowed for the concealment of more radical forms of irrationality. Hence we find the argument that civilization is emerging as "rationalized irrationality."[58] This kind of argument moved the Critical Theorists even further away from orthodox marxism, especially insofar as they began to place Marx more strongly within the Enlightenment tradition. Thus they argued that Marx placed too much emphasis on an objectivistic, instrumental concept of labor and that his view of a theory-praxis relationship presupposed the domination and control of nature.[59]

In the light of the Enlightenment degeneration of reason into positivistic, instrumental rationalization, the Critical Theorists conceived the need to recover the importance of "negation" and "negativity." Since the truth of a free human future was impossible to know by individuals who themselves were not yet free, the resting place of truth had to lie in negation.[60] The mentality of the Enlightenment, which had infused positivism, had systematically eliminated negation from language. This is apparent in the language of progressivism and rationalistic optimism. Thus it had substituted formulas for dialectical concepts and led to a form of nominalism. What emerges, therefore, is the evolution of a "one-dimensional" language and discourse which lack the element of negativity.[61] A one-dimensional language which does not express the negative is thus incapable of "criticism" and becomes simply another tool of the existing social forces of domination, predicated on the rationalizing domination of nature.

To summarize, the transformation of Critical Theory led it to posit a new goal: the reconciliation of man with nature. A step toward that goal was overcoming the separation of the natural and social sciences, a separation which theoretically and ideologically perpetuated the alienation of man and nature. Again, the domination of nature and ultimately of man was seen by the Critical Theorists as intrinsically related to the development of technical and instrumental rationalism. Furthermore, the development of industrial-technological society guided and defended by objectivistic, instrumental rationality was threatening the annihilation of subjectivity and the individual. One of the goals of Critical Theory was perceived as the "recovery of the individual." However, the Critical Theorists were not arguing for a return to the atomistic bourgeois individual of "negative freedom," dominated by self-interest, but for the development of a newly synthesized individual of "positive freedom," who would constitute (in a rather Rousseauean manner) a unity of particular and universal interests. However, and here the Critical Theorists differed from Marx, the ultimate unity of particular and universal interest in positive freedom, and the reconciliation of man with man and man with nature, would always be impossible since the demands of the totality would destroy the finite and contingent. Again, the dialectic must remain always "negative."

In a sense, then, the utopian impulse which guided Critical Theory at its beginning is now seen to function as the paradigms of classical political philosophy. Any vision of the "good society" acts only as a standard of critical evaluation for existing reality; the theory-praxis relationship is vitiated. Indeed, the entire shift in Critical Theory from a focus on class struggle to one on the reconciliation of man and nature resulted in the dismissal of any possibility of a revolutionary subject in history. Thus the original imperative of a critical *political* praxis disappears from the domain of Critical Theory, which now seems to enter the stage of depoliticization of a critical theory of society. To be sure, Critical Theory becomes less and less capable of suggesting any critical praxis at all; perhaps all it can do is to act as a "corrective of history." Or, as one interpreter has it, "Theory, Horkheimer and the others seemed to be saying, was the only form of *praxis* still open to honest men."[62]

What can be concluded from this apparently depoliticized Critical Theory? First of all, it may be the case that the growing lack of political criticism in Critical Theory was due to the recognition of the Frankfurt School as a "school," and to its development as an accepted, established institution in society.[63] Radicalism wanes as a position becomes institutionalized or "respectable." Nevertheless, despite the depoliticization of Critical Theory and its abandonment of the essential tenets of orthodox marxism, it seems to have contributed in at least four important ways to the development of a dialectical theory of society. First, in the face of deterministic, positivistic and totalitarian marxism, the Frankfurt School theorists recovered the crucial philosophical foundations of dialectical marxism, and more specifically the focus on the importance of freedom. Second, they restored vitality to a critical theory of society by interpreting marxism as open-ended critique and not as a dogmatic collection of scientific truths. Third, they attempted to open the door to inquiry into the psychological dimension of a critical theory of society, which had been neglected by positivistic marxism. Finally, the Critical Theorists demonstrated the need to recover the importance and dynamic character of cultural life as something more than an epiphenomenal reflection of material existence.

The Frankfurt School leaves us with an ambiguous legacy. With all of its "dialectical recoveries," it ultimately abandoned the unity of theory and praxis as a real goal and thus leaves us still with the need to overcome the "gap" between theoretical knowledge and political practice. It is here that Critical Theory's dialectic falters.

Habermas and the Future of Critical Theory

Jürgen Habermas, who has been compared in our time to Hegel, represents a major turning point in the development of Critical Theory.[64] As the most important and influential heir to the Frankfurt School, he deserves special mention in light of the development of a dialectical and critical theory of society. It has been said that with Habermas Critical Theory has entered its fourth and current phase.[65] His undertaking is, in a sense, to complete the basis for a critical theory of society by going beyond the work of Horkheimer, Adorno, and Marcuse to demonstrate the epistemological foundations and problems of "traditional theory" which not only justify but necessitate the transition to critical theory.

At the core of this effort lies Habermas's attempt to demonstrate that theory and practice are capable of a profound and radical unification *epistemologically*. Thus he develops a theory of the intrinsic epistemological connection of knowledge and human interest. His reformulation of the relationship between theory and practice in these terms, grounded in the notion of "cognitive interest," is perhaps the most important and innovative contribution Habermas offers to the evolution of dialectical theory and contemporary political inquiry. It is impossible here to deal adequately with the whole of Habermas's monumental effort—which draws on Kantianism, Hegelianism, Marxism, phenomenology, Wittgensteinian linguistic analysis, empirical-analytical sciences, systems theory, and historical hermeneutics—and I shall focus upon this argument for the connection of knowledge and interest, and its importance for dialectical theory. First, however, we must begin where Habermas begins, with his critique of Marx.

Epistemology and the Critique of Marx

Habermas's work stands in a critical relation to Marx, a relation not of absolute negation but of dialectical *Aufheben*. Hence he is interested in developing in Marx what is rightfully important and relevant for a critical theory of society, given the historical transformations of advanced industrial society, and in critically rejecting what seems to have lost its validity in the development of marxism, as it is rooted in Marx's thought itself. At one level, this means revising the categories of the radical critique of political economy (especially the "theory of crises").[66] At the most fundamental level, perhaps, this means recovering the epistemological dialectic from the instrumental and positivistic tendencies in Marx's thought which have prevailed in the development of the dominant self-understanding of marxism. Since Marx never explicitly reflected on the nature of "critique," his self-proclaimed mode of inquiry, he failed to distinguish it sufficiently from both traditional philosophy and "positive science" and hence allowed the dissolution of the dialectic into positivism.[67] Habermas attempts to recover the epistemological dialectic in Marx by developing a theory of cognitive interests, to which I shall turn in a moment.

For Habermas, Marx's critique of Hegel developed in such a way as to prevent him from seeing the entire dialectical impact and import of his own work. Marx's recovery of the object from Hegel's one-sided dialectic revealed itself primarily in Marx's development of an objectivistic concept of labor.[68] As we recall, for Marx social labor is the materialist synthesis of man and nature; it is thus a two-sided movement involving consciousness-subject and nature-object. What occurs in the development of the materialist synthesis, however, is a twofold reduction. On the one hand, the concept of "labor" becomes increasingly reduced to a narrower definition of "work," understood as instrumental, productive activity which dismisses the importance of interaction and social organization. On the other hand, the emphasis on the "recovery of the object" from Hegel results in the reduction of reflection itself to labor, understood as instrumental action.[69] It is this reduction of the process of reflection to instrumental action that disturbs Habermas, since it is Marx's emphasis on the instrumental nature of knowledge that permits the degeneration of his dialectic into pragmatism and the pretense of natural science.[70] Thus labor, which has the function of synthesis, is reduced to "production," which in turn becomes the epistemological framework for both productive activity and consciousness.

In other words, the two moments of Marx's material synthesis are reduced to one. There seem to be two aspects to Marx's view of the evolution of human society through material synthesis. On the one hand, man reproduces his existence through material labor (work) and productive activity. On the other hand, man becomes self-conscious, through an understanding based on interaction, of the self-formative process of his own history. The latter moment of the synthesis involves self-understanding which is mediated through historical and cultural forms and cannot be reduced to the moment of technical productive activity. This self-consciousness takes the historical and social form of "class consciousness." Both the moment of productive activity and of class consciousness are dialectically involved in the material synthesis of social labor which reveals the possibility of human emancipation. However, a reduction does seem to take place which reveals a contradiction in Marx, which in turn reveals the unclarified status of his dialectic. This appears in the two seemingly disparate views of ideology in Marx's thought. At certain times, ideology appears in the form of "false consciousness" in need of critical abolition through a process of reflexive critique which cannot be reduced to the instrumental activity of work. At other times, ideology appears simply as the vulgar reflection of the material substructure of society.[71] The latter view is the basis for a deterministic and positivistic marxism.

What concerns Habermas is how this contradiction reveals an alienation of Marx's own method of critique and his self-understanding of it, and what the consequences of this alienation are. As we noted in chapter 2, Marx's own "material investigations" in his critique of society take account of social praxis broadly conceived as the self-constitution of man, which encompasses both productive work and communicative interaction (involving reflection and consciousness), whereas at the level of the self-understanding of critique his view is reduced: "Self-constitution through social labor is conceived at the *categorial level* as a process of production, and instrumental action, labor in the sense of material activity, or work designates the dimension in which natural history moves."[72] The alienation in Marx of the practice of inquiry from the philosophical self-understanding of inquiry entails that the latter neglects the fact revealed by the former: that the "processes of history" are mediated both by productive activity and by men's organization of their interrelations. The medium for the regulation of these relations is the "cultural tradition," which forms the "linguistic communication structure" on the basis of which men interpret both nature and themselves in their environment.[73] What is lacking in Marx's philosophical self-understanding is the cultural moment of the dialectic, or the importance of cultural mediation grounded in communicative interaction. Here we see the basis for Habermas's "communication theory of society."

The consequences of a latent positivism in Marx are disastrous in the view of Habermas. Methodologically, marxist critique is reduced to materialistic scientism, in which the evolution of society is economistically and deterministically conceived on the basis of an objectivistic concept of productive activity. In terms of praxis, the nature of the emancipatory struggle is reduced to the formulation of instrumental strategies.[74] The only way to counter these consequences, for Habermas, is to re-establish the dialectic of work and interaction in the philosophical self-understanding of the critique of society. Thus we must begin with the recognition that there are two important processes of development at work in the evolution of social life. First, there is the self-constitution of mankind in the dimension of labor, the goal of which is emancipation from external natural contraints perpetuated by the capitalist system of production. Second, there is the self-formation of mankind on the interactive level that takes place in the struggle between social classes, the goal of which is emancipation from various repressions of the "internal nature" of mankind. The end of this often neglected second development is the "organization of society linked to decision-making processes on the basis of discussion free from domination."[75]

These two levels of development Marx often called the "forces of production" and the "relations of production," and he tried to establish a dialectic between them. For Habermas, however, that dialectic remains unclarified as long as "the materialist concept of the synthesis of man and nature is restricted to the categorial framework of production."[76] This kind of reduction conflates work and interaction and submits to positivism:

> If Marx had not thrown together interaction and work under the label of social practice (Praxis), and had he instead related the materialist concept of synthesis likewise to the accomplishments of instrumental action and the nexuses of communicative action, then the idea of a science of man would not have been obscured by identification with natural science.[77]

Instead, because Marx succumbed to equating critique with natural science, he ended by disavowing the very idea of "a science of man" and its critical-epistemological framework:

> Materialist scientism only reconfirms what absolute idealism had already accomplished: the elimination of epistemology in favor of unchained universal 'scientific knowledge'—but this time of scientific materialism instead of absolute knowledge.[78]

Habermas wants to complement marxism with a critical analysis, not simply of exploitation in capitalist society, but also of systematically distorted communication in industrial organization. What is needed is the development of a critical theory of society which can re-establish the dialectical relation between these two moments of the synthesis and engage actively in a critique of both the restraints on productive activity and the distortion of communicative praxis.[79] In order to understand the import of Habermas's contribution, however, we have to go beyond his critique of Marx to his theory of cognitive interests.

The Dissolution of Epistemology and Cognitive Interests

Habermas conceives the goal of critical theory to lie in the self-emancipation of mankind guided by the processes of self-reflection. This goal becomes intelligible only in light of the "dissolution of epistemology" after Kant.[80] With Kant and the birth of "critical philosophy," there existed the practice of critical reflection whereby philosophy had a sovereign role in relation to science and was still the basis for understanding the constitution of possible objects of knowledge and for evaluating various forms of knowledge. The dissolution of the Kantian conception of critique of knowledge took place beginning with Hegel and Marx but was completed in the emergence of positivism and the philosophy of science, especially in the work of Comte and Mach. The result has been the development of "positive sciences" whose concerns are methodological and no longer epistemological—which is to say that the critical-transcendental dimension has receded. The reduction of the theory of knowledge to philosophy of science begun by early positivism was interrupted by both C. S. Peirce and Wilhelm Dilthey, who expressed the philosophical self-reflection of the logic of inquiry in the natural and cultural sciences respectively.[81] Peirce and Dilthey brought the self-reflection of science to the point where its "knowledge-constitutive interests" were made visible.[82] But since neither one conceived his methodological reflections as the self-reflection of science, both of them missed the point where knowledge and interest are united.

To combat the dissolution of epistemology into methodology, Habermas conceives the need to recover the Kantian notion of an "interest of reason."[83] According to Habermas, in Kant we find the notion that reason has an inherent interest in emancipation insofar as it either arises from or awakens a need to be fulfilled. This interest is "cognitive" since it is part of the process of reflection itself. The interest of reason in emancipation and fulfillment is frustrated, however, by the Kantian distinction between theoretical and practical reason. Only if the speculative interest of reason is conceived as not simply residing in the theoretical faculty but as a pure practical interest, can Kantian theoretical reason connect with the practical interest of reason. It is this step that Habermas sees Fichte taking: conceiving the act of reason as a reflected action that returns into itself and "makes the primacy of practical reason into a principle." In other words, with Fichte reason becomes immediately practical in the form of original self-reflection itself.[84] In Fichte's declaration of the identity of theoretical and practical reason, self-reflection becomes "at once intuition and emancipation, comprehension and liberation from dogmatic dependence."[85] The point of this argument is as follows:

> The development of the concept of the interest of reason from Kant to Fichte leads from the concept of an interest in actions of free will, dictated by practical reason, to the concept of an interest in the independence of the ego, operative in reason itself.[86]

This unity of interest and reason rejects the traditional concept of theory reformulated in positivism:

> This *unity of reason and the interested employment of reason* conflicts with the contemplative concept of knowledge. As long as the traditional meaning of pure theory severs the cognitive process from life contexts in principle, interest must be viewed as something foreign to theory, coming to it from without and obscuring the objectivity of knowledge.[87]

The notion of a knowledge-constitutive interest emerges, then, in the view that in interested self-reflection, the interest embedded in reason becomes constitutive for both knowing and acting.[88]

However, unlike the absolute self-positing of ego in Fichte, or the absolute movement of mind in Hegel, the self-formative process of a species-subject does not simply take place as an unconditioned movement of reflection. Such a process is dependent on contingent conditions of both subjective and objective nature. Hence the self-formative process of the human species, in which reason's interest in emancipation is invested, aims at realizing conditions of "instrumental action" (conditions of the "material exchange" of man with nature) and of "symbolic interaction" (conditions of the interaction of men with men). What Habermas wants to do is to reinterpret the concept of the "interest of reason" (a cognitive interest) materialistically so that the emancipatory interest is contingent upon and embedded in the development of life processes of interaction and work. All of this is intended to demonstrate the necessity of recovering the dimension of self-reflection in which reason grasps itself as interested.[89]

Again, the goal of critical theory is liberation through the process of self-reflection. In the search for critical consciousness, we must first understand preceding consciousness which constitutes the legitimation of current conditions. This means that there must be self-reflection on the self-formative process of the species-subject. In this light, Habermas's aim is to recover the movement of liberating self-reflection which Hegel had grasped, and, as one interpreter has is, "to show how the dynamics of self-reflection are relevant for a critical understanding of contemporary social and political reality."[90] It is the movement of self-reflection that has been uncritically abandoned by the positivist dissolution of epistemology.

Habermas is aware that simply liberating ourselves from various mystifications (as in Hegel's notion of self-reflection), by way of a critical examination of the legitimation of a positivistic self-understanding of knowledge and science, is not sufficient for a radical praxis directed toward human emancipation. Nonetheless, he believes it is necessary for such a praxis. This involves nothing less than a fundamental rethinking of the nature of science and knowledge. We need to recover the interests that guide various modes of inquiry, which means reconceptualizing theory itself as active and constructive. In other words, we must develop a new view of the relation of theory and practice in terms of the interests of cognition. For Habermas, this view cannot be developed by positivistic marxism or by the positivistic orthodoxy in contemporary liberal society. It can only be developed by a critical theory of knowledge and human interests.

Theoria, Praxis, and Technē

In order to understand the basis and purpose of Habermas's theory of cognitive interests, we have to examine, first, his view of the historical transformation of the concept of "theory," and second, his conception of the relation of the "practical" and the "technical."

The classical concept of *theoria,* which emerged with Greek philosophy, referred to the "contemplation of the cosmos." The endeavor of *theoria* was founded on the distinction between Being and time and involved the search for the eternal and timeless nature of reality; this search defines classical ontology. Classical *theoria* embraced two primary assumptions and an intrinsically related claim: first, the "disinterested" theoretical attitude; second, an objectively structured and well-ordered cosmos independent of human knowledge; and third, the view that knowledge of the immortal order of the cosmos leads the philosopher to bring his life into accord with the harmonic proportions discovered there.[91] In other words, knowledge leads the philosopher to reproduce internally the harmony of the cosmos and to order his psyche accordingly. By manifesting these harmonic proportions he forms himself through mimesis and likens the soul to the order of the cosmos. For classical *theoria,* then, theory enters the conduct of life, molding life to its form, and there is an intrinsic connection between knowledge and ethical life. This constitutes the essence of Aristotle's argument for the connection of political knowledge and ethical practice.

In the seventeenth century, with the "metaphysically neutral" physics of Copernicus and Newton conceived as irrelevant to ethical life, the connection between knowledge and interest began to be severed. The emergence of a natural scientific model for all valid knowledge culminates in the positivism of the nineteenth century. Positivism, we know, is based on the rejection of all metaphysics, especially classical ontology (which Comte even placed in the "theological" stage of history). But here Habermas notices a problem: the positivistic understanding of science which has invaded the social sciences does not recognize its connection to traditional ontology and classical *theoria*. Indeed, positivistic science retains the two elemental assumptions of classical theory: the methodological assumption of disinterested, neutral observation as the mode of inquiry and the ontological assumption of an objectively structured cosmos. Yet it destroys in its process of inquiry the classical claim of *theoria:* that knowledge inherently provides cultivation of the individual which liberates him from the bonds of conventional wisdom.

Hence positivistic science abandons the connection between *theoria* and *kosmos,* and *mimesis* and *bios theoretikos.* It abandons the connection of knowledge and human interest, theory and practice, as intrinsic to the process of inquiry. It might be noted parenthetically that this was the "crisis of theory" that concerned both Horkheimer and Husserl. The classical claim of theory becomes methodologically prohibited by the "scientific" demands of science.[92] Furthermore, the subsequent separation of knowledge and interest serves as an ideological legitimation of existing conditions. The purpose of critical theory is to reestablish the connection between knowledge and human interests by means of the concept of knowledge-constitutive or cognitive interests so that theory retains its emancipatory interest.

Habermas is also concerned with the liberation of the "practical" realm of life and inquiry from domination by the "technical." As we have seen, the classical view of politics held as central the question of "the good life." Political life concerned questions of praxis, not *technē,* and was directed toward cultivation of individual character; *phronesis,* or "prudence," was a central virtue of political life. The modern conception, at least since Hobbes, evolves a view that social philosophy can be scientifically grounded. The translation of knowledge into practice is a technical problem, and the human behavior of political life is the material for scientific engineering.[93] This dismal state of affairs has succeeded in translating political questions of practice (in the broad sense) into those of technics. The attempt to attain rational consensus among citizens concerned with the ends of political life (praxis) has been replaced with an interest in technical control by the "perfection of administration."[94] Thus problems of action and praxis have been reduced to those of technical control and manipulation, resulting in a serious depoliticization of the public.[95] As one interpreter has it:

> The problem has become urgent in our time not only because science and technology are the most important productive forces in advanced industrial society, but because a technological consciousness increasingly affects all domains of human life, and serves as a background ideology that has a legitimating power.[96]

Thus Habermas is concerned with overcoming technical rationality based on the repression of the practical nature of political life. This requires a revitalization of a form of unconstrained, reflective communicative action. In order to overcome the domination of *technē*, the practical (communicative interaction) must be liberated from the technical. Habermas is concerned here with the Hegelian interest in "mutual recognition" of intersubjective understanding, which has been suppressed by technical rationality. The rationality of *technē* has expanded the realm of control and manipulation of objects according to technical rules and has bypassed the practical dimension of human political life. The growth of technical rationality has thus weakened communicative interaction and repressed the interest in emancipation through a system of distorted communication. This relation of the meaning of "practical" and "technical" is crucial for Habermas's theoretical schema of cognitive interests.

The Three Cognitive Interests

As we have seen, the central concept in Habermas's systematic understanding of knowledge is that of cognitive, or knowledge-constitutive, interest. A cognitive interest is an interest in life processes which guides and constitutes the process of inquiry and the nature of knowledge. The status of such an interest is a peculiar one in Habermas. It is quasi-transcendental and quasi-empirical. On one hand, cognitive interest is empirical insofar as it is rooted in and oriented toward life processes involved in the reproduction and self-constitution of the human species. But it cannot be naturalistically reduced to a mere function of the reproduction of social life and neither can it be seen to aim merely at the gratificaiton of immediate empirical needs.[97] On the other hand, a cognitive interest is transcendental (in the Kantian sense) insofar as it involves the transcendental-logical conditions for the possibility of knowledge itself; in this sense it has a categorical epistemological status. But it cannot be conceived separately from life processes, and hence knowledge is not the act of "a pure rational being removed from the context of life in contemplation."[98] Thus the concept of cognitive interest, or so it seems to me, is a radically *dialectical* concept.

For Habermas, there are three categories of knowledge resultant of a process of inquiry, each of which incorporates a particular cognitive interest, and each of which is grounded in and oriented toward a fundamental dimension of human social life. Each type of knowledge is constituted by the deep interest of the human species in its evolution. The empirical-analytical (natural) sciences incorporate a technical cognitive interest, are grounded in "work," and are oriented toward technical control of natural processes. The historical-hermeneutical (cultural) sciences incorporate a practical cognitive interest, are grounded in language, and are oriented toward maintenance of communicative intersubjectivity and symbolic interaction. The critical social sciences (rescued from their positivistic dissolution into empirical-analytical sciences) incorporate an emancipatory cognitive interest, are grounded in power, and are oriented toward the liberation of the subject from forms of domination and confinement.[99] In a sense, the emancipatory cognitive interest is derived from the other two, which constitute the dialectic of work and interaction, but at the same time it is the basis for the implicit goals of both the technical and practical interests.[100]

One recalls that it was Peirce who discovered the roots in "interest" of empirical-analytical or natural scientific knowledge, without reflecting on it as such or developing the concept of knowledge-constitutive interest.[101] The empirical-analytical sciences are guided by a technical cognitive interest, which is to say, an interest in technical control of our environment (in this sense they reflect our organic constitution and the need for the adaptation of the environment). This interest is necessitated by the very form of empirical-analytical knowledge: the isolation of objects and events into dependent and independent variables by which one can investigate the regularities among them. Furthermore, empirical-analytical knowledge is based on the model of negative feedback in which there can be confirmation and falsification of hypotheses.[102] Again, this form of knowledge is grounded in an instrumental orientation to nature which is quasi-transcendental; despite its historical mediation, it has a certain logical invariance to it.

Thus empirical-analytical inquiry takes place within the framework of a behavioral system of instrumental action. The methodological framework of the natural sciences dictates that the validity of knowledge lie in the formulation of universal propositions about reality which lead to technical recommendations for the control of observed processes of nature. Hence the meaning of knowledge resides in prediction. Since empirical-analytical knowledge is predictive knowledge, its ultimate meaning and interest lie in the "technical exploitability" of knowledge, which is to say, in technical control.[103] Its apparently pure "description" of reality conceals this interest.

The empirical-analytical sciences are subject, then, to the transcendental conditions of instrumental action. Therefore there are categorical limits, defined by the behavioral system of instrumental action, to empirical-analytical knowledge. It cannot, as Peirce himself could not, account for a type of action (communicative interaction) which is distinct from instrumental manipulation. Empirical-analytical knowledge is grounded in and oriented toward the dimension of social life that Marx called "substructure," only now it is understood as the "purposive-rational action system" (work and production) into which science itself is incorporated. Its categorical limits (due to its cognitive interest) dictate that it cannot be the measure of all legitimate knowledge.

The historical-hermeneutical or cultural sciences, for which Dilthey played the philosophically self-reflective role, are guided by an incorporated practical cognitive interest in the understanding and transmission of meaning through interpretation and communication. This interest reveals that the basic role of language and culture is just as central to social evolution (the reproduction of forms of life) as is technical control of nature. Historical-hermeneutic inquiry takes place within a framework of tradition-bound structures of symbolic interaction (cultural traditions). It aims at the clarification of practically effective knowledge and is thus interested in maintaining the intersubjectivity of mutual understanding.[104] Thus the cultural sciences proceed, not on the level of instrumental action, but on that of communicative interaction. This is a form of action which is irreducible, yet cannot be isolated from the realm of work and labor as a totally independent process. Nonetheless, communicative action exhibits a certain autonomy, insofar as the empirical-analytical sciences cannot give an account of themselves if they are limited to concepts shaped by technical interests.[105]

Because the historical-hermeneutic process of inquiry in the cultural sciences takes place within communicative action, its transcendental framework lies in the grammar of ordinary language, which links symbols, actions, and expressions. For cultural scientific knowledge, the counterpart of the verification of lawlike hypotheses in empirical-analytical science is the interpretation of texts (broadly understood). Its interest is in attaining rational consensus among actors in the context of self-understanding derived from tradition.[106] This is the practical interest which guides historical-hermeneutic inquiry and is grounded in and oriented toward the communicative intersubjective dimension of social life.

Thus the cognitive interest which guides symbolically mediated orientations to life processes, which themselves involve patterns of interaction necessary for communication and intersubjective cooperation, is epistemologically related to systems of symbolic interaction—not to systems of instrumental action. There can be no reduction of the norms which guide human activity in the reproduction of our cultural and communicative life to "technical rules."[107] This is to say that there can be no reduction, because of the categorical distinction of technical and practical interest, of symbolic interaction to instrumental or "purposive-rational" action. To be sure, there can be no "free and open communication," at which the practical interest aims, without the transformation of social institutions which either release or distort communication. Yet the achievement of the latter, which involves transformation of productive activity, is no automatic guarantee for the achievement of the former. By demonstrating the specific connection between the logical-methodological rules and knowledge-constitutive interests in the process of inquiry, Habermas recovers the twofold epistemological model for the marxian synthesis—which is to say that the synthesis involves two kinds of "action systems" (instrumental/work and communicative/symbolic interaction) in a position of mutual relation, neither of which is reducible to the other.

The process of inquiry for the critically oriented social sciences "incorporates the *emancipatory* cognitive interest that, as we say, was at the root of traditional theories."[108] In the process of inquiry, Habermas wants to recover the epistemological status and political import of this interest from its death at the hands of positivism. The emancipatory interest is both a derivative and a basic cognitive interest. In one sense, it is derived from the implicit meaning of the technical and practical interests, yet it is also the hidden presupposition of those interests. As Bernstein puts it:

> Implicit in the knowledge guided by the technical and practical interests is the demand for the intellectual and material conditions for emancipation, i.e., the ideal state of affairs in which nonalienating work and free interaction can be manifested.[109]

Unlike the technical and practical interests, the emancipatory cognitive intrerest pursues reflection. Thus the "methodological framework" determining the validity of critical knowledge is established by the concept of self-reflection; the process of self-reflection "releases the subject from dependence on hypostatized powers."[110]

What is crucial here is the way in which the emancipatory interest serves as a synthesis of the technical and the practical. In a sense, Habermas takes Marx's original dialectical struggle against the two fronts of idealism and materialism and radicalizes it at the level of cognitive interests. We recall that cognitive interests are neither wholly empirical or naturalistic nor wholly transcendental principles. Rather, they both serve as the transcendental conditions for knowledge (whether technical, practical, or emancipatory) and are grounded in the life orientations of the historical self-formative process (whether work, interaction, or power). Therefore, the methodological processes of the natural and cultural sciences are "blind" to the underlying frameworks of instrumental and communicative action which constitute the interest of the evolving species-subject. But once the constitution of knowledge is seen to originate in the interest structures of work and symbolic interaction (language), the need arises to supply the missing dimension of synthesis for these two interests: that is, the dimension of power expressed in the emancipatory interest which engenders the realization of the technical and practical cognitive interests. It is critical theory which guides the inquiry of the social sciences into the nature of the historically evolved restraints on emancipation, which is already rooted in the two moments of the synthesis.

From this perspective, both the technical and practical interests, which seem basic, can be seen as moments in the emancipatory "interest of reason." However, unlike Kant, Habermas does not interpret this interest of reason idealistically since he sees reason as inhering in the interests of the self-formative process of the human species. To be sure, there is no guarantee that emancipation will result automatically from "technical progress," as is often assumed, yet the pursuit of reflection at which the emancipatory cognitive interest aims can only be realized in and through the concrete social and political lives of human beings. It is in this sense Habermas asserts that the self-reflection engendered by the marxian "critique of ideology" and by psychoanalysis can render currently accepted "laws" (which are actually ideologically frozen relations of dependence) inapplicable, but such critically mediated knowledge cannot through reflection alone render such "laws" inoperative.[111] Nonetheless, reason's emancipatory goal, inherent in the interest structures of human history, can only begin its realization through a process of "critique."

The kind of knowledge involved in the social sciences is thus not simply technical or practical, but also critical; the process of inquiry of the social sciences is "critique." Again, there is an innate human interest in autonomy and emancipation by way of self-reflection. This is presupposed in Marx's theory of revolutionary consciousness and the role of the critique of ideology. Furthermore, self-reflection is a social process, not simply an individual one. The goal of critique as a form of knowledge is to distinguish theoretically between "invariant regularities of social action" and apparent regularities which are "ideologically frozen relations of dependence." When this distinction enters the consciousness of men as both knowledge and interest, it becomes possible to recognize our possible emancipation from seemingly natural constraints. In emancipatory knowledge, then, interest and knowledge are identical.[112]

However, the realization of the emancipatory goal is only possible on the basis of unrestricted and undistorted universal discourse, which presupposes and anticipates an "ideal speech situation" and which Habermas models after the Socratic dialogue, the possibility of which has been suppressed by historical developments of domination. It is this presupposition and goal of an ideal speech situation, which Habermas also develops from the Wittgensteinian analysis of "language games," that forms the basis of his theory of communicative competence and his elaboration of a "communication theory of society." Habermas's most recent work investigates the conditions and claims involved in the possibility of Socratic dialogue and undistorted communication in relation to social theory.[113] A major task of critical theory is to analyze in their historical concreteness social structures which prohibit an ideal speech situation.

To conclude this summary of Habermas's theory of cognitive interests, let us take note of the five "theses" which appear at the conclusion of *Knowledge and Human Interests*.[114] Habermas presents them in light of the demonstration that there are only three perspectives from which to apprehend reality, grounded respectively in orientations toward (1) technical control, (2) mutual understanding in the conduct of life, and (3) emancipation from seemingly natural constraints. His first thesis claims, against Kant, that the standards and methodological criteria of knowledge are not totally transcendent and independent from the human interests rooted in the evolution of mankind: "The achievements of the transcendental subject have their basis in the natural history of the human species." However, this is not to claim that knowledge can be reduced to the adaptation of man to his environment for the purpose of survival alone. There exists in the history of society an urge "toward utopian fulfillment" which is evident in various culturally reproduced definitions of social life and the quest for the "good life." Thus Habermas's second thesis states that "knowledge equally serves as an instrument and transcends mere self-preservation."

The third thesis argues that the three viewpoints from which we apprehend reality (the three cognitive interests) originate in the interest structures of mankind radically connected to specific means of social organization. Thus "knowledge-constitutive interests take form in the medium of work, language, and power." However, the relation of knowledge and interest is not the same in all three categories of knowledge. It is only the emancipatory cognitive interest that pursues reflection as such; and since in self-reflection "knowledge for the sake of knowledge" is equivalent to the interest in autonomy, thesis four states that "in the power of self-reflection, knowledge and interest are one." The realization of the truth of this thesis is dependent, however, upon historically created structures which liberate free and open communication; emancipation through self-reflection is not a "given" but a task. Thus we note the fifth thesis: "the unity of knowledge and interest proves itself in a dialectic that takes the historical traces of suppressed dialogue and reconstructs what has been suppressed."

Habermas's theory of cognitive interests provides us with a new conception of the dialectical relation of subject and object, and of theory and practice. It is inspired by an attempt to show the illusory separation of theory and practice in the positivistic self-understanding of the process of inquiry, a separation which is epistemologically unfounded. Furthermore, this positivistic divorce of knowledge and human interests is seen to serve an ideological function preventing inquiry into, and hence legitimating, a system of domination and one-dimensionality. This is no less true of a positivistic degeneration of marxism: "Bureaucratically prescribed partisanship goes only too well with contemplatively misunderstood value freedom."[115] Thus the objectivism of the positivistic self-understanding of inquiry must be combated for both theoretical and practical reasons. But objectivism cannot be eliminated simply through the renewal of classical *theoria;* it can only be eliminated through demonstrating what the objectivism of pure theory and positivism conceals: the connection of knowledge and interest. In the spirit of Marx's pronouncement that philosophy can only realize itself by abolishing itself (in the sense of *Aufheben*), Habermas concludes, "Philosophy remains true to its classic tradition by renouncing it."[116]

Habermas's Legacy

How does Habermas's development of critical theory fare in light of the attempt to reconstitute the social sciences on the basis of dialectical theory? There are major achievements as well as major problems. Above all, his achievement lies in the monumental effort of demonstrating the dialectical unity of theory and practice *epistemologically* through his development of a theory of cognitive interests. This is a major step in the development of a dialectical theory of knowledge. In his search for the metatheoretical principles which guide dialectical social theory, and in his attempt to understand the dialectic of social evolution, Habermas has developed a profound critique of positivistic social theory and of its relations to the developments in advanced industrial society.

The development of a radical and critical method for understanding the problem of human freedom and community in contemporary society has required a revision of historically developed marxism. Hence Habermas has attempted to develop the marxian dialectic by returning to its roots in Kant and Hegel as well as by extending it to encompass the problems raised by contemporary philosophy and social science. In the face of Marx, Habermas has attempted to demonstrate the way in which systematic restrictions and distortions of communicative interaction have helped to sustain the domination of the productive forces of capitalist society. By recovering the relationship between the dialectic, self-reflection, and emancipation, grounded in human symbolic interaction, he has sketched a critical method for analyzing the peculiar forces of domination in a highly developed technological civilization. This is especially the case in his attempt to combat the subordination of critical thought to a scientific positivism which powerfully justifies the existing state of affairs. In all of these ways, Habermas has contributed to an expansion of the interpretive scope of original critical theory in Horkheimer (and even in Marx), and his thought therefore marks an advance in the evolution of dialectical theory and contemporary political inquiry.

But there are problems. For example, it has been rightly pointed out that in his attempt to prevent the conception of knowledge-constitutive interests from degenerating either into the notion of mere empirical, naturalistic interests or into something rooted in an ahistorical, transcendental subject, Habermas has left the epistemological status of the three cognitive interests extremely unclear.[117] There are two possible reasons for his failure to justify sufficiently the categorical distinction of the three cognitive interests. First, at the metatheoretical level, the inquiries of postempiricist philosophy and history of science seem to be questioning the possibility of categorically distinguishing the natural from the historical-hermeneutical sciences.[118] Second, therefore, in terms of the *practice* of inquiry in the natural sciences, there may be a less than clear boundary between the technical-informational knowledge produced by empirical-analytical science and the "practical knowledge" Habermas reserves for the cultural sciences.[119]

Perhaps just as important is the unresolved problem of praxis. For example, critical theory is supposed to provide enlightenment for a praxis of emancipation. However, as one critic has it, what seems to be lacking in Habermas is illumination on the problem of human motivation and agency. Hence certain questions remain unanswered: When will the agents of change understand their historical situation in order to overcome it? What are the concrete dynamics of this process? Who will become the agents of change?[120]

It may also be that Habermas's goal of the "ideal speech situation" is too formalistic. In a sense, he may be retreating to a reformulated position of a Kantian "categorical imperative," which posits a priori the primary "noble ideal" for a rational human life. Indeed, Habermas states at the end of *Knowledge and Human Interests* that "autonomy and responsibility," which are presupposed by the ideal speech situation, "constitute the only Idea . . . we possess in the sense of the philosophical tradition."[121] Both Hegel and Marx showed how such "noble ideals" become impotent in the course of concrete history, and thus "in the final analysis we must honestly confront the gap that has always existed—and still exists—between the ideal of such a critical theory of society and its concrete practical realization."[122]

The problem of praxis is finally revealed in the charge that the recovery of the "cultural moment" of the marxian synthesis has been overextended to the point where critical theory is too distanced from any critique of political economy. This is partly due to the obsession of critical theory (of which the present study is not totally free) with recovering and reconstructing continually its own philosophical roots, leading to theory which is perhaps "introgenetic" in its concerns and hence more removed from a concern with praxis and even more inaccessible to comprehension.[123]

Habermas offers us an ambiguous legacy, although the term "legacy" may be premature. The promises of a comprehensive dialectical theory of the relation of knowledge and interest, of theory and practice, abound from the ambition of his project. What appears on the horizon in the form of a "communication theory of society" holds forth even greater expectations. Yet these promises and contributions are fraught with problems and unresolved uncertainties, which is not to say that immediate assistance is emerging from other quarters. Habermas's development of critical theory to its present phase has involved advances in the development of dialectical theory and has produced an important voice in the dialectic of contemporary political inquiry. The issues entailed in an alternative dialectical epistemological orientation for future political inquiry have been compellingly set forth. Thus Habermas has contributed to the revelation of the dangers and the tasks that face the dialectical reconstitution of political science.

7 Prologue to the Future

Dialectical Theory and Political Inquiry

Voltaire, that sharp-witted master of the Enlightenment, had some rather strong words to say about the nature of philosophy: "La superstition met le monde entier en flammes; la philosophie les éteint." Nothing could be further removed from the spirit which has guided this study than the notion that philosophy "quenches the flames that superstition ignites throughout the world." Although one would hardly want to eulogize superstition, what we glean from the emergence of dialectical theory is a rather different view of the nature of philosophy and truth. The spirit of the Enlightenment fueled the later development of positivism, which today still dominates the pursuit of political inquiry. For the Enlightenment, truth was conceived as something straightforward and "factual," something to be rescued from the grasp of metaphysical and religious superstition by the noble, inexorable, and clarifying power of philosophy and rational thought. In dialectical thought truth appears as something uncertain and fleeting, and philosophy is not quite so confident about its efforts to understand and change the world; *les philosophes* become philosophers again. That is why my endeavor is underlined with the belief that we can be assisted by a way of examining the world which allows us to incorporate those dimensions of life and experience that defy the unequivocal grasp of purely rational or scientific thought. It may well be that "truth" is somewhat magical, and not simply the "fact" we have always thought it to be.

Recapitulation: The Shape of Dialectical Theory

As I mentioned at the beginning of this work, there appears to be an ever-growing awareness of the need to reconstitute or restructure political science. This seems to be no less true among those individuals working within the broad classical tradition of political theory than it does among those who draw their inspiration from the movements of language analysis, phenomenology, and critical theory. The latter are most obviously represented in Richard Bernstein's *The Restructuring of Social and Political Theory,* to which I have already had occasion to refer, and also in a work like Hwa Yol Jung's *The Crisis of Political Understanding.* The former are exemplified by Lee McDonald, who is concerned with the reconciliation of private and public ethics on the basis of a fully developed theory of political education. At the conclusion of his paper on ethics and political science, we find the following statement: "I end with a question: can political science as presently constituted be the basis for such a developed theory of political education?"[1] These kinds of awareness inspired this study.

In light of the various competing efforts to clarify the epistemological status of political inquiry, I have tried to isolate three general orientations worthy of our attention: (1) the recent positivist orthodoxy in political science, especially in the form of behavioralism; (2) the theoretical and philosophical enterprise associated with the classical tradition of political theory, especially in the form of its revival; and (3) the evolution of post-Kantian dialectical and critical theory of knowledge and society, especially in the forms of marxism, existential phenomenology, and critical theory. Although there is a certain arbitrariness and simplification to this categorization, it seems to represent accurately some of the major choices we face in trying to understand the past, present, and future of political inquiry. Furthermore, these general orientations to, or self-understandings of, political inquiry do not stand in static isolation from each other. There is a continual, although often implicit, dialectic between them which allows us to take note of their relationships to each other.

For the purposes of this study, that dialectic "begins" with the critique of behavioralism and positivistic social science offered by the revival of political theory. Accordingly, I dealt in chapter 1 with the dominant critique of the positivistic understanding of political inquiry as expressed by Leo Strauss, whose impact on current political theory has been considerable. Special attention was paid to Strauss's attack on the fact-value distinction, which lies at the heart of positivist dogma and scientific epistemology. Although Strauss's argument on behalf of classical political philosophy appeared sufficient for exposing the theoretical narrowness and inadequacies of behavioralist political science, we also noted some of its shortcomings, especially in view of the need to develop a dialectical epistemological framework for a critical science of politics, which requires a focus on the unity of theory and practice.

It was at this point that I introduced a third voice or "moment" in the dialectic of contemporary political inquiry—"dialectical theory" itself. If we can locate the distant historical origins of behavioralist epistemology in Humean empiricism, and if we can locate those of the revived tradition of political theory in classical *theoria* and noetic inquiry, then we can find in Kant the beginnings of dialectical theory. It was Kant, we observed, who forcefully and clearly challenged the presupposed division of subject and object in both the rationalist and the empiricist impulses in the history of human inquiry. The debate between those epistemological inclinations has continued to be elaborated in the methodological debates of current political science. In order to clarify the dialectical critique of both rationalism and empiricism, and of both classical theory and behavioralism, it seemed helpful to reconstruct the origins of such a critique in the epistemological reflections of Kant, Hegel, and Marx.

Chapter 2 summarized those original developments in light of the fundamental effort to effect a synthesis of epistemological subject and object. Kant began by dialectically closing the gap between subject and object with his concept of the synthetic activity of mind. His failure, in the eyes of Hegel, Marx, and subsequent dialectical theorists, lay in maintaining the nondialectical separation of phenomenon and noumenon, and of theoretical and practical reason. Hegel's "phenomenological radicalization" of Kantian epistemology introduced the connection of dialectic, logic, and history. He attempted to elaborate a dialectical synthesis of subject and object both in the stages of reflection and in the unity of logic and history, which is central to a dialectical critique of how rationalism and empiricism stand in a divided relation to the object. Above all, Hegel's effort to overcome the alienation of subject and object expanded the character of the Kantian knowing subject. However, the argument for the recovery of the unity of theoretical and practical reason was vitiated by the "positivism" of Hegel's method, which rendered philosophy and human consciousness politically impotent.

Hegel's contribution to a dialectical theory of knowledge and society consisted of many elements: (1) the historicity of the conditions of knowledge, which radicalized Kant's search for presuppositionless transcendental-logical conditions; (2) the unity of theory and practice at the level of a moral-knowing subject; (3) an ontological totality conceived in terms of internally mediated relations; (4) the historical and nonstatic relation of knower and known; and (5) a universal subject which "labors" to "make" history, a concept which nonetheless runs the risk of being mystified and objectified, leading to a metaphysical singularism and determinism. The dialectical achievements of Hegel were undermined, however, by other elements in his thought, most notably: (1) the overspiritualization of the human consciousness-subject; (2) the conception of philosophy as retrospectively contemplative; and most important of all, (3) the presupposition of absolute knowledge; and (4) the reliance upon a philosophy of identity, which transforms the critical role of epistemology into one of ontology and dissolves the dialectic in the process of human inquiry. Ultimately, Hegel's attempt to make the synthesis radical entailed making it absolute, presupposing the absolute unity of subject and object, and thus revealed a form of closure untenable for an open and vitalizing dialectical theory.

In this light, it is apparent how Marx endeavored to overcome alienated subject and object by introducing the synthetic activity of human praxis, rather than simply of theoretical consciousness or moral-knowing subject. Marx attempted to root and resolve Kant's notion of synthetically active consciousness and Hegel's notion of self-formative phenomenological movement of mind in the concrete totality of social life. Knowledge would thus emerge as something active, historical, moral, and social. In trying to recover what I have termed "the concrete epistemological-practical human dialectic," Marx aimed at recovering from Hegel the importance of the sensuous, concrete object, or the objectivity of the human subject conceived in terms of social labor as the synthetic activity which overcomes the alienation of subject and object. This effort resulted in Marx's dialectical notion of a "real *Aufhebung*" in knowledge, which goes beyond the abstract unity of theory and practice, and in his argument for replacing Hegel's spiritual metasubject with the laboring praxis of the self-formative human species. Ultimately, Marx's criticism of the Kantian and Hegelian epistemological adventures gave a new shape to dialectical theory by conceiving the synthesis as practical and human, and therefore as fundamentally relative and open. The union of subject and object becomes neither impossible (as with Kant) nor guaranteed (as with Hegel), but a human historical task always threatened by contingency. Unfortunately, Marx's obsession with the recovery of objectivity allowed the subsequent degeneration of his theory into various forms of scientism, materialism, positivism, and determinism, all of which threatened subjectivity.

On the basis of these germinal philosophical movements, it is possible to make more intelligible some twentieth-century developments of dialectical theory. This was the intention of chapters 3 and 4. In chapter 3, we observed some of the central dialectical elements of Marx's theory as they emerged in his philosophy of internal relations, epistemology, methodology, and conception of history and praxis. In terms of dialectical theory, a continual vigilance is required to distinguish dialectical from positivistic marxism. Some important examples of individuals who have held such a vigil include Gramsci, Lukács, Merleau-

Ponty, and Kolakowski. There is still much to be learned from their efforts.

In chapter 4, a brief reconstruction of the history of phenomenology from its origins in Husserl's transcendental philosophy to its existential elaboration in Heidegger, Sartre, and Merleau-Ponty revealed a certain stratum of thinking which provides another twentieth-century source and expression of dialectical theory. Without committing too great an interpretive sin, it seems possible to distinguish a dialectical existential phenomenology from both transcendental and nondialectically existential phenomenology. Here Merleau-Ponty emerges as the thinker who most coherently and self-consciously expressed possible "dialectical directions" in phenomenology. In light of the discussion in chapter 2, Merleau-Ponty is seen to recover the importance of the prereflective, interior, and intersubjective dimensions of human knowledge and experience which are neglected and occluded in the objectivistic deterioration of Marx's dialectical theory.

The emerging shape of contemporary dialectical theory was the focus in chapters 5 and 6. In particular, two movements or directions were isolated which seem important to our current views of political inquiry. First, the confluence of marxism and phenomenology, examined in chapter 5, appears as one of the most important and fruitful developments of dialectical theory in our time. We witnessed some of the conditions, problems, and promises of such a union in the thought of Sartre and Merleau-Ponty. Merleau-Ponty's adventures in this realm seem the most significant and hopeful for the future of social and political inquiry.

Beyond the efforts of Sartre and Merleau-Ponty, we noted briefly more recent and diverse adventures in the confluence of marxism and phenomenology. In the first place, contributions of existential phenomenology in general to political science were outlined in the following areas of inquiry: (1) the foundational nature of the *Lebenswelt;* (2) the nature of "radical empiricism"; (3) the self-reflexivity of theory which speaks to the need for a philosophical self-understanding of political science; (4) the unity of subject and object; (5) the meaning of intentionality in human action; and (6) the centrality of sociality. In the second place, we saw that amid the diversity of individuals self-consciously working within the marxian-phenomenological union, certain important commonalities are apparent: (1) a view of theory as critical theory; (2) an opposition to all forms of objectivism; (3) a focus on the dialectic of subject and object; (4) a rejection of all forms of rationalism and empiricism; (5) a view of human nature which assumes man as a constituted-constituting being who is open and unfinished and never all that he can be; and (6) an effort to unite theory and practice in the service of human emancipation. These recent adventures are still at an early stage and offer one possible future for dialectical theory.

In chapter 6, a second direction of contemporary dialectical theory was noted in the evolution of the Frankfurt School. Although it is partially grounded in and closely related to the expressions of dialectical theory examined in chapters 3, 4, and 5, Critical Theory has emerged in its own distinctive form. After examining its general origins, especially its foundations in Horkheimer, and its transformation into the second half of the twentieth century, I discussed central dialectical elements in the thought of Habermas, the Frankfurt School's most powerful contemporary heir. Of particular importance are Habermas's epistemological contributions in his critique of Marx and his theory of cognitive interests. It seems credible to isolate Habermas's theory of cognitive interests, which tries to unite epistemologically knowledge and human interests, or theory and practice, in the logic and process of inquiry, as one of the most significant contributions current dialectical theory offers to our view of the philosophical foundations of political inquiry. It is possible that Habermas today is providing the same kind of dialectical turning point for "marxism" that Merleau-Ponty provided for phenomenology.

Current Political Science: The View in Light of a Dialectical Critique

The insights revealed by tracing the contours of the emergence of dialectical theory offer a new view of recent debates in political science. If we bring those insights to bear on the debates between behavioralism and the revival of political theory, not only do we discover an alternative understanding of the broad philosophical orientation of political inquiry, but we also can see how positivist behavioralism and revived classical theory implicitly converge on a number of theoretical issues. To be sure, by looking at the recent fray in this manner, with a rather sweeping view upon epistemological orientations and inclinations, we ignore the many crucial and fundamental differences between the two, and especially the richness and profundity of classical theory. Nonetheless, it is instructive to note the similarities in order to emphasize the alternative sensitivity that emerges from a broad conception of dialectical theory.

Perhaps what is held most in common between positivism and revived political theory is an objectivistic conception of reality, either in implicit or in explicit formulations. In classical political theory, this is apparent in the assumption of a permanent and intelligible nature that can be known by reason. The quest for objectivity is a quest for an objective standard of truth. In a sense, this presumption is apparent even in Kant (although the objective structure of "ultimate" reality is inaccessible to human knowledge) and especially in Hegel's concept of absolute spirit as objectively structured metasubject. With Kant, the objective standard of knowledge becomes the "sure march of science," and the standard for human action and life is the objective moral "categorical imperative."[2] With Hegel, absolute knowledge serves the role of objective criterion for knowledge, while absolute spirit embodied in the ethical state serves it for "practice." There is an objectivism of sorts even for the harbingers of "dialectical theory."

For certain leaders of revived political theory, truth presumes objectivity. Otherwise, the resolution of subject and object would be impossible, since there would be no objective order or truth with which to bring the knowing subject into accord. With Leo Strauss, this assumption takes the form of "natural right" and the rationally discoverable truth of the "whole."[3] With Eric Voegelin, it takes the form of an objectively ordered transcendent-divine ground of being to which the human psyche can "attune itself."[4] Such objectivism, for all its richness and seriousness, runs the risk of denying a concrete dialectic of subject and object where the human subject actually participates in creating reality itself through knowledge and praxis. The assumption that in order for knowledge to be possible there must be an objectively ordered reality, with an ontological independence from human knowing and acting, can culminate in a nondialectical metaphysical realism.

When classical political theory is brought to a criticism of behavioralism it is not a critique of objectivity as such. The critique of behavioralism's empiricism and positivism is directed at the "pseudoobjectivity" attained when we rest content with an analysis of the material and behavioral world. This objectivity is ultimately illusory because it is grounded in an incomplete conception of reality, and because it ignores the heights and depths of experience of man's interior life, which is no less real or true than his "outer" life. Indeed, the ontological assumption in classical theory entails an absolute epistemological standard, which is related to an objective ethical standard. This is more than behavioralism is willing to offer, since for methodological reasons it admits no connection at all between its objective standards of knowledge and ethical-practical life. Nonetheless, both of these general orientations to human inquiry share an objectivistic view of an already ordered reality awaiting the gaze of the knowing subject. From a dialectical perspective, all forms of objectivism are fundamentally suspect.

The revived tradition of political theory and behavioralism also share a quality of abstraction. For the former, the subject as knowing consciousness is often detached or abstracted *from* the world in such a way as to leave it untouched after knowing it. For the latter, the subject as sensorial observer is abstracted *within* the world so that he must ignore cognitively the nonobservable dimensions of human experience and reflection. Both stances miss the totality of reality, by removing the knower either from the concrete, historical, lived world of experience or from the nonmaterial, nonbehavioral ways in which man constitutes his life and shares the meaning of being human.

What seems to be required of the knower or inquirer by the sensitivity of dialectical theory is the critical self-examination of his epistemological inherence in praxis, nature, and the world, an integral part of the process itself of knowing. This requires that we recover qua inquirers our concrete, sensuous, and perceptually relative and relational roots in the world. It requires that we remember that we *exist* in all our wholeness before, during, and after we *reflect,* that our detachment presupposes our attachment, and that in this attachment we recover and reapproach ourselves and the world for what they really are. To be sure, "political theory" correctly reminds behavioralism and positivism that in their dismissal of subjectivity, in their bifurcation of fact and value, they ignore their own roots as principles and as ideas (their own subjectivity) and thus truncate reality unrealistically. Yet political theory is often guilty of a similar transgression whenever it neglects its own dialectical, existential, and radical inherence in the sensuous everyday world. There is something one-sided and abstract in both of these endeavors. Furthermore, both behavioralism and revived political theory, with their respective emphases on the authority of empirical observation and of reason, too often preclude the experience of "unreason" and prereflectivity—a crucial dimension of human life presupposed by consciousness. The experience of prereflection and primordial, preconscious perception needs to be taken into account in any self-critical, self-reflexive theory of knowledge that underpins political inquiry.

These preliminary considerations indicate how the concretely critical function of political inquiry is often dismissed. For behavioralism, with its empiricist impulse, political knowledge is uncritical because "scientific knowledge" should be objectively descriptive and explanatory; for knowledge to be critical of life would result in subjectivism or emotionalism. For revived political theory, knowledge is only uncritical practically, because the criticism it forms in its process of inquiry is self-consciously disengaged from the ongoing practical process of social life. It is not uncritical in intent, at least not always, but only in effect. To incorporate concrete, practical criticism in the process of inquiry would mean clearly taking sides in everyday struggles of life and would be considered "unphilosophical." It always remains to be taken another day, and wearing a different hat. The conception of human inquiry as a solely contemplative process aimed at objects leads us to ignore the level at which there is a dialectical interaction of thinking and doing, reflecting and being. If we fail to recognize that praxis is involved in the enterprise of knowing, we do not allow for our critical function to be practical or even moral as well as theoretical.

In other words, the process of human inquiry is an act; it is as much an integral, practical, and existentially creative act as it is a contemplative and theoretically reflective act. Without this dialectical corrective, the epistemological subject becomes, in the process of knowing, a static creature; he becomes, as it were, frozen in a moment of knowing. He is no longer a part of the world and of history in which he is continually "caught up." We run the risk of forgetting that knowledge is historically and practically relative and perspectival, and that the knowing subject is engaged in the world and the movement of history at every moment in his knowing. Furthermore, insofar as our experience as inquirers is a whole experience, wherein every dimension of our being is engaged in knowing, it is impossible to restrict ourselves epistemologically to the observable "facts" of the world; such an inquirer would be something other than human. Therefore, to the extent that positivist behavioralism entails abstraction from the totality of human experience, and to the extent that current political philosophy entails abstraction from the concrete, lived world in which we participate and struggle every day, both remain incomplete.

The foregoing remarks provide only an indication of how some of the issues involved in political science's internal debates can be seen in light of dialectical theory, and of how it is possible to note points of convergence between the two dominant participants in those debates. Although it is overly schematic and merely suggestive, a dialectical critique of some of the disagreements over epistemological orientation in recent political science might be summarized in the following preliminary theses.

I

The classical philosophical basis/bias of the revival of political theory is often critical of empiricist behavioralism for its transformation into historicism, a form of relativism. Behavioralism is seen to lack some historically or situationally transcendent objective standard of the truth of the whole of reality. One aspect of this criticism points up the pseudoobjectivity of the empiricist method and its resultant inability to face up to all of the dimensions of political reality. But it is a criticism only of a reduced, one-dimensional objectivity, and not of objectivity as such. Thus there is a shared "structure" of objectivism to the two orientations, although the substance of each is drastically different.

II

From Lukács: "Every contemplative, purely cognitive stance leads ultimately to a divided relationship to its object."[5]

III

Empiricism and materialism cannot be established *in* principle but only *on* principle. Materialism cannot establish itself materially; empiricism cannot establish itself empirically. Its self-critical reflection would reveal empiricism's self-contradictory nature. Empiricism must return to reason for a formulation; it is ultimately another lesser and impoverished form of rational philosophy.

IV

In political theory, we often confront the contingency of history with a sense of disquiet. Political theory often entails a desire for an absolutely rational structure of the world. Although behavioralism is criticized for the reductionist, pseudoobjective character of its quest for scientific certainty, political theory too runs the risk of being caught up in an unending desire for certitude and an "absolute basis in experience or reason." Witness the fear of one current proponent of classical theory that "the theorist [be] left with no solid base on which to stand"; if there is no "fixed" human nature, the argument continues, then what basis exists for general assertions about the structure of human action and consciousness?[6]

V

Therefore, whereas behavioralism often reduces its theme to its current historical situation, political theory faces the temptation to abstract its theme from the situation. The temptation reflects the theorist's apprehension at being imprisoned by (or responsible for?) his own time and social context. The lure of the absolute is strong when we face with trepidation irrationality and contingency. Perhaps when we begin to equate the contingent or the relative with the arbitrary we reveal a fear of taking full responsibility for history and the future.

VI

There is an irony in political theory's recurrent fear that historicism, especially marxist materialism, presupposes a determinism which eliminates man's freedom and capacity for individual responsible action. As Merleau-Ponty puts it, "Marxism not only tolerates freedom and the individual but, as 'materialism,' even gives man a dizzying responsibility, as it were."[7] Indeed, it may be that a dialectical historicism, which conceives knowledge itself as a matter of human praxis, requires too much human responsibility and cooperation to create a world that is just. The irony is reflected in the fact that the individuals in political theory today who argue that historicism's determinism destroys critical and responsible thought are often the same ones who are surprisingly uncritical of the American constitutional-democratic political order. It is often argued that in such a regime, the principles of "natural right" themselves are most closely approximated or embodied. There is a strange kind of historicism in this claim.

VII

In searching for an objective basis upon which to stand, positivism truncates reality and ignores or "brackets" its subjective components. However, traditional political theory often faces the hazard, in searching for its own objective basis, of abstracting itself from history and from the concrete unity of thought and existence, by finding that basis outside of the historically relative world.

VIII

The revival of political theory criticizes behavioralism for merely describing and explaining what we should also be criticizing and evaluating. Thus it reminds us of the unity of "is" and "ought," and that we should continually offer new visions of reality. In other words, it reminds us of the whole of human political experience and knowledge. However, the revived tradition of political theory runs the risk of excluding epistemologically (though not always pragmatically) the historicity of human praxis and its potential union with philosophy. Thus its critical evaluation is often impotent.

IX

"Going beyond historicism and positivism" does not necessarily entail only a restoration of the tradition of political theory. Dialectical theory, which could be seen loosely as a form of historicism, also tries to go beyond positivism and historicism, especially insofar as it sees the latter as degenerating into a nondialectical form of objectivism.[8]

X

It is possible to view historicism and political theory as agreeing upon the necessity for evaluation in political inquiry. It is also possible to view positivism and political theory as agreeing upon the possibility of knowing an objective world. This latter thesis reveals a shared ontological assumption in the classical and positivist conceptions of theory. But the former ignores how a dialectical theory cannot remain epistemologically contemplative or isolated from praxis in its criticism and evaluation.

XI

Political theory reminds behavioralism and positivism of their own metaphysical roots. We need to remind political theory of its own prereflective, historical, and practical roots.

XII

Again, both political theory and positivist behavioralism can result in abstract approaches to understanding and to changing political reality. The latter abstracts itself from the totality of real human experience, while the former often abstracts itself from the concrete, lived world in which we exist, labor, love, and die.

XIII

The fear of ambiguity lies at the heart of both rationalism and empiricism.

Conclusion: Toward a Philosophy of Ambiguity and Commitment

> What we call the beginning is often the end
> And to make an end is to make a beginning.
> The end is where we start from.
>
> We shall not cease from exploration
> And the end of all our exploring
> Will be to arrive where we started
> And know the place for the first time.
> > T. S. Eliot, "Little Gidding"

Sounding very much like Hegel in the *Phenomenology of Spirit,* Eliot's words mark the spirit of the end of the present journey. In the beginning, I took note of what seem to be the two major voices in recent debates over the nature of authentic political science or theory: positivist behavioralism and the revival of political theory. It was suggested that for the past few decades these debates have missed a third and important voice which emerged from post-Kantian philosophy: the voice of dialectical theory. In our brief journey through the evolution of a dialectical theory of knowledge and reality, I hope I have clarified some of the questions and issues, problems and promises, raised by that voice in light of the pursuit of political inquiry. By reaching the end of our tour, we have returned to the beginning, but it is a new beginning, one hopes, mediated and enriched by the experience of the journey itself. Much like the path traveled by spirit in Hegel's *Phenomenology,* we return to the beginning "uttering the same creed," but as it emerges from our lips now, it contains a new meaning.

Thus it is hoped that the term "dialectical theory" now conjures up a richer and more intelligible picture than it did in the opening pages of this study. It has not been my primary intention in this volume to introduce a collection of new and unknown thinkers to political science or to put forward radically new interpretations of their thought—although to the extent that either of these services has been performed, that much more will the work gratify my efforts. Rather, I have tried to interpret and clarify a complex tradition of philosophical thought, which is unheralded in contemporary American political science, by unifying that tradition around the concept of dialectic. Although many of the individuals considered throughout this study never regarded themselves primarily as dialectical theorists, or as contributing to the evolution of a dialectical theory, I believe it is precisely their varying degrees of sensitivity to a dialectical theory of knowledge and reality, especially their attentiveness to a dialectic of epistemological subject and object, that unite them in the face of positivism and the revival of political theory.

In particular, if we interpret those individual thinkers in light of the emergence of dialectical theory, it allows us to assemble and clarify a lot of what has simply been called "historicism." It seems unfair and inaccurate to exile all those thinkers who stand outside positivism and revived classical theory to the monolithic ideological prison of historicism. Yet this is precisely what is often done. In a recent article on current political science, one finds the following individuals placed within the province of historicism: Kant, Hegel, Marx, Nietzsche, Husserl, Spengler, Dewey, G. H. Mead, Bergson, Sartre, Dilthey, Mannheim, Heidegger, Merleau-Ponty, Wittgenstein, Cassirer, Kuhn, Hwa Yol Jung, John Gunnell, and Henry Kariel—just to name a few figures, both major and minor.[9] This is quite a collection, and one that is not altogether helpful. Furthermore, it ignores the importance of distinguishing the dialectical strands of thought within this "movement," especially those that resist extreme relativism and historicism. Again, the thinkers I have assembled under the banner of "dialectical theory" are not terribly new to us, but perhaps this way of organizing and viewing them is.

In arguing for a discernible evolution of dialectical theory, I have not intended to suggest that this movement ought to replace current forms of the pursuit of political inquiry or usurp the throne of "authentic political science." To the contrary, much of what has been examined in this study is not political inquiry proper, but philosophical inquiry. Thus I have argued only that this philosophical tradition can condition, shape, and enrich our view of the domain, method, and spirit of political inquiry, and it can alter our general way of pursuing political study in terms of the assumptions and conclusions, means and ends, of our research. In light of our study, it is possible to outline several elements that emerge from a broad dialectical theory that might act as theoretical and practical guideposts or leaveners for future political inquiry. These form what we might call the marks of authentic dialectical theory relevant to political science. Finally, each of the following marks or elements reflects a differing degree of generality or specificity from the others, regarding the spirit, method, or goal of research.

1. *Self-critical and self-reflective theory.* Informed by dialectical theory, political inquiry would be involved in continual reflection on the assumptions and nature of its enterprise. Insofar as we take a critical stance toward reality, we must also take a critical stance toward our own theory and criticism. This means that we are always in a state of beginning anew in confronting the world for the sake of comprehension. As Merleau-Ponty has it:

> The philosopher . . . is a perpetual beginner, which means that he takes for granted nothing that men, learned or otherwise, believe they know. It means also that philosophy itself must not take itself for granted, in so far as it may have managed to say something true; that it is an ever-renewed experiment in making its own beginning.[10]

Although on the face of it, this sounds none too difficult, such a stance would require constant and prodigious vigilance against the dangers of self-closure, "scientific" overconfidence, and unreflectiveness in political science.

2. *Totality.* We glean from dialectical theory a conception of reality as a totality of internal relations. This is especially true of social and political reality, where those relations are mediated by human beings caught up in a nexus of historical, natural, and communal ties. The ontological assumption of a relational totality instructs us to recognize in our research the interconnectedness and radical openness of any "factor" of society and politics we choose to investigate. It militates against a "methodological individualism" or "anarchism," which would not see the whole in the parts, and hence would ignore how the parts themselves are constituted by the relations of the whole.

3. *Beyond causality.* An intriguing aspect of dialectical theory, rooted in Kant himself and taken up again by Marx, is the suggestion that relationships between man (or knowing subject) and reality (or known object) are not simple causal ones, but involve an element of codetermination and cocreation. Furthermore, we find a suggestion that it may be misleading to approach reality in terms of linear causal relations, when we should rather view the two poles of apparent "cause" and "effect" as two terms which mutually express two sides of a common reality and relation. This is the sense in which Marx speaks of the sun

existing as an "object" for the plant, and the plant as an "expression" of the sun's life-giving powers. In the same way, private property is not seen to cause alienated labor any more than alienated labor is seen to cause private property; the two mutually express different aspects of a common whole. We may do well to think of relations in the world in terms of manifestations, expressions, reflections. To view the world primarily in terms of cause and effect blinds us to the rich complexity and openness of our natural and social relations.

4. *Prereflectivity and perception.* Certain developments in dialectical theory reveal the importance of the prereflective dimension of human knowledge, experience, and life. It is imperative to keep in mind the preconscious perceptual character of our everyday life as well as the prereflective foundation of our conscious and rational thought. This dimension must not only become an object of inquiry, but must also be reincorporated in our theory of knowledge. Our prereflective perceptual rootedness in the world reveals the presence of the world to us in its most original form and reveals an essential unity of consciousness and body that is often neglected or distorted in scientific and philosophical representations. The open horizon of the world revealed in perception, as our primary act in the world, impels our effort to recover the unreflected and to recognize our perceptual situatedness in time and space. This notion has no minor consequences for objectivistic theories of truth.

5. *The critique of objectivism.* As we have repeatedly seen, the individuals involved in the emergence of dialectical theory are almost unanimous in their stance against ontological and epistemological objectivism. Although one could view dialectical theory as equally opposed to all forms of rationalism, empiricism, idealism, materialism, determinism, and so forth, it seems consistently to focus its attention on various assumptions of "objective reality" or "objective truth" as they occlude the ascendency of subjectivity and the dialectic of subject and object. As one current phenomenological critic, who calls for the "triumph of subjectivity," has put it, "The crisis of political understanding is the crisis of objectivity without subjectivity."[11]

6. *Creative activity of consciousness.* Closely related to the critique of objectivism is the notion that human consciousness participates in the creation of reality, of that which is often assumed to exist objectively beyond our efforts at changing and knowing the world. Consciousness is not simply the passive receptacle of sensations or the creative author of ideas detached from the empirical world. This notion originates in Kant's argument for the synthetic activity of consciousness which creatively orders the manifold of sense experience. It is taken much further in Marx's identification of consciousness with man's practical process of shaping and changing reality itself. This is not to

argue that human consciousness creates reality totally and at will, nor to argue that all transformation of reality, such as that produced by the technological impulse of domination, is praiseworthy or emancipatory. It is rather to argue, against behavioralism for example, that behind man's behavior lies a dialectic of subject and object whereby what we take to be reality is always partially constituted by us. Still, such a metastatic conception of reality always runs the risk, as Voegelin, Germino, and others have pointed out, of degenerating into untrammeled messianism and oppression, and, as the Critical Theorists have indicated, of permitting the domination of man and nature in the name of "the achievements of humanity." This is the ever-threatening dark side of dialectical theory.

7. *Historicity of knowledge.* Furthermore, there seems to be agreement in most dialectical theory that the conditions of knowledge are fundamentally historical in character. This notion is most strongly rooted in Hegel's theory of the continual *Aufhebung* of past forms of consciousness and knowing which produces new conditions of knowledge, and in the view that there are no absolute transcendental-logical conditions of knowledge. There is a historical and nonstatic relation of the knower and the known, so that all claims to have discovered *the* condition of what counts as knowledge, or to possess a monopoly on truth, are suspect. There is always a danger in this view of losing any standard of knowledge at all. This is why the dialectical concept of *Aufhebung* is so important, for it reminds us of the need to preserve, negate, and transcend simultaneously the standards and conditions that have evolved through the self-formation of the self-reflective human species. Finally, we must always protect against the danger that history itself be made an absolute condition.

8. *Universal subject of history.* The notion of a "metasubject" of history emerges from Hegel's concept of laboring absolute spirit. It is developed by Marx as the laboring proletariat, which forms the historical subject-object, and it is opened up by dialectical marxism and critical theory, as in Habermas, as the laboring praxis and self-reflection in the self-formation of the human species through history, and in interaction with nature and symbols. The importance of this concept is twofold: it recognizes that history is a product of a laboring subject, and it identifies that subject as something greater than isolated individuals and events. History is no longer seen either as the absolute determining source of all reality or as the mere recording of events or as the mere context of unconnected and disparate contacts with reality. There is a discernible logic and meaning to history, which nonetheless is constantly threatened by contingency and non-sense.

9. *Philosophy as forward-looking.* One element that emerges from dialectical theory is the view that knowledge is oriented toward the

future. This is not to say we are interested in scientistic "futurology" or crystal-gazing. It is to say that philosophy is more than a retrospective, contemplative enterprise, that knowledge is oriented not only to what is past but essentially to what is yet to come—that knowledge has an interest in the future based upon its understanding of the past and of the immanent tendencies of the present. As Ernst Bloch has it, "Only the horizon of the future," as it is brought into knowledge and related to the past as the corridor to the future, "gives reality its dimension of reality."[12] Or in Merleau-Ponty's words: "Philosophy is not the reflection of a pre-existing truth, but, like art, the act of bringing truth into being."[13]

10. *Philosophy as life*. Dialectical theory seems to evoke, among all its participants, a sense that philosophy is grounded in, and interested in, concrete, everyday life. Thus it always maintains a practical aim of the emancipation of man from various forms of intellectual and practical domination and control. Furthermore, philosophy emerges as a way of life which does not flee the world of everyday life; it involves simply another, more intense, way of living that life. Philosophy thus must not forget its rootedness and interest in life, and indeed should find itself returning there often. Philosophy, as Merleau-Ponty once put it, involves a way of saying what we already know well. And it needs to be said, continually.

11. *The unity of theory and practice*. We have seen how the epistemological unity of theory and practice has formed the focus of much of dialectical theory. Beginning with Hegel's attempt to unify theory and practice in the phenomenologically reconstructed moral-knowing subject, the focus shifted with Marx to the level of a concrete epistemological-practical human subject. In the dialectical theory of Habermas, we find one of the most powerful efforts in our time to unite theory and practice epistemologically in the process of inquiry itself, by way of a theory of cognitive interests. The notion that knowledge and human interests in emancipation are joined together in the act of knowing is a significant insight for a critical science of politics. The quest for a unity of theory and practice is a simultaneously moral, epistemological, and practical one. The unity of theory and practice does not entail a pragmatistic notion that an idea is true because it is useful, but argues that it is useful because it is true. "The concrete idea," writes Bloch, "becomes the illumination for the act," and the act "becomes the crown of truth."[14]

12. *Dialectic as corrective*. There is a sense in which a dialectical sensitivity plays a role in inquiry that is as much "negative" as it is "positive." Rather than view dialectical theory as a set of positive operating instructions and insights for political inquiry, it is helpful to view it as a corrective, which continually prevents us from moving to extremes. Much in the spirit of Kant's notion of the "regulative use of the ideas of pure reason," dialectical theory may be able to guide

our inquiry in such a manner that we avoid the extremes of rationalism and empiricism, of immanentism and transcendentalism, of freedom and determinism, of all absolutes and certainties, including the temptation to make the "dialectic" absolute and objective. At the same time, as we saw with Kolakowski, the dialectic maintains the tension between the poles of various absolute positions, thus never denying the possible validity of either. This means that there can be no absolute relativism. In a sense, what makes the concept of dialectical theory so difficult to pin down is precisely this "negative" role it assumes so well, and its unwillingness to decide for either pole of our many abstract dualities. Merleau-Ponty puts it strikingly:

> Any dialectical philosophy will always resist being labeled, since, according to Plato, it sacrifices nothing willingly and always wants 'both.' And so the philosophical effort to get past abstractions is sometimes challenged in the name of matter and sometimes in the name of Spirit. Everyone keeps the bee in his bonnet.[15]

13. *Radical openness.* Perhaps what is prized most highly in the evolution of dialectical theory is the emergence of a spirit of radical openness. We sense a rejection of all forms of closure of thought and action. "That we disavow reflection is positivism," writes Habermas.[16] In this terse statement, we discover a call for the openness of reflection, which opposes all closed systems of thought regardless of their metaphysical bases. Dialectical theory recognizes not only the need for human inquiry to remain open to reflection, to the past and future, and to all modes of knowing and expressing, but also the need to remain open to the movement of concrete, practical life itself. Gramsci was endeared to humanist marxists and non-marxists alike not only for his openness to Crocean idealism, but as well for his openness to Catholicism and other experiences of the concrete life of his day which revealed elements of meaning and humanity. Finally, radical openness requires that the synthesis which dialectical theory seeks is never finished. What is appealing about the interpretation of Marx offered in this work is that it focuses upon the open-endedness of his synthesis. The synthesis always remains to be made generation after generation, with new and different meaning revealed in each effort.

14. *Ambiguity and commitment.* Finally, a crucial mark of authentic dialectical theory lies in the mutual, yet apparently contradictory, claims of ambiguity and commitment. Most of the individuals involved in the evolution of a dialectical theory of knowledge and society have cried out for human inquiry to become committed to the creation of a truly human world, where man is free from domination and control and emancipated to fulfill that which he is and can become. At the same time, the need for a sense of commitment in philosophy and political

inquiry is measured against the recognition of the fundamental ambiguity of human knowledge and life. There are never any guarantees that we can ever fully understand the world, much less change it in the direction of truth. Yet somehow the need to make the effort remains with us. To act out of ambiguity is one of the most difficult tasks imaginable; our actions are always threatened with paralysis. Without the act, our inquiry remains ghostly and impotent, but without the recognition of ambiguity, our knowledge degenerates into ideology and our acts so easily lead to systems of totalitarian oppression, irrational indifference, and human sorrow—all justified on the basis of certainty and special insight. The attempt to unite the need for radical commitment with the awareness of fundamental ambiguity is most starkly evident in Merleau-Ponty's view of marxism:

> Boiled down to its essence, Marxism is not an optimistic philosophy but simply the idea that another history is possible, that there is no such thing as fate, that man's existence is open-ended. It is the resolute try for that future which no one in the world or out of the world can know will come or, if it comes, what it will be.[17]

Contemporary political inquiry has been shaped by various philosophical traditions, most importantly by classical philosophy and positivism. Its future holds forth the possibility of greater sensitivity to the tradition of dialectical theory that I have sketched in this study. That possibility, however, is contingent upon the further development of the points summarized in the past few pages. On the one hand, I believe it is necessary to reconstruct and reinterpret the emergence of dialectical theory. But on the other hand, we cannot remain content with this kind of enterprise. We desperately need the revitalization of the philosophical spirit itself within political science, a spirit which thirsts after the new and the undiscovered, the nontrivial and the inspiring. Over thirty years ago, Merleau-Ponty, whom I believe later generations will discover as the greatest dialectical thinker of our century, made some remarks which seem distressingly appropriate to political science today:

> For to philosophize is to seek, and this is to imply that there are things to see and to say. Well, today we no longer seek. We 'return' to one or the other of our traditions and 'defend' it. Our convictions are founded less on perceived values and truths than on the vices and errors of those we do not like. We love very few things, though we dislike many. Our thinking is a thought in retreat or in reply.[18]

That this state of affairs exists today is evident in the pages of our journals of political science.

To learn from dialectical theory is to recognize that it is always unfinished theory. As I have understood and presented it, dialectical theory does not elaborate a set of fixed propositions or a formula that can simply be applied to our research in political science. It is not a new model or paradigm in that sense. Rather, it marks a new sensitivity in our pursuit of political knowledge and informs us of a particular spirit and goal of research. For those who are dissatisfied with the lack of a clear-cut and precise definition of the dialectic and dialectical theory, I can only offer my own shared sense of dissatisfaction. This is a problem, or perhaps an achievement, which seems inherent in the very concept of dialectic. It may be that the dialectic is somewhat like the neutrino recently "discovered" by nuclear physics. We cannot precisely measure or clearly define its mass, yet we know that somehow it moves us.

This work is primarily addressed to those individuals in political science who are deeply discontented with the present state of affairs. We have recently been told of the withdrawal of political theorists in the face of the success of behavioralism in defining political science.[19] But it does not seem inexorable that political science turn either to public policy analysis or to the clarification of the antiquated conception of science accepted by behavioralism. It is careless to ignore the debate of the past few decades in political science. That debate is neither dead nor won; it merely smolders.

Dialectical theory is in search of a political science and a politics that fit our lived experience and the highest potential that lies within us. The pretense of a scientific study of politics reveals an interest in removing ambiguity from human life, and it both reflects and helps to create the same kind of politics: a politics of technological solutions, of carefully managed dissent and debate, a politics where the "intolerable burden" of freedom is gradually being lifted from the backs of citizens. Political science is often prosaic and it reflects a politics which has become prosaic. As the character of our political knowledge and political life descends into the prose of information and mere survival, the need emerges for a political science equally philosophical and empirical, equally poetic and prosaic. T. S. Eliot once posed an interesting question that could just as well be directed to contemporary political inquiry:

> Where is the Life we have lost in living?
> Where is the wisdom we have lost in knowledge?
> Where is the knowledge we have lost in information?
> Choruses from *The Rock*, I

Our responsibility as political scientists is to take up again the banner of humanity in our quest for political knowledge. Political theory has limitations; it alone cannot save the world. But by the same token, it should do what it can to illuminate the possibilities of political emancipation and, by the act of its knowing, engage itself in a world in the making. We should not take too much joy in retreating to our studies to discover eternal verities or universal laws. What Merleau-Ponty wrote about freedom at the end of his last work on political theory could well be applied to our responsibility and commitment to the social and political world: our pursuit of political knowledge and our responsibility to truth is not only our own thing, our secret, our pleasure, our salvation—it involves everyone else.[20]

Our excitement in pursuing political inquiry for the sake of human emancipation and community is always threatened by our recognition of the dialectical ambiguity of knowledge and reality, by the awareness that we live, act, and know in the "shadow" that falls between the idea and the reality. For one last time, Eliot's words of over fifty years ago, interpreted in light of our present concern, serve to caution a dialectical political theory radically committed to human life and political practice in the interest of changing the world:

> Between the idea
> And the reality
> Between the motion
> And the act
> Falls the Shadow
>
> Between the conception
> And the creation
> Between the emotion
> And the response
> Falls the Shadow
>
> Between the desire
> And the spasm
> Between the potency
> And the existence
> Between the essence
> And the descent
> Falls the Shadow

"The Hollow Men, V"

So long as we do not retreat in fear or despair from the shadow, and so long as we continue to express and create in spite of the shadowy uncertainty of our efforts, then we can begin to pursue a political theory which is a philosophy both of ambiguity and of commitment. Dialectical theory, as one possibility, does not find the solution to the human condition either in man alone or in the world alone, either in discovery alone or in creation alone, either in history alone or outside of history. A truly dialectical theory would amend Hegel's words in expressing the ultimate goal of our inquiry. We must be involved in nothing less than the discovery and creation of a world worthy of the human spirit to inhabit, as well as the discovery and creation of a human spirit worthy of the world.

Notes

Chapter One

1. Richard J. Bernstein, *The Restructuring of Social and Political Theory* (New York: Harcourt Brace Jovanovich, 1976).

2. Dante Germino, *Beyond Ideology: The Revival of Political Theory* (New York: Harper and Row, 1967; reprint ed., Chicago: University of Chicago Press, 1976). All references are to the 1967 edition.

3. I have chosen not to capitalize the term marxism. My intent is not to be idiosyncratic, but to make a point about marxism as a philosophical movement. The kind of marxism I am presenting in this study is broad, rich, open, diverse, and constantly evolving. It has taken on a character and significance that have transcended any mere association with the name Marx (as well as Engels). My purpose is thus to register my resistance against any tendency to reify something that has become so richly complex as marxism.

4. Of the many examples of this attitude, see, for example, Eugene Meehan's desire to eliminate "the mystical, the metaphysical, the meaningless" from political science in *The Theory and Method of Political Analysis* (Homewood, Ill.: Dorsey Press, 1965), 260. See also the interpretation of political philosophy presupposed in Harold D. Lasswell and Abraham Kaplan, *Power and Society* (London: Routledge and Kegan Paul, 1952), 118. Or see the attitude characteristic of a work like Felix Oppenheim's *Moral Principles in Political Philosophy* (New York: Random House, 1968).

5. For just a few examples of the continuing currency of such debates, see the collected papers in Maria J. Falco, ed., *Through the Looking-glass: Epistemology and the Conduct of Inquiry, an Anthology* (Washington, D.C.: University Press of America, 1979); see also, John G. Gunnell, *Philosophy, Science, and Political Inquiry* (Morristown, N.J.: General Learning Press, 1975); and Dante Germino, "The Fact-Value Dichotomy as an Intellectual Prison," *Modern Age* 23, no. 2 (Spring 1979): 140–44.

6. On the "behavioral persuasion," see Heinz Eulau, *The Behavioral Persuasion in Politics* (New York: Random House, 1964). For other examples of positivism in the philosophy of science and social science see Rudolf Carnap, *The Unity of Science* (London: Routledge and Kegan Paul, 1934); A. J. Ayer, *Language, Truth, and Logic,* 2d ed. (London: Gollancz, 1958); Barbara Wooten, *Testament for Social Science* (New York, 1951); Arnold Brecht, *Political Theory: The Foundations of Twentieth-Century Political Thought* (Princeton: Princeton University Press, 1959); Ernest Nagel, "Problems of Concept and Theory Formation in the Social Sciences," in *Science, Language, and Human Rights,* Symposia papers for annual meeting of Eastern Division of the American Philosophical Association (Philadelphia: University of Pennsylvania Press, 1952), and *The Structure of Science* (New York: Harcourt, Brace and World, 1961). On the revival of political theory, see Germino, *Beyond Ideology.*

7. By "traditionalist" I mean that critique which derives insight and inspiration from the classical tradition of political theory, focusing on the epistemological authority of reason. It opposes the empiricist-scientific approach to political inquiry, which dominates political science today. The meaning of this characterization will emerge throughout this study.

8. Apart from classical formulations of "historicism," more recently "relativism" has come to include such diverse perspectives as analytic-linguistic philosophy, pragmatism, postempiricist philosophy and history of science, existentialism, phenomenology, neo-marxism, and "critical theory." I return to this issue in chapter 7.

9. See, again, Bernstein, *The Restructuring of Social and Political Theory,* and Germino, *Beyond Ideology.* See also the accounts of behavioralism and empirical theory in Hwa Yol Jung, *The Crisis of Political Understanding: A Phenomenological Perspective in the Conduct of Political Inquiry* (Pittsburgh: Duquesne University Press, 1979); and in Fred R. Dallmayr, *Beyond Dogma and Despair: Toward a Critical Phenomenology of Politics* (Notre Dame: University of Notre Dame Press, 1981).

10. See, for example, Germino, *Beyond Ideology,* 67–87, 187–214. I shall focus simply on a few major figures whose influence has been strongly felt in political science, specifically Easton, Eulau, and Meehan.

11. David Easton, *The Political System: An Inquiry into the State of Political Science* (New York: Alfred A. Knopf, 1953), 3–4.

12. Ibid., 38ff.

13. Meehan, *Theory and Method,* 237.

14. Easton, *The Political System,* 40.

15. Brecht, *Political Theory,* 481.

16. See Easton, *The Political System,* 233–65.

17. Ibid., 236.

18. Ibid., 78.

19. Meehan, *Theory and Method,* 12.

20. Eugene J. Meehan, *Value Judgment and Social Science: Structures and Processes* (Homewood, Ill.: Dorsey Press, 1969), 12 (emphasis added).

21. Easton, *The Political System,* 66.

22. Eulau, *Behavioral Persuasion,* 7.

23. Meehan, *Value Judgment,* 147.

24. Easton, *The Political System,* 45.

25. Ibid., 78, 86.

26. Ibid., 89.

27. Eulau, *Behavioral Persuasion,* 133.

28. Ibid., 136.

29. Easton, *The Political System,* 221.

30. Alan Isaak, *Scope and Methods of Political Science: An Introduction to the Methodology of Political Inquiry* (Homewood, Ill.: Dorsey Press, 1969), 25–30. Isaak's work is an example of the simplistic extremes to which a behavioralist and positivist view of political inquiry can be taken.

31. Easton, *The Political System,* 225.

32. See Robert A. Dahl, *Modern Political Analysis* (Englewood Cliffs, N.J.: Prentice-Hall, 1963), 101–7.

33. Easton, *The Political System,* 225–26.

34. Isaak, *Scope and Methods,* 56.

35. See Dallmayr's comment in *Beyond Dogma and Despair,* vii.

36. Meehan, *Value Judgment,* 7–8.

37. Ibid., 11.

38. Ibid., 51–52.

39. Ibid., 5, 12, 110.

40. David Papineau, *For Science in the Social Sciences* (New York: St. Martin's Press, 1978), 1.

41. Ibid., 36. See the classic work of T. S. Kuhn, *The Structure of Scientific Revolutions,* 2d ed. (Chicago: University of Chicago Press, 1970). See also, Paul Feyerabend, *Against Method* (London: New Left Books, 1975); and the provocative collection of writings in Imre Lakatos and Alan Musgrave, eds., *Criticism and the Growth of Knowledge* (Cambridge: Cambridge University Press, 1970).

42. Papineau, *For Science,* 2.

43. Ibid., 46.

44. Ibid., 159–60.

45. Ibid., 173–74.

46. Warren Miller, "The Role of Research in the Unification of a Discipline," *American Political Science Review* 75 (March 1981): 9.

47. Ibid., 10.

48. Ibid.

49. Ibid., 12.

50. Thus, for example, Hegel's *Philosophy of Right* can be seen as the elaboration of a political paradigm in the tradition of Plato's *Republic.* See Michael Foster, *The Political Philosophies of Plato and Hegel* (Oxford: Clarendon Press, 1935); and especially Dante Germino, *Machiavelli to Marx: Modern Western Political Thought* (Chicago: University of Chicago Press, Phoenix Books, 1979), 320–43.

51. For the declaration of the dismal fate of traditional political theory, see the following works: Alfred Cobban, "The Decline of Political Theory," *Political Science Quarterly* 68 (September 1952): 321–37; David Easton, "The Decline of Modern Political Theory," *Journal of Politics* 13 (February 1951): 36–58, and *The Political System,* chap. 10; Peter Laslett, Introduction to *Phi-*

losophy, Politics, and Society, 1st ser. (New York: Barnes and Noble, 1957); Robert Dahl, "Political Theory," *World Politics* 11 (October 1958): 89–102. For some of the responses to this declaration, see the following works: the essays by Jacobson, Sibley, and especially Carl Friedrich, in Roland Young, ed., *Approaches to the Study of Politics* (Evanston: Northwestern University Press, 1958); Isaiah Berlin, "Does Political Theory Still Exist?" *Philosophy, Politics, and Society,* 2d ser. (New York: Barnes and Noble, 1962), 1–22; Germino, *Beyond Ideology.* See also the essays in Herbert J. Storing, ed., *Essays on the Scientific Study of Politics* (New York: Holt, Rinehart, and Winston, 1962); and in George Graham, Jr., and George Carey, eds., *The Post-Behavioral Era: Perspectives on Political Science* (New York: David McKay Co., 1972).

52. See, for example, the discussion in Dante Germino, "Some Observations on Recent Political Philosophy and Theory," *Annals of the American Academy of Political and Social Science* (Philadelphia) 400 (March 1972): 140–48.

53. For example, see Eric Voegelin, *The New Science of Politics* (Chicago: University of Chicago Press, 1952); Leo Strauss, "What Is Political Philosophy?" *Journal of Politics* 19 (August 1957), and "An Epilogue," in Storing, *Essays.* See also his "Political Philosophy and the Crisis of Our Time," in Howard Spaeth, ed., *The Predicament of Modern Politics* (Detroit: University of Detroit Press, 1964). For examples of other respondents to positivistic and behavioralist political science who have produced metatheoretical reflections on the nature of political inquiry, see George H. Sabine, "What Is a Political Theory?" *Journal of Politics* 1 (February 1939): 1–16; from an analytic-empiricist perspective, George E. G. Catlin, "Political Theory: What Is It?" *Political Science Quarterly* 72 (March 1957): 1–29; Christian Bay, "A Critical Evaluation of Behavioral Literature," *American Political Science Review* 59 (March 1965): 39–61; Germino, "Two Conceptions of Political Philosophy," in Graham and Carey, *Post-Behavioral Era,* 243–57; and Gunnell, *Philosophy, Science, and Political Inquiry.*

54. Strauss, "What Is Political Philosophy?" 345.

55. Strauss, "An Epilogue," 311.

56. Strauss, "What Is Political Philosophy?" 345.

57. Strauss, "An Epilogue," 316.

58. Ibid. Against Strauss, it may be noted that the claim of a prescientific awareness of people as people and things as things, about which there is no argument from one's peers, may be seen as a political claim rather than an epistemological one. Social authority and agreement tell us little about the epistemological question of how we know people as people, etc.

59. Ibid., 317. Here we discover the intriguing influence of Husserl on Strauss's thought. See, for example, Strauss, "Philosophy as Rigorous Science and Political Philosophy," *Interpretation* 2 (Fall 1971): 1–9. See also the discussion in Jung, *Crisis of Political Understanding,* chap. 8.

60. Strauss, "An Epilogue," 317.

61. Here we find evidence of the objectivistic motivations and tendencies of the traditionalist critique.

62. Ibid., 321.

63. Ibid., 322.

64. Ibid.

65. Strauss, "What Is Political Philosophy?" 347. A conceptualization of value as preference can result in some dubious equivalencies. One is reminded of Sartre's example where the moral condemnation of slavery or evil or the praise of freedom or good becomes cognitively equivalent to the statement "I like oysters." The latter may be a statement of value only if the concept of value is demoralized and understood economistically.

66. For example, the positing of a distinction between "democratic" and "authoritarian" behavior is possible only if one understands what it is that constitutes each characteristic, which in turn depends upon how one judges the nature of each. Thus judgment is intrinsic to the process of research. Against this, see Ernest Nagel's sophisticated objection which distinguishes between "characterizing value judgments" and "appraising value judgments." The former is permissible in social science research, while the latter involves opinions of approval and disapproval and is not permitted. See his development of the logical independence of these two types of value judgment in *The Structure of Science*.

67. Karl Deutsch, "The Limits of Common Sense," *Psychiatry* 22, no. 2 (May 1959): 105–12. Interesting to note by contrast is Jürgen Habermas's reference to the critical social scientist as a nonmanipulative social psychoanalyst or psychotherapist in *Knowledge and Human Interests*, trans. Jeremy J. Shapiro (Boston: Beacon Press, 1971).

Strauss explains with the following example: In order to define what is political (related to the *polis*), it is necessary to search for what constitutes a particular society; to define a society's "constitution" it is required to make reference to its purpose, thereby admitting a standard in the light of which political actions and institutions are judged. Thus the constitutive purpose of a society necessarily functions as a standard of judgment of societies. Hence "value-free" political science is impossible.

68. Strauss, "What Is Political Philosophy?" 354.

69. Strauss, "An Epilogue," 322–24.

70. Ibid., 324.

71. Ibid., 325.

72. Ibid.

73. Ibid., 326.

74. Ibid., 327.

75. Strauss, "What Is Political Philosophy?" 362–63.

76. Ibid., 363.

77. Ibid., 368.

78. The following paragraph refers to Germino, *Beyond Ideology*, 160.

79. See Strauss's expressed purpose in the introduction to *On Tyranny: An Interpretation of Xenophon's Hiero* (New York: Free Press, 1948), and in "The Literary Character of the *Guide for the Perplexed*," in Wittmayer Baron, ed., *Essays on Maimonides* (New York: Columbia University Press, 1964).

80. See, for example, the abysmal consequences in Oppenheim, *Moral Principles in Political Philosophy*, of the interpretive distortion which Strauss fears. See also Lasswell and Kaplan, *Power and Society*, especially 118.

81. Dante Germino makes a vaguely similar argument in *Beyond Ideology*; see especially 17.

82. For examples of these three arguments (and there are numerous others), see respectively, Leo Strauss, *Natural Right and History* (Chicago: University of Chicago Press, 1953); Eric Voegelin, *The New Science of Politics,* and the four-volume *Order and History* (Baton Rouge: Louisiana State University Press, 1956–75); and Germino, *Beyond Ideology.*

83. Although, for example, Voegelin deals with some problems of epistemology in certain of his essays collected in *Anamnesis: Zur Theorie der Geschichte und Politik* (Munich: Piper Verlag, 1966). See also some of Strauss's epistemological concerns in "What Is Political Philosophy?"

84. For a popular classic statement of this position, see Ayer, *Language, Truth, and Logic.*

85. See Gilbert Ryle's assertion that to speak of any nonphysical consciousness is to speak of a "ghost in the machine," *The Concept of Mind* (London: Hutchinson, 1949).

86. See T. D. Weldon, *Vocabulary of Politics* (London: Penguin Books, 1953). See also the contributions of A. R. Louch, *Explanation and Human Action* (Berkeley: University of California Press, 1966).

Chapter Two

1. For some recent efforts, see Susan Shell, *The Rights of Reason: A Study of Kant's Philosophy and Politics* (Toronto: University of Toronto Press, 1979); William A. Galston, "Kant and Contemporary Political Theory" (Paper presented to the APSA in Washington, D.C., 1–4 September, 1977; and Hans Reiss, ed., *Kant's Political Writings* (Cambridge: Cambridge University Press, 1971).

2. Throughout the following discussion I refer to Norman Kemp Smith's well-known translation of Kant's *Critique of Pure Reason* (London: Macmillan and Co., 1929), with reference to the original when necessary. In line with Smith's translation, the following notes refer to Kant's first edition pagination as A and to the second edition (1787) pagination as B. My reading of Kant has been aided by the following works: Smith's *A Commentary to Kant's "Critique of Pure Reason"* 2d ed. (London: Macmillan and Co., 1923); Robert Paul Wolff's commentary on the Transcendental Analytic, *Kant's Theory of Mental Activity* (Cambridge: Harvard University Press, 1963); and Justus Hartnack's brilliantly succinct *Kant's Theory of Knowledge,* trans. M. Holmes Hartshorne (New York: Harcourt, Brace and World, 1967).

3. See Hume's "epistemological" inquiries in the *Treatise of Human Nature* (1737), where he attempts to develop Lockean empiricism and analysis of human experience to its extreme logical conclusion.

4. One consequence of Hume's empiricism is the denial of causality, since there can be no foundation for causation if all we have access to is an endless succession of sense impressions. From a dialectical perspective, Kant's attempt to prove the principle of causality is ironic, since that principle becomes important for positivist social science.

5. It should be mentioned that both Hume and Kant accepted the logical distinction between analytic a priori and synthetic a posteriori judgments. It

is a mistaken to assume, as an otherwise astute dialectical critic like Trent Schroyer does, that "Hume did not make the logical distinction between analytic and synthetic judgments" (*The Critique of Domination: The Origins and Development of Critical Theory* [Boston: Beacon Press, 1975], 109). More precisely, it was the distinction between synthetic a posteriori and synthetic a priori judgments, the latter introduced by Kant, that Hume never conceived.

6. *Critique of Pure Reason,* A 57, B 81–82, 95–116.

7. A 97–98.

8. For a discussion of the distinction between subjective and objective deductions, see Smith's *Commentary,* 234–45.

9. B 132–36. It would appear to be more accurate to speak of the transcendental "I" *(das Ich)* rather than of the transcendental "ego." One of Kant's main arguments concerns the impossibility of objectifying transcendental apperception of the "I." The term "ego" presupposes objectification, whereas the term "I" connotes the kind of transcendental, pure "subjectivity" of which Kant is speaking.

10. Thus Kant states that "the categories do not afford us any knowledge of things; they do so only through their possible application to *empirical intuition*" (B 147–48).

11. B 266.

12. The notion of an "interest of reason" in Kant's theory is crucial for Habermas's development of critical theory. Habermas explores the notion in chapter 9 of his *Knowledge and Human Interests.*

13. See B 350–55, esp. 354.

14. See A 370–71.

15. This distinction, which is cricial for Kant's argument in the Transcendental Dialectic, is first systematically raised in the Transcendental Analytic at B 295–315.

16. See B 307.

17. See B 311.

18. See B 532. Kant distinguishes between dialectical and analytical oppositions. With the former, both sides of the opposition may be false, while with the latter, one side must be true. This narrow and technical use of the term "dialectical" is not the one I hope to elaborate in this book.

19. A 504–5; B 532–33.

20. See A 643; B 537, 671.

21. B 671–73, 679.

22. See, for example, the opening lines of Galston's interesting paper, "Kant and Contemporary Political Theory."

23. See Habermas, *Knowledge and Human Interests,* 13–15.

24. All references to the *Phenomenology* will be made to J. B. Baillie's translation, *The Phenomenology of Mind,* 2d ed. (London: George Allen and Unwin, 1931). As is well known, the difficult German term *Geist* has been translated both as "mind" and "spirit." There is no problem in using the two terms interchangeably so long as one keeps in mind that as Hegel's supreme principle, *Geist* should not be reduced to "mind" in the sense of mere individual mental operations and functions, nor should it be taken to mean "God" in the usual sense. Occasionally I use the term "mind" when referring to the more

clearly epistemological aspects of Hegel's reflections, and the term "spirit" when referring to the more clearly active, ontological aspects.

For examples in current Hegel scholarship of the argument that the *Phenomenology* can only be fully understood in critical relationship to Kantian epistemology in the *Critique of Pure Reason*, see the following: Hans-Georg Gadamer, *Hegel's Dialectic*, trans. Christopher Smith (New Haven: Yale University Press, 1976), esp. 35, where he writes, "the beginning of the *Phenomenology* cannot be comprehended at all without direct reference to Kant's philosophy"; Quentin Lauer, S.J., *Essays in Hegelian Dialectic* (New York: Fordham University Press, 1977), e.g., 140, where he claims that the *Phenomenology* "can be looked upon as the Hegelian counterpart of—and answer to—Kant's *Critique of Pure Reason*"; and Werner Marx, *Hegel's Phenomenology of Spirit*, trans. Peter Heath (New York: Harper and Row, 1975), e.g., xix–xx, where he argues Hegel's adherence to the structure of Kant's transcendental apperception and the importance of the subject-object identity. A similar argument underpins Habermas's *Knowledge and Human Interests*. For Hegel's own most specific critical references to Kant's *Critique*, see chapter 4, entitled "Second Attitude of Thought to Objectivity," in the *Science of Logic*, part 1 of *The Encyclopedia of Philosophical Sciences*. See William Wallace's translation, *The Logic of Hegel* (Oxford: Clarendon Press, 1892), 82–121. Unless otherwise noted, all future references to Hegel's *Logic* are made to Wallace's translation.

25. *Phenomenology*, 132–33.

26. *Logic*, 84.

27. Ibid., 84–85.

28. *Phenomenology*, 133.

29. *Logic*, 83–84, 90, 94.

30. Ibid., 92–93; see *Phenomenology*, 112; cf. also W. Marx, *Hegel's Phenomenology*, 9–12.

31. *Phenomenology*, 135; see also 136–45.

32. Ibid., 142.

33. See the *Logic*, 119–20; the *Phenomenology*, 80, 133ff.

34. See the *Phenomenology*, 131–32.

35. See the opening remarks of the *Phenomenology*, 67; see also 70, 137–38.

36. See Gadamer's claim in "Hegel's 'Inverted World,' " in his *Hegel's Dialectic*, 37.

37. Note the structure of the first four chapters of the *Phenomenology*.

38. See the *Phenomenology*, 234–39.

39. In this connection see Schroyer, *Critique of Domination*, 112; and Jürgen Habermas, *Theory and Practice*, trans. John Viertel (Boston: Beacon Press, 1973), especially the chapter on Hegel's "Jena" *Philosophy of Mind*, 142–69.

40. *Phenomenology*, 797.

41. *Logic*, 4.

42. Ibid., 28–30. It is important to note that, *contra* Kant, logic for Hegel deals not in terms of judgments but in terms of concepts first and foremost. Recall that for Hegel "ideal" means the absolute rationality of the whole of

reality. Thus there is a certain equivalency of terms to "idea," "truth," and "absolute." See *Logic*, 352–53.

43. Ibid., 29.

44. *Phenomenology*, 82. As we shall note, it is precisely this circularity which so disturbs Habermas in his critique of Hegel.

45. *Logic*, 375.

46. See the *Phenomenology*, 267, 273, 276, 457, 460. For another account of this development, see Quentin Lauer's "Hegel's Critique of Kant's Theology," in his *Essays in Hegelian Dialectic*, 137–52.

47. As Jeremy Shapiro puts it in a note to his translation of Habermas's *Knowledge and Human Interests*, "The philosophy of identity is that which postulates the identity of thought and being, of subject and object. German Idealism attempted to overcome Kant's separation of the subject and the thing-in-itself by asserting that the realm of nature and objects was a mere externalization of an absolute subjectivity" (320, n. 5).

48. Hegel summarizes this development at the end of the *Phenomenology*, esp. 790–93.

49. Ibid., 798–90.

50. See Baillie's Introduction to the *Phenomenology*, 50.

51. This is the underlying view of Kant's *Critique of Pure Reason*.

52. Hegel, *The Encyclopedia of Philosophical Sciences*, trans. Gustav Emil Mueller (New York: Philosophical Library, 1959), 82.

53. See Alexandre Kojève, *Introduction to the Reading of Hegel*, ed. Allan Bloom, trans. James H. Nichols, Jr. (New York: Basic Books, 1969). The work was originally published as *Introduction à la lecture de Hegel* (Paris: Gallimard, 1947).

54. *The Encyclopedia*, 82. See also the *Logic*, 147–48.

55. See *The Encyclopedia*, 82–83; *Logic*, 147–48.

56. *Phenomenology*, 112.

57. See Kojève, *Reading of Hegel*, 176.

58. *Phenomenology*, 142.

59. For a creative account of this development, see Kojève, *Reading of Hegel*, 179–83; for a good collection of essays on the general topic, see J. J. O'Malley, K. W. Algozin, F. G. Weiss, eds., *Hegel and the History of Philosophy* (The Hague: Martinus Nijhoff, 1974).

60. See Gadamer, *Hegel's Dialectic*, 9.

61. See the *Phenomenology*, 458–61; see also 80.

62. Ibid., 82, 114.

63. Ibid., 115: "that fixed and stable existence carries the process of its own dissolution within itself."

64. See ibid., 86.

65. See Kojève, *Reading of Hegel*, 202; see also *Logic*, 152.

66. *Phenomenology*, 80–81.

67. For an excellent discussion of Hegel's critique of Kant's three presuppositions, see Habermas, *Knowledge and Human Interests*, 14–18. Note the number of times Kant refers in the *Critique of Pure Reason* to a progressivistic criterion of knowledge, "the secure path of science." In the preface to the second edition alone, for example, see B vii–xii, xiv, xv, xix, xxiii, xxx, xxxvi,

and so on. Here and elsewhere Kant uses interchangeably the following terms: secure path, sure path, sure march, highway, secure progress, sure road. Like much of contemporary positivist methodology, Kant contends that even metaphysics must be judged against the standard of cognitive progress in mathematics and physics. For this reason he claims that we must "revolutionize" metaphysics in agreement with the "example set by the geometers and physicists" (B xxii).

68. We often find epistemologists recognizing the one ego in Kant's theory, and social and political theorists, the other. Hegel outlines his attempt to reunite these egos, for example, in the *Phenomenology*, 613–14.

69. Habermas, *Knowledge and Human Interests*, 17.

70. Hegel, *Science of Logic*, trans. W. H. Johnston and L. G. Struthers (London: George Allen and Unwin, 1929), 2:147.

71. Ibid., 145.

72. Ibid., 146, 147. See also *The Encyclopedia*, 118: "In every distinguishing situation, each pole is for itself that which it is; it also is not for itself what it is, but only in contrasting relation to that which it is not. If the *relativity* is rejected, each pole *seems* to be independent."

73. See the *Logic*, 160; see also Joseph C. Flay, "The History of Philosophy and the *Phenomenology of Spirit*," in O'Malley, Algozin, and Weiss, *Hegel*, 59; and John N. Findlay, "Hegelianism and Platonism," in ibid., 85.

74. *Phenomenology*, 81–82.

75. On this problem, see Flay, "The History of Philosophy," and J. Smith, "Hegel's Critique of Kant," in O'Malley, Algozin, and Weiss, *Hegel*, esp. 59, 113.

76. *Phenomenology*, 91.

77. As Habermas reminds us in *Knowledge and Human Interests*, 10.

78. *Phenomenology*, 797, 801.

79. Ibid.,

80. See W. Marx, *Hegel's Phenomenology*, xix–xxi.

81. *Phenomenology*, 806; see also Kojève, *Reading of Hegel*, 174.

82. *The Encyclopedia*, 133.

83. *Logic*, 94.

84. *The Encyclopedia*, 158; *Phenomenology*, 804.

85. See Karl Marx, *Theses on Feuerbach*, V, VIII, and esp. I.

86. From the *German Ideology*, in *Karl Marx: Selected Writings*, ed. David McLellan (Oxford: Oxford University Press, 1977), 167.

87. "Private Property and Communism," in *Karl Marx: Early Writings*, trans. and ed. T. B. Bottomore (New York: McGraw-Hill, 1964), 162. Unless otherwise noted, all references to Marx's *Economic and Philosophical Manuscripts*, or the *Paris Manuscripts*, will be made to Bottomore's edition.

It seems important to emphasize that Marx views the overcoming of subject and object to be not only an epistemological problem. Rather than viewing Marx as wanting to do away with philosophy altogether in favor of an unreflective praxis, it seems more helpful if we see his effort as reconceptualizing the nature of philosophy and its relation to human life and praxis, by which he does not seem to mean mere technical, instrumental activity.

88. See Marx, from the *German Ideology*, in McLellan, *Karl Marx*, 167.

89. Marx, "Critique of Hegel's Dialectic and General Philosophy," in Bottomore, *Karl Marx,* 200. Unless otherwise noted, all references to this work will be designated simply as "Critique."

90. Georg Lukács, *History and Class Consciousness: Studies in Marxist Dialectics,* trans. Rodney Livingstone (Cambridge: MIT Press, 1971), 204.

91. Marx, "Critique," 195.

92. The view that Marx remains indebted to the framework of dialectic and philosophy of internal relations bequeathed to him by Hegel is argued nowhere so clearly and concisely as in Bertell Ollman, *Alienation: Marx's Conception of Man in Capitalist Society,* 2d ed. (Cambridge: Cambridge University Press, 1976); in this regard, see chaps. 1–6 and apps. 1 and 2; see esp. chap. 3: 31–36.

93. Marx, "Critique," 197. For Feuerbach's critique of Hegel, see his *The Philosophy of the Future (Grundsätze der Philosophie der Zukunft,* 1843).

94. See Marx, "Critique," 198.

95. Marx uses the term "alienation" (*Entäusserung* or *Entfremdung,* also meaning "estrangement") in at least two senses when discussing Hegel. First, in discussing Hegel's view of the dialectic of subject and object, Marx defines alienation as the process of the externalization or objectification of the subject; when he criticizes the alienation of pure thought he refers to the loss of the real, sensuous object in Hegel, for whom objectivity is merely the externalization of subjectivity. Second, Marx uses the term to refer to the real condition within which Hegel's entire philosophical development takes place. Therefore, alienation can refer either to epistemological externalization and objectification or to the ontological condition of separation and abstraction. This point will emerge more clearly throughout the following discussion. See Marx, "Critique," 200–201.

96. Ibid., 201.

97. Ibid., 202.

98. Ibid.

99. Ibid., 202–3.

100. Or "spiritual." Here again we encounter the difficulty of translating the term *Geist* (at this point *geistige*); see Marx, *Die Frühschriften* (Stuttgart: A. Kroener, 1953), 270.

101. Marx, "Critique," 203.

102. Ibid., 204.

103. Ibid., 205.

104. Ibid., 206.

105. See ibid. I think, however, that it may be mistaken to claim too strongly, as Habermas does, that Marx is "caught" in naturalism. See *Knowledge and Human Interests,* 26. Although true to a certain extent, such a claim ignores the seriousness of the dialectic when Marx speaks of "naturalism *or* humanism," and the particular meaning Marx attaches to the term.

106. Concerning Marx's adherence to the philosophy of internal relations, see his famous example which describes the nature of the plant as lying in the sun and that of the sun as lying in the plant, or rather in the relation of the two ("Critique," 207).

107. Ibid., 208.

108. Ibid.

109. Here, as throughout his critique, Marx clearly is not "turning Hegel on his head." Nowhere is Marx's critique of Hegel a matter of simple inversion.

110. See the account in Habermas, *Knowledge and Human Interests*, 29.

111. From the *German Ideology*, in McLellan, *Karl Marx*, 172–73. See Marx, *Die Frühschriften*, 368.

112. See Marx, Theses I and V on Feuerbach.

113. Marx, "Critique," 209.

114. Ibid., 210.

115. See Hegel's introductory argument in his *Lectures on the Philosophy of History* (1837), translated as *Reason in History* by R. S. Hartman (Indianapolis: Bobbs-Merrill, Liberal Arts Press, 1953).

116. A reminder is in order to emphasize that Marx's actual word for "supersession" is *das Aufheben*. Supersession is thus dialectical, and not absolute negation. For confirmation of this point, see *Die Frühschriften*, 278.

117. See Marx, "Critique," 211.

118. Ibid., 212.

119. Ibid., 213.

120. For an interesting discussion of the relation of theoretical and practical humanism, see Louis Althusser's "Marxism and Humanism," especially the "Complementary Note on 'Real Humanism,' " in *For Marx*, trans. Ben Brewster (New York: Random House, 1970), 221–47.

121. Marx, "Critique," 213.

122. Ibid., 213–14, and from the *German Ideology*, in McLellan, *Karl Marx*, 171–75. Cf. also Habermas, *Knowledge and Human Interests*, 31.

123. Marx, "Critique," 214. As Marx puts it in the *Holy Family:* "In Hegel the Absolute Spirit of history already treats the mass as material and finds its true expression only in philosophy." It is worth citing at length how Marx continues to criticize the merely retrospective function of philosophy in Hegel:

> But with Hegel, the philosopher is only the organ through which the creator of history, the Absolute Spirit, arrives at self-consciousness by retrospection after the movement has ended. The participation of the philosopher in history is reduced to this retrospective consciousness, for real movement is accomplished by the Absolute Spirit unconsciously, so that the philosopher appears *post festum*.
>
> Hegel is doubly inconsistent: first because, while declaring that philosophy constitutes the Absolute Spirit's existence he refuses to recognize the real philosophical individual as the Absolute Spirit; secondly, because according to him the Absolute Spirit makes history only in appearance. (McLellan, *Karl Marx*, 144)

124. Marx, "Critique," 214.

125. Ibid., 215.

126. Ibid., 216, 217, 218–19.

127. From the *German Ideology*, in McLellan, *Karl Marx*, 175.

128. As we shall see, there is a sense in which dialectical theory in general possesses a kind of "in-between" character, or ambiguity, in its self-constitution and inquiry. The quality of *metaxy* in a classical context is dealt with centrally in current thought by Eric Voegelin; see Dante Germino, "Eric Voe-

gelin's Framework for Political Evaluation in His Recently Published Work," *American Political Science Review* 72 (March 1978): 110–21. In marxism, a different kind of *metaxic* quality militates against any absolute materialism or determinism. In his last book, Marcuse, for example, recognizes this point in dialectical aesthetic theory; see *The Aesthetic Dimension: Toward a Critique of Marxist Aesthetics* (Boston: Beacon Press, 1978).

129. See Habermas, *Knowledge and Human Interests,* 324, n. 28, where he cites Alfred Schmidt's observation on this point in *Der Begriff der Natur in der Lehre von Marx* (Frankfurt am Main, 1962), 103.

130. Note, for example, Marx's remark in "Private Property and Communism," which is surprisingly often neglected by his followers and detractors alike: "Communism is the necessary form and the dynamic principle of the immediate future, but communism is not itself the goal of human development— the form of human society" (167). What precisely that goal is, Marx never says.

131. The most sophisticated form of this criticism is found in Habermas, *Knowledge and Human Interests,* 42–63.

132. See Richard Bernstein's remarks in this connection, in his *The Restructuring of Social and Political Theory,* 260, n. 30, where he argues that Habermas's criticism of Marx rests on the categorial distinction between work and interaction, which Habermas sees Marx merging and reducing. Bernstein suggests, "Rather than charging Marx with some sort of category mistake, a more penetrating interpretation would indicate that Marx is calling into question the very categorial distinction that Habermas takes to be fundamental." The danger of Habermas's criticism lies in the reawakening of "idealism."

Chapter Three

1. See John G. Gunnell, *Political Theory: Tradition and Interpretation* (Cambridge, Mass.: Winthrop Publishers, 1979), 10.

2. Including the nondialectical variants of marxism, existentialism, and phenomenology themselves, relativist positions can be found in such movements as pragmatism, ordinary- or contextual-language philosophy, structuralism, hermeneutics, and even "postempiricist" history and philosophy of science. For examples of this last interesting development, see Gunnell, *Philosophy, Science, and Political Inquiry,* and see the "manifesto" of this development, Kuhn, *Structure of Scientific Revolutions.* See also the works of Stephen Toulmin and Paul Feyerabend.

3. For examples of the arguments both for and against the idea of a tradition, see respectively, Germino, *Beyond Ideology,* and Gunnell, *Political Theory.* For Marx's pivotal role, see, for example, Hannah Arendt, *Between Past and Future: Eight Exercises in Political Thought* (New York: Viking Press, 1961), 17–40.

4. See Habermas's interesting discussion in his essay "Between Philosophy and Science: Marxism as Critique," *Theory and Practice,* trans. John Viertel (Boston: Beacon Press, 1973).

5. See, for example, Germino, *Machiavelli to Marx,* 357–85.

6. Perhaps the closest semblance to a major political development that might find sympathy with dialectical marxism is the still nebulous emergence of Eurocommunism, especially with the Italian Communist party, due in part to the original influence of Antonio Gramsci. The theoretical lessons of Poland's Solidarity movement still await us.

7. One of the best accounts of Marx's ontology is Ollman's *Alienation*. Ollman draws frequently from Marx's introduction to the *Critique of Political Economy*, which is often referred to as the *General Introduction to the Grundrisse*. The *Grundrisse* is a central work for understanding Marx's dialectical theory. For another excellent discussion of Marx's thought in this regard, see Carol Gould, *Marx's Social Ontology* (Cambridge, Mass.: MIT Press, 1978).

8. See Ollman, *Alienation,* 14–16.

9. Ibid., 17–18.

10. See ibid., 12, 17, 28. Regarding even the physical world, see Marx, "Critique of Hegel's Dialectic," 207.

11. See Marx, from the *General Introduction to the Grundrisse,* in McLellan, *Karl Marx,* 356.

12. For one example, current "interactional analysis" (and this applies equally to "systems analysis") is nondialectically faulty if it deals with interaction between things or people only in terms of external relations. For Marx, interaction is also, and more fundamentally, "*inner*action," because the "external" relations are contained internally in each unit. See Ollman, *Alienation,* 16–17. As we shall later note, the concept of intentionality in phenomenology also does away with a notion of interaction based solely upon external relations.

13. Ibid., 45. For Marx's argument that the fact-value distinction itself is an expression of alienation in capitalist society, see his "Needs, Production, and Division of Labor," in Bottomore, *Karl Marx,* 173.

14. Ernst Bloch, *On Karl Marx,* trans. John Maxwell (New York: Herder and Herder, 1971), 150.

15. Ibid.

16. Of the many treatments of Marx's dialectic, see for example, the good analysis of its development in Dick Howard, *The Development of the Marxian Dialectic* (Carbondale: Southern Illinois University Press, 1972).

17. The following three paragraphs refer summarily to Ollman's direct treatment of the dialectic and method, *Alienation,* 52–69.

18. See Marx, *German Ideology,* trans. R. Pascal (London, 1942), 35.

19. This is how Marx states his goal in the preface to the *Economic and Philosophical Manuscripts,* in Bottomore, *Karl Marx,* 63. For an example of his perception of the maze of interconnections with which to be dealt, see "Alienated Labour," in ibid., 121. See also Marx, *Capital,* trans. Samuel Moore and Edward Aveling (Moscow, 1958), 1:19.

20. This is the sense in which Marx speaks of his own writings as an artistic whole. See *Selected Correspondence,* trans. and ed. Dona Torr (London, 1941), 204.

21. For an example of how Marx does this, see Ollman's account of the metamorphosis of value in *Alienation,* 187–94.

22. On Marx's use of language, see the chapter "With Words that Appear Like Bats," in ibid., 3–11.

23. See Norman D. Livergood, *Activity in Marx's Philosophy* (The Hague: Martinus Nijhoff, 1967), 6. Livergood's essay is also a fair introduction into the centrality of "activity" in Marx's materialism, epistemology, and philosophy.

24. Bloch, *On Karl Marx,* 111.

25. For some of Marx's comments on freedom, see, for example: *The Holy Family,* where he speaks of it as the expression of true individuality; *The German Ideology,* where he speaks of the realization and cultivation of talents in community as "personal freedom"; see also the selections from *The German Ideology* on artistic talent and free development, in McLellan, *Karl Marx,* 154, 189–91.

26. The most notable omission is the Frankfurt School of critical theory—Horkheimer, Adorno, Marcuse, Habermas, and others—an omission which is remedied in chapter 6. Another notable omission is the prolific and interesting Yugoslavian Praxis Group of neomarxists, to whom I shall have occasion to refer in chapter 5.

27. For an excellent account of Gramsci's life, thought, and politics, see Giuseppe Fiori, *Antonio Gramsci: Life of a Revolutionary,* trans. Tom Nairn (New York: Schocken Books, 1973).

28. See Alastair Davidson, *Antonio Gramsci: The Man, His Ideas* (Australian Left Review Publications, 1968), 22. It should be mentioned that most attempts to revive dialectical marxism in the face of its positivistic degeneration (rooted in Russian marxism, if not in Engels) have often been labeled "neo-marxist." See further in Davidson, *Antonio Gramsci: Towards an Intellectual Biography* (London: Merlin Press, 1977). See also the excellent work by Carl Boggs, *Gramsci's Marxism* (London: Pluto Press, 1976).

29. Gramsci, in *Selections from the Prison Notebooks of Antonio Gramsci,* trans. and ed. Quinton Hoare and G. N. Smith (New York: International Publishers, 1971), 371. Hereafter this work is cited as *Prison Notebooks*. It should be noted that the term "philosophy of praxis" is used by Gramsci as synonymous with "marxism," not only to avoid censorship in prison, but also because Gramsci sees the philosophy of praxis as the central concept in marxism, which involves the union of theory and practice.

30. Ollman, for one, goes so far as to subsume the dialectic (which is a relational principle and framework) in the "philosophy of internal relations." Although he admits a certain interchangeability between "dialectic" and "relations," he prefers the "philosophy of internal relations" as a broader and more effective framework for understanding the elements of Marx's thought. See *Alienation,* 52, 60n.

31. See in Fiori, *Antonio Gramsci,* Gramsci's understanding of the movement of history (112, 114, 240), his understanding of the relation of historical means and ends (175), his treatment of party sectarianism and class alliances (105, 126, 143, 167, 237, 249), and his intellectual and personal development (94, 114). This quality of openness is so important and pervasive in Gramsci that his marxism has been termed an "open marxism." See Carl Marzani's annotated translation of Gramsci's work, *The Open Marxism of Antonio Gramsci* (New York: Cameron Associates, 1957).

32. Gramsci, *Prison Notebooks,* 171.

33. Ibid.

34. Ibid., 445.

35. See ibid., translators' note 92. Gramsci's view that the unity of subject and object is ultimately dependent upon the efforts of a historically united human race corresponds to Marx's development of the notion of a concrete, historical metasubject, or "universal subject."

36. Ibid., 446.

37. See ibid., 448.

38. Ibid., 168.

39. Ibid., 201.

40. Ibid., 233.

41. Ibid., 184.

42. Ibid., 336.

43. Ibid., 337.

44. See ibid., 243–44.

45. Ibid., 438, 442.

46. Ibid., 172.

47. See ibid., 171.

48. Antonio Gramsci, "Critical Notes on an Attempt at a Popular Representation of Marxism by Bukharin," *The Modern Prince and Other Writings,* trans. Louis Marks (New York: International Publishers, 1957), 109–10.

49. See *Prison Notebooks,* 388.

50. Lukács's intellectual career spanned over sixty years and is a complex one. To give an indication of dialectical tendencies in his work against positivistic marxism, I focus here on *History and Class Consciousness* (1923), which is his most "dialectical" work in political theory, even though it is highly debatable (especially given his later renunciation of it) whether it is representative of his thought.

51. See ibid., 4, 6, 9, 11–13.

52. Ibid., 5.

53. Ibid., 6–7.

54. Ibid., 24.

55. Ibid., 129.

56. Ibid., 134.

57. Ibid., 145, 156.

58. Ibid., 73.

59. Ibid., 250–51.

60. Ibid., 257.

61. Ibid.

62. Ibid., 311.

63. Ibid., 313.

64. Ibid., 292.

65. Ibid., 69.

66. See Maurice Merleau-Ponty, *Phenomenology of Perception,* trans. Colin Smith (London: Routledge and Kegan Paul, 1962), 434, 453.

67. Ibid., 442.

68. Ibid., 453.

69. Merleau-Ponty, "Marxism and Philosophy," in *Sense and Non-Sense,* trans. H. L. Dreyfus and P. A. Dreyfus (Evanston: Northwestern University

Press, 1964), 125–26. Hereafter I refer to this work as *SNS*. (*Sens et non-sens* was originally published by Nagel in 1948.)

70. Merleau-Ponty, *Phenomenology of Perception*, 443.

71. Ibid., 446.

72. Merleau-Ponty, "Concerning Marxism," *SNS*, 107.

73. Ibid., 108.

74. Ibid., 112.

75. Merleau-Ponty, "Crisis of the Understanding," in *The Essential Writings of Merleau-Ponty*, ed. A. L. Fisher (New York: Harcourt, Brace and World, 1969), 325, 326. See also 332.

76. Ibid., 331.

77. Ibid., 337.

78. Merleau-Ponty, *Humanism and Terror*, trans. John O'Neill (Boston: Beacon Press, 1969), xxxi.

79. Marx, *The Holy Family*, in *Karl Marx: Selected Writings in Sociology and Social Philosophy*, ed. T. B. Bottomore and Maximilien Rubel (New York: McGraw-Hill, 1964), 63.

80. Merleau-Ponty, "Concerning Marxism," 121.

81. Merleau-Ponty, *Phenomenology of Perception*, 449.

82. Ibid., 450.

83. The following remarks are inspired by Kolakowski's essay collection *Toward a Marxist Humanism: Essays on the Left Today*, trans. J. Z. Peel (New York: Grove Press, 1969). Because I am interested in presenting ruminations on the spirit and nature of dialectical marxism that have resulted from my reading of Kolakowski, I do not examine Kolakowski's "position," nor do I enter into the debates over whether he has a consistent position, or over whether he is an "empiricist," as George Lichtheim claims (see Lichtheim, *From Marx to Hegel* [New York: Seabury Press, Continuum Books, 1974], 44, n. 16). Lichtheim's charge certainly cannot apply to the contents of *Toward a Marxist Humanism*. Regardless of the outcome of these kinds of debates, I believe Kolakowski's book can stand on its own as it relates to and inspires contributions to a dialectical marxism. One could, for example, point to his three-volume *Main Currents of Marxism* (New York: Oxford University Press, 1978), in which he moves quite some distance away from his earlier position of dialectical marxism in the direction, some would argue, of positivism and scientism. Such a development does not negate for me the sensitivity of his earlier work.

84. See Kolakowski, "The Priest and the Jester," in *Toward a Marxist Humanism*, 9–37.

85. This point will be clarified in the following chapters.

86. See Merleau-Ponty, "Marxism and Philosophy," 134.

87. The following paragraph refers to Kolakowski's essay "Karl Marx and the Classical Definition of Truth," in *Toward a Marxist Humanism*, 38–66.

88. The following paragraphs refer to Kolakowski, "The Concept of the Left," in ibid., 67–83.

89. See above, chap. 2, n. 119, and for example, Garaudy's call for Marxism to open itself to dialogue with traditional philosophy, theoretical humanism,

and theology, in *The Crisis in Communism,* trans. Peter Ross and Betty Ross (New York: Grove Press, 1969).

90. The following four paragraphs refer to Kolakowski's four short essays collected under the title "Responsibility and History," and to the essay "Determinism and Responsibility," in *Toward a Marxist Humanism,* 87–157 and 188–210.

91. I refer here to Arthur Koestler's argument in *Darkness at Noon,* trans. Daphne Hardy (London: Jonathan Cape, 1940), that in order to become a Communist one must surrender all individual responsibility to the Party, which is the "correct" interpreter of a deterministic and theistic History.

92. The following paragraph refers to Kolakowski's "Intellectuals and the Communist Movement," in *Toward a Marxist Humanism,* 158–72.

93. One has to keep in mind here that Kolakowski's primary concern in this essay is the relation between academic intellectuals and political officials in Poland. But the implications of his concern certainly reach beyond Poland, as well as beyond the "totalitarian Communist world" itself.

94. The following paragraph refers to Kolakowski, "In Praise of Inconsistency," in ibid., 211–20.

Chapter Four

1. See the discussion of phenomenology, which focuses on Alfred Schutz, in Bernstein, *The Restructuring of Social and Political Theory,* 135–69.

2. For reasons of space limitations and the purpose of our present discussion, I shall not deal with the more recent developments in structuralism, hermeneutics, and deconstructionism, which owe something at least to phenomenology. In contemporary philosophy, I believe that phenomenology and the development of ordinary-language philosophy (from Wittgenstein and Austin to Louch, Pitkin, and others) provide two of the richest available sources of philosophical thought. This is not to argue that the influence of logical positivism, out of and against which linguistic philosophy developed, is by any means dead.

3. James M. Edie, Introduction to Pierre Thévenaz, *What is Phenomenology? and Other Essays,* trans. James M. Edie, Charles Courtney, and Paul Brockelman (Chicago: Quadrangle Books, 1962), 16–17.

4. One finds a notable exception in Habermas's attempt to construct a theory of communication which draws on both Continental philosophy and ordinary-language philosophy. See also the efforts of Hans-Georg Gadamer, who stands in critical relation to Habermas, in his *Philosophical Hermeneutics,* trans. and ed. David E. Linge (Berkeley: University of California Press, 1976), and his *Truth and Method* (New York: Seabury Press, 1975). For two attempts to deal with phenomenology and ordinary-language philosophy together, see Bernstein, *The Restructuring of Social and Political Theory,* and Maurice Roche, *Phenomenology, Language, and the Social Sciences* (London: Routledge and Kegan Paul, 1973). For an example of the continuing lack of communication between the two movements, see Anthony Quinton, "The Foundations of Knowledge," in R. F. Dearden, P. H. Hirst, and R. S. Peters,

eds., *Education and the Development of Reason* (London: Routledge and Kegan Paul, 1972). In this essay we find reference to the following works: Bertrand Russell's *Our Knowledge of the External World* and *Human Knowledge*, Moritz Schlick's *Allgemeine Erkenntnislehre*, Wittgenstein's *Tractatus*, Rudolf Carnap's *Logische Aufbau der Welt*, C. I. Lewis's *Mind and the World* and *Analysis of Knowledge and Valuation*, and A. J. Ayers's *The Foundations of Empirical Knowledge* (276). Yet in an essay dealing with the philosophical concern for the "foundations of knowledge," we find not one mention of the tradition of phenomenology!

5. For a few examples of approaching the issues of social science and political theory from the perspective of ordinary-language philosophy, see T. D. Weldon, *Vocabulary of Politics* (London: Penguin Books, 1953); A. R. Louch, *Explanation and Human Action* (Berkeley: University of California Press, 1966); and Hannah Pitkin, *Wittgenstein and Justice* (Berkeley: University of California Press, 1972).

6. Richard Zaner, *The Way of Phenomenology: Criticism as a Philosophical Discipline* (New York: Pegasus, 1970), 83, 202.

7. Ibid., 199.

8. For some good accounts of the history, development, and meaning of phenomenology, see the following works: Herbert Spiegelberg, *The Phenomenological Movement: A Historical Introduction*, 2 vols. (The Hague: Martinus Nijhoff, 1960)—the most comprehensive account I know—Marvin Farber, *The Foundations of Phenomenology: Edmund Husserl and the Quest for a Rigorous Science of Philosophy* (Cambridge: Harvard University Press, 1943); Zaner, *The Way of Phenomenology;* and Thévenaz, *What Is Phenomenology?*.

9. Of the many excellent treatments of Husserl and phenomenology see, for example, Maurice Natanson, *Edmund Husserl: Philosopher of Infinite Tasks* (Evanston: Northwestern University Press, 1973); Joseph Kockelmans, *A First Introduction to Husserl's Phenomenology* (Pittsburgh: Duquesne University Press, 1967); Quentin Lauer, ed., *Edmund Husserl: Phenomenology and the Crisis of Philosophy* (New York: Harper and Row, 1965); Edo Pivcevic, *Husserl's Phenomenology* (London: Hutchinson, 1970); Farber, *Foundations of Phenomenology;* Spiegelberg, *The Phenomenological Movement*, vol. 1; and the series of volumes published as *Analecta Husserliana: The Yearbook of Phenomenological Research* (Dordrecht: D. Reidel Publishing Co.).

10. Edmund Husserl, *The Crisis of European Sciences and Transcendental Phenomenology: An Introduction to Phenomenological Philosophy*, trans. David Carr (Evanston: Northwestern University Press, 1970), 99. Hereafter all references to this work are made to Carr's translation and cited as *Crisis*.

11. See Husserl, *Crisis*, 68.

12. Ibid., 97.

13. As Thévenaz puts it, "The problem that haunted Husserl from his *Philosophie der Arithmetik* (1891) until his death was that of foundations" (*What Is Phenomenology?*, 41).

14. Husserl, *Crisis*, 70.

15. On "intentionality" in Husserl, see, for example, his *Logical Investigations*, 2 vols., trans. J. N. Findlay (London: Routledge and Kegan Paul, 1970), and *Ideas: General Introduction to Pure Phenomenology*, trans. W. R.

Boyce Gibson (London: George Allen and Unwin, 1931). See also Spiegelberg, *The Phenomenological Movement* 1:107–10; Farber, *Foundations of Phenomenology*, 333–447; Pivcevic, *Husserl's Phenomenology*, 45–54; and Kockelmans, *A First Introduction*, 169–200.

16. On the "phenomenological reduction," see Husserl, *The Idea of Phenomenology*, trans. W. P. Alston and G. Nakhnikian (The Hague: Martinus Nijhoff, 1964); and *Ideas*, part 1. See also, for example, Kockelmans, *A First Introduction*, 133–68; Pivcevic, *Husserl's Phenomenology*, 64–73; and Spiegelberg, *The Phenomenological Movement* 1:133–38.

17. Husserl, *Ideas*, 99–100.

18. See Husserl, *Crisis*, 168.

19. For an example of the difference between the radical empiricism of Husserl and William James, see Spiegelberg, *The Phenomenological Movement* 1:129, n.1.

20. See Husserl, *Ideas*, 74–79.

21. Husserl, *Crisis*, 7.

22. Thévenaz, *What Is Phenomenology?*, 53.

23. Ibid.

24. On the *Lebenswelt*, see Husserl, *Crisis*, 103–89. See also Spiegelberg, *The Phenomenological Movement* 1:159–62; Kockelmans, *A First Introduction*, 250–80; and Pivcevic, *Husserl's Phenomenology*, 83–92.

25. See, for example, Husserl's "Vienna Lecture," appended to the *Crisis*, 295.

26. See Husserl, *Crisis*, 127–28, 130.

27. Ibid., 153.

28. Ibid., 176–77.

29. Husserl, "The Vienna Lecture," 299.

30. See Bernstein's comment on Husserl: "One is left with no basis for bridging the gap between theoria and praxis, for transforming social and political reality so that it would be in accord with Husserl's ideal of the life of reason" (*The Restructuring of Social and Political Theory*, 178).

31. Mention should be made, first, of the development from Husserl's transcendental, or "constitutive," phenomenology to the "phenomenology of essences" in the work of Pfänder (1870–1941), Geiger (1880–1937) and especially Scheler (1874–1928). See, for example, Alexander Pfänder, *Phenomenology of Willing and Motivation*, trans. Herbert Spiegelberg (Evanston: Northwestern University Press, 1967); and Max Scheler, *The Nature of Sympathy* (New Haven: Yale University Press, 1954).

32. See Martin Heidegger, *Sein und Zeit* (Halle: Niemeyer, 1927), 52–62.

33. It should be noted that although both Heidegger and Nietzsche are crucial to the developments of historicism and relativism in the twentieth century, I do not find them to be particularly dialectical thinkers. For this reason, and not because I underestimate the importance of their reflections on a myriad of other philosophical and political problems, Nietzsche and Heidegger are of minimal concern to our inquiry.

34. Heidegger, *Being and Time*, trans. John Macquarrie and Edward Robinson (Oxford: Basil Blackwell, 1962), 49–63.

35. See Heidegger's account of this in "What Is Metaphysics?" in *Existence and Being* (Chicago: Henry Regnery, Gateway ed., 1960), 325–49.

36. See Thévenaz, *What Is Phenomenology?*, 57.

37. for what I read as a hint of confirmation on this point, see Dallmayr, *Beyond Dogma and Despair*, 103–4, and esp. 168–69.

38. See Jean-Paul Sartre, *Being and Nothingness*, trans. Hazel Barnes (New York: Philosophical Library, 1956).

39. See Jean-Paul Sartre, *The Transcendence of the Ego*, trans. Forrest Williams and Robert Kirkpatrick (New York: Noonday Press, 1957), 40–49, 98–106.

40. The subtitle of *Being and Nothingness* is "An Essay on Phenomenological Ontology."

41. Maurice Roche, *Phenomenology, Language, and the Social Sciences*, 22.

42. See Sartre, *Being and Nothingness*, 431–556, esp. 431–38 and 475–80.

43. See, for example, ibid., 221–23 and 254–65.

44. For an example of this in Sartre's drama, see *No Exit* (New York: Alfred A. Knopf, 1947).

45. See Sartre's remarks on responsibility in *Being and Nothingness*, 553–56.

46. See Merleau-Ponty, *Phenomenology of Perception*, vii–xxi. For Merleau-Ponty's criticism of the *pour soi–en soi* dualism, see, for example, 369–409. For his conception of freedom in contrast to Sartre's, see 434–56.

47. Ibid., 430.

48. See ibid., xvi, xx.

49. See Thévenaz, *What Is Phenomenology?*, 88.

50. Merleau-Ponty, "The Primacy of Perception and Its Philosophical Consequences," in Fisher, *The Essential Writings of Merleau-Ponty*, 61.

51. Merleau-Ponty, *Phenomenology of Perception*, xix.

52. Merleau-Ponty, "For the Sake of Truth," *SNS*, 168.

53. Merleau-Ponty, "The Primacy of Perception," 61–62.

54. Merleau-Ponty, *Phenomenology of Perception*, xix.

55. Ibid., 373.

56. On Marx and "objectivity," see above, chap. 2.

57. Edie, Introduction to Thévenaz, *What Is Phenomenology?* 18. Edie's mention of "noetic" here refers to Husserl's concepts of *noesis* and *noema*. *Noesis* refers to the intentional and nonmaterial act or process of experiencing the world. *Noema* refers to that which is experienced, the intentional object, in terms of its content-meaning. This relationship has nothing to do with the sensory content of experience, but refers to the relational structure of the act of experiencing itself.

58. Zaner, *The Way of Phenomenology*, 107.

59. See Thévenaz, *What Is Phenomenology?*, 90.

60. Edie, Introduction to Thévenaz, *What Is Phenomenology?* 19.

61. Hwa Yol Jung, "The Political Relevance of Existential Phenomenology," *Review of Politics* 33 (October 1971): 540.

62. See, for example, Marx, "Critique of Hegel's Philosophy of Right" and "Private Property and Communism," in Bottomore, *Karl Marx*, 43, 158.

63. See Jung, "Political Relevance," 543.

64. See Zaner, *The Way of Phenomenology*, 37–38, 203.

65. Jung, "Political Relevance," 545.

66. Ibid., 546.

67. See the last chapter, "The Limitations of Phenomenology—Concluding Remarks," in Pivcevic's *Husserl's Phenomenology*, 145–54.

68. See ibid., 147.

69. Thévenaz, *What Is Phenomenology?*, 91; see Zaner, *The Way of Phenomenology*, 82, 203.

70. Again, see Zaner, *The Way of Phenomenology*, 112, 202–3.

71. Merleau-Ponty, "Hegel's Existentialism," *SNS*, 63.

72. See Quentin Lauer, *The Triumph of Subjectivity: An Introduction to Transcendental Phenomenology* (New York: Fordham University Press, 1958), 2.

73. See Herbert Spiegelberg, *Doing Phenomenology: Essays on and in Phenomenology* (The Hague: Martinus Nijhoff, 1975), 3.

74. See, e.g., Merleau-Ponty, *Phenomenology of Perception*, especially his discussion in the second part of the work on the "perceived world." The basis for this argument is formed in his earlier work *The Structure of Behavior*, trans. Alden Fisher (Boston: Beacon Press, 1963), especially in chapter 4, where he deals with the relation of soul and body and the concept of perceptual consciousness. For a recent attempt to provide a systematic account of Merleau-Ponty's philosophy, which nonetheless does not focus on his dialectical theory, see Samuel B. Mallin, *Merleau-Ponty's Philosophy* (New Haven: Yale University Press, 1979).

75. Merleau-Ponty, Preface to *SNS*, 3.

76. Ibid., 4.

77. Merleau-Ponty, "The Battle over Existentialism," *SNS*, 73.

78. Merleau-Ponty, "Hegel's Existentialism," 64.

79. Merleau-Ponty, "The Battle over Existentialism," 72.

80. Merleau-Ponty, "Marxism and Philosophy," *SNS*, 130.

81. Merleau-Ponty, "The Battle over Existentialism," 80. The reference here is to Marx's statement "The main defect of all previous materialism . . . is that things, reality, the sensible world, are conceived only in the form of *objects,* or of *observation,* but not as *sensuous human activity, praxis,* not subjectively," *Theses on Feuerbach,* I.

82. Merleau-Ponty, *SNS*, 77. Here Merleau-Ponty is explicitly referring to Henri Lefebvre's criticism of Sartre in "Existentialisme et Marxisme," *Action* 40 (8 June 1945). But one need not look very far to find that this form of marxism has dominated the self-understanding of orthodox marxist theory.

83. Ibid., 78–79.

84. Ibid., 78.

85. Ibid., 72.

86. Merleau-Ponty, "Marxism and Philosophy," 130, 134.

87. See Marx, "Critique of Hegel's Dialectic," 202–3.

88. See Merleau-Ponty's comment that Marx "situates synthesis in our future instead of outside time," in "The Battle over Existentialism," 79.

89. Merleau-Ponty, "Marxism and Philosophy," 129 (emphasis added).

90. Merleau-Ponty, "The Battle over Existentialism," 82. Here one notes a defense of Sartre.

91. Ibid. It is interesting to note in this regard that both Merleau-Ponty and Habermas appear to argue that there is a discrepancy between the practice of marxist theory by Marx and the usual understanding of marxist theory formulated in theoretical debates.

92. Merleau-Ponty, "The Metaphysical in Man," *SNS*, 97.

93. Merleau-Ponty, "Marxism and Philosophy," 133.

94. Ibid., 135.

95. Marx speaks of this in "The Critique of Hegel's Philosophy of Right," in Bottomore, *Karl Marx,* 50–51 and 58–59. Again, it should be emphasized that at both these places the word which is translated as "abolish," "abolition," is found in Marx as *aufheben, Aufhebung.*

96. Merleau-Ponty, "Marxism and Philosophy," 133.

Chapter Five

1. See Herbert Marcuse's 1928 essay, "Contributions to a Phenomenology of Historical Materialism," translated in *Telos,* no. 4 (Fall 1969): 3–24.

2. See Enzo Paci, *The Function of the Sciences and the Meaning of Man,* trans. Paul Piccone and James E. Hansen (Evanston: Northwestern University Press, 1972). For a recent attempt to suggest a union of critical marxism and phenomenology in political science, see Fred Dallmayr, "Beyond Dogma and Despair: Toward a Critical Theory of Politics," *American Political Science Review* 70 (March 1976): 64–79. See also Dallmayr's "Phenomenology and Marxism: A Salute to Enzo Paci," in George Psathsas, ed., *Phenomenological Sociology: Issues and Applications* (New York: John Wiley and Sons, 1973). His latest effort is *Beyond Dogma and Despair.* And see Bernstein, *The Restructuring of Social and Political Theory.*

3. This is the promise of Paci's work, for example. For further examples of the argument, see Paul Piccone and James E. Hansen, Translators' Introduction to Paci, *The Function of the Sciences,* esp. xxv–xxxv; and Dallmayr, "Phenomenology and Marxism," esp. 308–18.

4. See H. Stuart Hughes, *The Obstructed Path: French Social Thought in the Years of Desperation, 1930–1960* (New York: Harper and Row, 1968), chap. 5, which is a good account of the effect of this period on all aspects of French social and political thought.

5. For examples of the effects of the war, see Merleau-Ponty's essays "Concerning Marxism," "Faith and Good Faith," and "The War Has Taken Place," in *SNS.* See also Sartre's autobiographical reflections in *The Words,* trans. Bernard Frechtman (New York: Braziller, 1964), and his reflections throughout *Situations,* trans. Benita Eisler (New York: Braziller, 1965).

6. See Merleau-Ponty, *The Structure of Behavior,* esp. 185–224.

7. See Merleau-Ponty, *Phenomenology of Perception,* for example, 124.

8. See ibid., for example, 218–20.

9. See Sartre, *Being and Nothingness,* for example, lxiii; see also 617–25.

10. See ibid., for example, li, lvi.

11. Merleau-Ponty, "Marxism and Philosophy," *SNS*, 130.

12. See Sartre, *Being and Nothingness*, for example, xlv–xlviii.

13. For one of the earliest excellent accounts of Sartre's phenomenological ontology, see Maurice Natanson, *A Critique of Jean-Paul Sartre's Ontology* (The Hague: Martinus Nijhoff, 1973), originally published in 1951. See also Klaus Hartmann, *Sartre's Ontology: A Study of "Being and Nothingness" in the Light of Hegel's Logic* (Evanston: Northwestern University Press, 1966); and Jacques C. Salvan, *To Be and Not To Be: An Analysis of Jean-Paul Sartre's Ontology* (Detroit: Wayne State University Press, 1962).

14. This argument is prefigured in Sartre's *Transcendence of the Ego*, originally published in 1936.

15. See Sartre, *Being and Nothingness*, 221–302, esp. 252–302, concerning the "Look."

16. See Wilfrid Desan, *The Tragic Finale: An Essay on the Philosophy of Jean-Paul Sartre* (New York: Harper and Row, 1960), esp. 91–95. See also his *The Marxism of Jean-Paul Sartre* (New York: Doubleday, 1965).

17. Merleau-Ponty, "The Battle over Existentialism," 72.

18. Merleau-Ponty, "A Scandalous Author," *SNS*, 41.

19. Merleau-Ponty, "Hegel's Existentialism," 68.

20. Ibid., 69–70.

21. Merleau-Ponty, "Metaphysics and the Novel," *SNS*, 36.

22. Merleau-Ponty, "The Metaphysical in Man," *SNS*, 90.

23. Merleau-Ponty, "Marxism and Philosophy," 129. See Sartre, "Matérialisme et révolution," *Les Temps Modernes* 1, no. 9 (June 1946): 1537–63.

24. Merleau-Ponty, "Man, the Hero," *SNS*, 186.

25. For a good account of the development of Merleau-Ponty's existential and social thought, see Albert Rabil, *Merleau-Ponty: Existentialist of the Social World* (New York: Columbia University Press, 1967).

26. Merleau-Ponty, "The War Has Taken Place," 140.

27. See Simone de Beauvoir, *Force of Circumstances*, trans. Richard Howard (New York: G. P. Putnam's Sons, 1965), 5.

28. Sartre admits that his attraction to marxism was based on practicality and not on a theoretical understanding of Marx. See *Search for a Method*, trans. Hazel Barnes (New York: Alfred A. Knopf, 1967), 17–18.

29. See Merleau-Ponty, *Signs*, trans. Richard McCleary (Evanston: Northwestern University Press, 1964), 20. See also Hughes's account in *The Obstructed Path*, 197. In the same work, Hughes comments that although Merleau-Ponty's original interests were nonpolitical, his development of marxian theory was one of the most insightful in all France: "One of the curious features of the vicissitudes of Marxism in postwar France was that its most sophisticated interpreter and critic should have been an heir of the phenomenological tradition whose original writings seemed to have nothing to do with ideology" (192).

30. See, for example, Merleau-Ponty, "For the Sake of Truth," *SNS*, 160.

31. See H. L. Dreyfus and P. A. Dreyfus, Translators' Introduction to *SNS*, xxiv.

32. Sartre, *Situations*, 287.

33. See ibid., 288.

34. Ibid., 295.

35. See Merleau-Ponty, *Adventures of the Dialectic,* trans. Joseph Bien (Evanston: Northwestern University Press, 1973), 95–201.

36. For a recently translated examination of Sartre, existentialism, and marxism, see Pietro Chiodi, *Sartre and Marxism,* trans. Kate Soper (New York: Humanities Press, 1976), which contains a good analysis of the *Critique of Dialectical Reason.* For a few other examinations of these relations, see Desan, *The Marxism of Jean-Paul Sartre;* Walter Odajynk, *Marxism and Existentialism* (New York: Anchor Books, 1965); Jacques Salvan, *The Scandalous Ghost: Sartre's Existentialism as Related to Vitalism, Humanism, Mysticism, Marxism* (Detroit: Wayne State University Press, 1967); and Mark Poster, *Existential Marxism in Postwar France: From Sartre to Althusser* (Princeton: Princeton University Press, 1975). See also Poster's *Sartre's Marxism* (Cambridge: Cambridge University Press, 1982). For a comparison, see David Archard, *Marxism and Existentialism: The Political Philosophy of Sartre and Merleau-Ponty* (Belfast: Blackstaff Press, 1980).

37. See Hughes, *The Obstructed Path,* 197; see also Rabil, *Merleau-Ponty,* 81–84.

38. See Merleau-Ponty, "Marxism and Philosophy," 128, and Hughes, *The Obstructed Path,* 209.

39. Merleau-Ponty, *Humanism and Terror,* trans. John O'Neill (Boston: Beacon Press, 1969), xiv–xv.

40. Ibid., 179. For a brief reflection on the content of this work, see Merleau-Ponty, *Adventures of the Dialectic,* 228–30.

41. Merleau-Ponty, *Adventures of the Dialectic* and *Signs,* especially the Introduction, 3–13.

42. Ibid., 9–10.

43. See ibid., 11–13.

44. Merleau-Ponty, *Adventures of the Dialectic,* 4.

45. Ibid., 5.

46. Ibid., 5–6.

47. The names refer to the subject matter of the five chapters of the *Adventures of the Dialectic.*

48. Ibid., 204.

49. Ibid., 6.

50. Ibid., 206.

51. Ibid., 231. Some critics might argue that Merleau-Ponty's later dialectical relativization of marxism marks a break from marxism altogether. This only makes sense if one operates on the basis of a closed, fixed view of dialectical marxism. For an example of Merleau-Ponty's continuing contribution to the evolution of a broad dialectical theory, see his provocative discussion of "philosophical interrogation" and the "dialectic," in his posthumously published *The Visible and the Invisible,* ed. Claude Lefort and trans. Alphonso Lingis (Evanston: Northwestern University Press, 1968), chap. 2, e.g., the discussion of the "bad" and "good" dialectic, 93–95.

52. Merleau-Ponty, *Adventures of the Dialectic,* 233.

53. Again, see the major argument of Zaner, *The Way of Phenomenology.*

54. Sartre, *Critique of Dialectical Reason,* trans. Allan Sheridan-Smith (London: New Left Books, 1976).

55. See Sartre's arguments in ibid., 15–41, esp. 34. Also, Sartre does acknowledge a certain debt to Merleau-Ponty in his essay "Merleau-Ponty" in *Situations.*

56. Merleau-Ponty, *Adventures of the Dialectic,* 205.

57. Perhaps the best example of such an encounter before Sartre and Merleau-Ponty occurs in Lukács. See, for example, the brief introductory account of such encounters in Dallmayr, "Phenomenology and Marxism"; and Piccone and Hansen, Translators' Introduction to Paci, *The Function of the Sciences.*

58. See Jung, "Political Relevance." A longer version of this essay is found as the introductory essay to Hwa Yol Jung, ed., *Existential Phenomenology and Political Theory: A Reader* (Chicago: Henry Regnery Co., 1972), xvii–lv. Hereafter I shall quote from and refer to this second version. For Jung's most recent effort, see his *The Crisis of Political Understanding.*

59. Paul Ricoeur, *Husserl,* trans. E. G. Ballard and L. E. Embree (Evanston: Northwestern University Press, 1967), 212.

60. Jung, *Existential Phenomenology,* xix, xx.

61. Ibid., xxx.

62. Ibid., xxiii.

63. Ibid., xxxii. One might add that "background" is perhaps too tenuous a term. "Foundation" might be better.

64. See ibid., xxiii–xxiv.

65. Ibid., xxvi.

66. See ibid., xxviii–xxix. It is interesting to note that Jung's paragraphs on the relations between existential phenomenology and marxism are absent in his first version of the article, which appeared in the *Review of Politics.* Indeed, in the earlier version there is not even a mention of Marx, although the connections are implicit.

67. The investigation and establishment of the relations between phenomenology and the social sciences is a great contribution of Alfred Schutz. See, for example, *The Phenomenology of the Social World,* trans. George Walsh and Frederick Lehnert (Evanston: Northwestern University Press, 1967). See also, for example, his *Collected Papers I: The Problem of Social Reality,* ed. Maurice Natanson (The Hague: Martinus Nijhoff, 1962), esp. parts 1 and 2. What Schutz seems to lack most in his treatment of phenomenology and social science is a *critical* theory of society.

68. Jung, *Existential Phenomenology,* xxix–xxx.

69. Merleau-Ponty makes this argument in "The Philosopher and Sociology," *Signs,* 98–113.

70. As his example Jung criticizes the approach taken by Heinz Eulau in *The Behavioral Persuasion* and in *Micro-Macro Political Analysis* (Chicago: Aldine, 1969), 148–65 and 370–90.

71. Jung, *Existential Phenomenology,* xxx.

72. Ibid., xxxviii. See also John Wild, Foreword to Merleau-Ponty, *The Structure of Behavior,* xiv–xvi.

73. Jung, *Existential Phenomenology,* xl.

74. Merleau-Ponty, "The War Has Taken Place," 152.

75. Jung, *Existential Phenomenology,* xl.

76. Ibid., xlii–xliii.
77. Ibid., xliv.
78. Ibid., xlvii.
79. Ibid.
80. Ibid., xxi.
81. Ibid., xxii.
82. Among them one could include Richard Bernstein, Fred Dallmayr, Enzo Paci, Barry Smart, Karel Kosik. See Kosik, *Dialectics of the Concrete: A Study on Problems of Man and World,* trans. Karel Kovanda with James Schmidt (Dordrecht: D. Reidel Publishing Co., 1976). One could also include Paul Piccone, John O'Neill, and Pier Aldo Rovatti. See Rovatti's short essay "Critical Theory and Phenomenology," *Telos,* no. 15 (Spring 1973): 35–40. For an interesting attempt to unite marxism and phenomenology by way of formulating Marx's own method (especially in the *Grundrisse*) as one of dialectical phenomenology, see Roslyn Wallach Bologh, *Dialectical Phenomenology: Marx's Method* (London: Routledge and Kegan Paul, 1979). I should also mention here what has often been called the Yugoslavian "Praxis Group," a group of philosophers interested in the development of a dialectical, anti-positivist marxism. They include such thinkers as Gajo Petrović, Mihailo Marković, and Svetozar Stojanović. Although I have chosen not to focus on their thought, it would be inexcusable to ignore their various attempts to revive a dialectical critical marxism, as well as to attempt a marxist-existentialist dialogue. For example, see the discussion in Petrović, *Marx in the Mid-Twentieth Century* (Garden City, N.J.: Anchor Books, 1967), 17. See further in the following works: Marković, *From Affluence to Praxis* (Ann Arbor: University of Michigan Press, 1974); Stojanović, *Between Ideals and Reality: A Critique of Socialism and Its Future,* trans. Gerson S. Sher (London: Oxford University Press, 1973), and *In Search of Democracy in Socialism: History and Party Consciousness,* trans. Gerson S. Sher (Buffalo, N.Y.: Prometheus Books, 1981). For a marvelous collection of essays by numerous members of the group, see the following work: Marković and Petrović, eds., *Praxis: Yugoslav Essays in the Philosophy and Methodology of the Social Sciences,* trans. Joan Coddington et al., Boston Studies in the Philosophy of Science, ed. Robert S. Cohen and Marx W. Wartofsky, vol. 36 (Dordrecht: D. Reidel Publishing Co., 1979).
83. See Dallmayr, "Beyond Dogma and Despair," 65. See also his "Phenomenology and Marxism," 306.
84. Efraim Shmueli, "Consciousness and Action: Husserl and Marx on Theory and Praxis," in Anna-Teresa Tymieniecka, ed., *The Crisis of Culture: Analecta Husserliana,* vol. 5 (Dordrecht: D. Reidel Publishing Co., 1976), 345. For more of Shmueli's thoughts on this matter, see his "Can Phenomenology Accommodate Marxism?" *Telos,* no. 17 (Fall 1973): 164–80.
85. Paci, *The Function of the Sciences,* 71.
86. Ibid., 60.
87. Ibid., 202–3.
88. It is the argument that social and political theory need to be critical in this manner (and, indeed, that if theory is not critical of the quality of social and political life, it is not theory) which underlines and guides the entire ar-

gument of Bernstein's *The Restructuring of Social and Political Theory,* see especially the Conclusion, 225–36.

89. See Paci, *The Function of the Sciences,* 44.

90. Paci himself often seems to fall into the category of those who view phenomenology as a "science of the subject." See ibid., 262.

91. See, for example, Dallmayr's argument in "Beyond Dogma and Despair," 70.

92. Paci, *The Function of the Sciences,* 172, 175. On this problem see further, 161–65, 255–59.

93. Ibid., 294.

94. Ibid., 398.

95. See Dallmayr, "Beyond Dogma and Despair," 69–71. For Dallmayr's discussion of the subject-object relation in Paci, see "Phenomenology and Marxism," 323–25.

96. See Shmueli, "Consciousness and Action," 360, where he argues for this tension of subject and object. I disagree with his conclusion, however, that this tension is absent in Marx.

97. See ibid., 366.

98. See Dallmayr, "Beyond Dogma and Despair," 69.

99. See, for example, the argument of the *Theses on Feuerbach.*

100. Paci, *The Function of the Sciences,* 251–52.

101. See Marx, "Private Property and Communism," 162.

102. Paci, *The Function of the Sciences,* 252 (Paci's emphasis).

103. See Dallmayr, "Beyond Dogma and Despair," 66.

104. See, for example, Bernstein, *The Restructuring of Social and Political Theory,* 229–30.

105. See Dallmayr, "Beyond Dogma and Despair," 75–79.

106. Ibid., 75.

107. Shmueli, "Consciousness and Action," 346. For a discussion of the limits of the attempt to unify theory and practice in Husserl and Marx, see further, 369–76.

108. See Piccone and Hansen, Translators' Introduction to Paci, *The Function of the Sciences,* xxvii.

109. See Paci, *The Function of the Sciences,* 295–99. It is interesting to note that Paci ends this section on critical marxism with a quote from Gramsci attacking dogmatic marxism.

110. Ibid., 315.

111. Ibid., 323.

112. See Piccone and Hansen, Translators' Introduction to Paci, *The Function of the Sciences,* xxv.

113. Paci, *The Function of the Sciences,* 447. For one critique skeptical of the ease of this union, see Shmueli, "Can Phenomenology Accommodate Marxism?"

114. For a few examples of this emphasis see Paci, *The Function of the Sciences,* 53–55, 107–8, 242. See also Dallmayr's critical evaluation of Paci in "Phenomenology and Marxism."

115. See, for example, Paci, *The Function of the Sciences,* 325–26, 328–29, 346. This same criticism of Merleau-Ponty's "philosophy of ambiguity" is

found in Paul Piccone, "Phenomenological Marxism," *Telos,* no. 9 (Fall 1971): 11. For a fairly recent defense of Merleau-Ponty's fusion of marxism and phenomenology, see the brief discussion in Laurie Spurling, *Phenomenology and the Social World: The Philosophy of Merleau-Ponty and Its Relation to the Social Sciences* (London: Routledge and Kegan Paul, 1977), chap. 4.

116. See Dallmayr's "Beyond Dogma and Despair."

117. See Bernstein, *The Restructuring of Social and Political Theory,* 235. I shall return to Bernstein in chapter 6, in terms of his interpretation of critical theory and the restructuring of political theory.

118. See ibid., 135.

Chapter Six

1. Although it violates my inclination against hypostatizing philosophical movements to render them in upper-case letters, I will nonetheless use "Critical Theory" and "Critical Theorists" when referring to the specific efforts of the Frankfurt School, in order to distinguish it from the general dialectical and critical theory which has formed the object of inquiry in previous chapters.

2. By far the best account of the history and nature of the Frankfurt School from its origins to the middle of the century is Martin Jay's *The Dialectical Imagination: A History of the Frankfurt School and the Institute of Social Research, 1923–1950* (Boston: Little, Brown and Co., 1973). For another account of the Frankfurt School which focuses upon Adorno and his relation to Walter Benjamin, see Susan Buck-Morss, *The Origin of Negative Dialectics* (New York: Macmillan Publishing Co., Free Press, 1977). See also Schroyer, *The Critique of Domination.*

3. Of the many discussions of the nature and importance of the eastward shift of the socialist "center of gravity," see, for example, Dick Howard, "The Historical Context," and Martin Jay, "The Frankfurt School and the Genesis of Critical Theory," in Dick Howard and Karl Klare, eds., *The Unknown Dimension: European Marxism since Lenin* (New York: Basic Books, 1972)— indeed, the entire book, which includes articles on Lukács, Bloch, Korsch, Gramsci, W. Reich, W. Benjamin, Marcuse, Habermas, Sartre, Lefebvre, Della Volpe, Althusser, Serge Mallet and Andre Gorz, is a good testament of the response to the eastward shift of socialist orthodoxy. From another perspective, see Perry Anderson, *Considerations on Western Marxism* (London: New Left Books, 1976). For an interesting comparison, see Merleau-Ponty's chapter " 'Western' Marxism" in *Adventures of the Dialectic.* See also Russell Jacoby, *Dialectic of Defeat: Contours of Western Marxism* (New York: Cambridge University Press, 1981).

4. The effects of this development become a theme in the later work by Max Horkheimer and Theodor Adorno, *Dialectic of Enlightenment,* trans. John Cumming (New York: Herder and Herder, 1972), which was originally published in 1944. Also, the development of state interventionism becomes one of the bases for Marcuse's theory of the "self-reflexivity of capitalism." See his argument, for example, in *One-Dimensional Man: Studies in the Ideology of*

Advanced Industrial Society (Boston: Beacon Press, 1964) and in *An Essay on Liberation* (Boston: Beacon Press, 1969).

5. See, for example, Horkheimer's discussion of these structural transformations in capitalism in "Traditional and Critical Theory," in Horkheimer, *Critical Theory: Selected Essays,* trans. Matthew J. O'Connell et al. (New York: Herder and Herder, 1972), 234–36. The essay was written in 1937 and was published as part of the two-volume essay collection *Kritische Theorie,* (1968).

6. See Jay, *The Dialectical Imagination,* 43.

7. Indeed, after World War II, Horkheimer organized a collection of essays under the title *Critique of Instrumental Reason,* trans. Matthew J. O'Connell et al. (New York: Seabury Press, 1974). For a good treatment of the centrality in Critical Theory of a critique of instrumental reason, see the work by the contemporary heir to the Frankfurt School, Albrecht Wellmer, *Critical Theory of Society,* trans. John Cumming (New York: Seabury Press, 1971), esp. 121–39. This was originally published as *Kritische Gesellschaftstheorie und Positivismus,* (1969).

8. The theme of the reciprocal relationship between scientistic positivism and the legitimation of an oppressive and alienating society forms a major focus for such Frankfurt thinkers and heirs as Marcuse and Habermas. It is the dominant theme of Marcuse's *One-Dimensional Man.* See Jürgen Habermas's "Technology and Science as 'Ideology,' " in *Toward a Rational Society: Student Protest, Science, and Politics,* trans. Jeremy J. Shapiro (Boston: Beacon Press, 1970). See also his *Legitimation Crisis,* trans. Thomas McCarthy (Boston: Beacon Press, 1975).

9. See my discussion of Gramsci and Lukács above, chapter 3. The major early works involved in this recovery of the philosophical dimension of marxism which influenced the Frankfurt Critical Theorists were Lukács's *History and Class Consciousness* and Korsch's *Marxism and Philosophy,* trans. Fred Halliday (New York: Monthly Review Press, 1971). Both works were originally published in 1923. For a concise discussion of Korsch's work, see Mihaly Vajda, "Karl Korsch's 'Marxism and Philosophy,' " in Howard and Klare, *The Unknown Dimension,* 131–46.

10. This is one reason why George Lichtheim entitles his essay collection on Western Marxism *From Marx to Hegel.*

11. This reconstruction is a major theme of Habermas's *Knowledge and Human Interests.*

12. See Jay, *The Dialectical Imagination,* 41–43. As Jay points out, the philosophical origins of Critical Theory find their true source in the Left Hegelianism of the 1840s.

13. On this see Habermas's discussion in *Knowledge and Human Interests,* 25–42. See also Wellmer's excellent treatment of Marx's latent positivism and objectivism in *Critical Theory of Society,* esp. 67–119. These two sources of marxism's dogmatic reification relate to my earlier discussion of the opposition of dialectical marxism to a metaphysical determinism applied to history and to an economic determinism, both of which form the core of positivistic marxism. See chapter 3 above.

14. One of the members of the Frankfurt School who was most "culturally" oriented was Walter Benjamin. See, for example, his *Illuminations: Essays and Reflections,* ed. with Introduction by Hannah Arendt, trans. Harry Zohn (New York: Schocken Books, 1968). Also see Shierry M. Weber, "Walter Benjamin: Commodity Fetishism, the Modern, and the Experience of History," in Howard and Klare, *The Unknown Dimension,* 249–75; and Buck-Morss, *The Origin of Negative Dialectics.* For an example of Theodor Adorno's exercises in "cultural criticism and society," see his *Prisms,* trans. Samuel Weber and Shierry Weber (London: Neville Spearman, 1967).

15. It should be mentioned, however, that the relationship between Critical Theory and phenomenology is a problematical one. Critical Theory developed from its origins in a somewhat hostile relation to phenomenology, especially to Husserl. For the most hostile attack on Husserl, see Adorno's *Zur Metakritik der Erkenntnistheorie: Studien über Husserl und phänomenologischen Antinomien* (Frankfurt am Main: Suhrkamp Verlag, 1970). The work was actually sketched out between 1934 and 1937. See the critique in Horkheimer and Adorno, *Dialectic of Enlightenment.* See also, for example, Marcuse, "The Concept of Essence," in his *Negations: Essays in Critical Theory,* trans. Jeremy J. Shapiro (Boston: Beacon Press, 1968). For a brief but interesting comparison of the two movements, see Rovatti, "Critical Theory and Phenomenology," 25–40. See also the summary in Jeremy Shapiro, "The Dialectic of Theory and Practice in the Age of Technological Rationality: Herbert Marcuse and Jürgen Habermas," in Howard and Klare, *The Unknown Dimension,* 276–303.

16. See Jay, *The Dialectical Imagination,* 3–5.

17. This is the theme of Horkheimer's "Traditional and Critical Theory."

18. See my discussion of Husserl in relation to the *Crisis* in chapter 4 above. See also Horkheimer's "Notes on Science and the Crisis," in *Critical Theory,* 3–9.

19. On the critique of Husserl, apart from Adorno's *Zur Metakritik der Erkenntnistheorie,* see also his "Husserl and the Problem of Idealism," *Journal of Philosophy* 27, no. 1 (January 1940).

20. See the account in Schroyer, *The Critique of Domination,* 132–37.

21. Horkheimer, "Traditional and Critical Theory," 188–243.

22. For an example of Horkheimer's concern with individuality, see his chapter "Rise and Decline of the Individual" in *The Eclipse of Reason* (New York: Oxford University Press, 1947), in which he relates the crisis of reason with the crisis of the individual. It should be mentioned also that this concern for individuality was a major impetus for the attention paid by the Frankfurt School to the problems of mass society and mass culture. See, for example, Horkheimer's "Art and Mass Culture," *Studies in Philosophy and Social Sciences* 9, no. 2 (1941). See also their chapter "The Culture Industry: Enlightenment as Mass Deception," in Horkheimer and Adorno, *Dialectic of Enlightenment.*

23. See my discussion of the philosophy of identity and Hegel's relation to Kantian epistemology, and of Marx's critique of the Hegelian philosophy of identity in chapter 2 above. For examples of Horkheimer's critique, see his "Thoughts on Religion," *Critical Theory,* 129–31 (where he criticizes the con-

cept of absolute justice) and his "Hegel und die Metaphysik," in *Festschrift für Carl Grünberg: Zum 70. Geburtstag* (Leipzig, 1932). See also his "Materialism and Metaphysics," *Critical Theory*, 27–28.

24. On Horkheimer's relation to the *Lebensphilosophen*, see Jay, *The Dialectical Imagination*, 48–53.

25. On the degeneration of *Lebensphilosophie*, see Horkheimer's critique in "Zum Rationalismusstreit in der gegenwartigen Philosophie," *Zeitschrift für Sozialforschung* 3, no. 1 (1934).

26. See Jay, *The Dialectical Imagination*, 48.

27. See ibid., 51.

28. See Horkheimer's arguments in "Materialism and Metaphysics," where he argues, for example, that materialism seeks historical comprehension of spiritual phenomena (39) and that materialism cannot be reduced to formal traits which oppose it to idealistic metaphysics (45).

29. See Jay, *The Dialectical Imagination*, 53.

30. Again, see the argument of "Materialism and Metaphysics." In particular see 38, where Horkheimer addresses this criticism to the "predictive" claim of scientistic positivism.

31. See Jay, *The Dialectical Imagination*, 54. It is interesting to recall here Merleau-Ponty's criticism that to treat consciousness as a "by-product of being" or as an "epiphenomenon" is to use language that has never been marxist and to reject dialectical philosophy; see his "The Battle over Existentialism," 77–78.

32. Horkheimer, *Eclipse of Reason*, 176–77.

33. Ibid., 187.

34. This is the argument of Horkheimer's "The Latest Attack on Metaphysics," in *Critical Theory;* see, for example, 153–60, 164–65, 182–83.

35. One recalls again the criticism of Husserl in Adorno's *Zur Metakritik der Erkenntnistheorie* and in his "Husserl and the Problem of Idealism."

36. It should be pointed out here that Horkheimer equates traditional theory with positivism. In my previous discussions of political theory, I have used the term "traditional theory" to refer to the classical tradition of political theory and its current revival. To avoid confusion this distinction should be kept in mind while examining Horkheimer's critique of traditional theory.

37. Horkheimer, "Traditional and Critical Theory," 188.

38. Ibid., 188–89.

39. Ibid., 194.

40. Ibid., 209–10. This is the same criticism aimed at social science positivism by the rational-philosophical critique in Strauss, for example. See my discussion in chapter 1 above.

41. Ibid., 190.

42. Ibid., 206–7.

43. Horkheimer, "The Social Function of Philosophy," *Critical Theory*, 270.

44. See Horkheimer, "Traditional and Critical Theory," 213–14.

45. Ibid., 231–32.

46. See Joseph Gabel, *False Consciousness: An Essay on Reification*, trans. Margaret A. Thompson (New York: Harper, 1975).

47. See the comments in Jay, *The Dialectical Imagination*, 81.

48. On this issue see the comments in Bernstein, *The Restructuring of Social and Political Theory,* 180.

49. See Horkheimer, "Traditional and Critical Theory," 231. The following discussion is drawn from this article. See in particular 196–97, 213, 215–16, 242.

50. Ibid., 221. See also 223–24.

51. This is Bernstein's criticism of Horkheimer in *The Restructuring of Social and Political Theory,* 182–83.

52. The most important work to emerge from this interest was, of course, Theodor Adorno et al., *The Authoritarian Personality* (New York: Harper and Brothers, 1950). See also Horkheimer, "Traditional and Critical Theory," 207, and Jay, *The Dialectical Imagination,* 84–85. The attempt to provide a psychological link between superstructure and substructure with the aid of Freud has been a major concern of many of the Critical Theorists. One of the most influential of such attempts is Marcuse's *Eros and Civilization: A Philosophical Inquiry into Freud* (New York: Random House, Vintage Books, 1962).

53. The following brief summary of the transformation of the Frankfurt School during and following the Second World War is heavily indebted to Jay's analysis in *The Dialectical Imagination,* 253–99. It should also be kept in mind that during the war years, and the postwar years until Horkheimer's final return to Germany in 1949, the Institut was situated in the United States.

54. The necessity for a critical theory of society to transform itself as society and history change had already been spelled out by Horkheimer; see, for example, "Traditional and Critical Theory," 233–38.

55. Recall that Horkheimer originally identified critical theory with the "dialectical critique of political economy." See "Traditional and Critical Theory," 206, n. 14. In the essay he also relies on the framework of class conflict.

56. See the argument of the chapter "The Revolt of Nature," in Horkheimer's *Eclipse of Reason.*

57. See Jay, *The Dialectical Imagination,* 257–58. See also Horkheimer, *Anfänge der bürgerlichen Geschichtsphilosophie* (Stuttgart, 1930).

58. See, for example, Horkheimer, *Eclipse of Reason,* 94. This is also the argument of Marcuse's *One-Dimensional Man.*

59. This problem in Marx is indirectly an object of criticism in Horkheimer and Adorno, *Dialectic of Enlightenment.* It is more explicitly attacked in Habermas, *Knowledge and Human Interests,* and it finds its most developed and strongly argued criticism in Wellmer, *Critical Theory of Society,* 67–119, in "The Latent Positivism of Marx's Philosophy of History."

60. Indeed, in an essay collection he issued in 1965, Marcuse argued for the importance of "negative thinking" and gave his work the title *Negations.* At about the same time, Adorno published a work in which he claimed that dialectics can only be negative, and tried to purge dialectics of its "affirmative traits." See Adorno, *Negative Dialectics,* trans. E. B. Ashton (New York: Seabury Press, 1973), originally published in 1966.

61. See Marcuse, *One-Dimensional Man,* 84–120, where he deals with the "closing of the universe of discourse."

62. Jay, *The Dialectical Imagination,* 280. See Horkheimer, *Eclipse of Reason,* 183–87.

63. See Jay, *The Dialectical Imagination,* 288.

64. See Lichtheim, *From Marx to Hegel,* 175.

65. See Jeremy Shapiro's excellent summary of the Frankfurt School in his book review "The Critical Theory of Frankfurt," *Times Literary Supplement,* 4 October 1974. He distinguishes four phases of Critical Theory: first, its genesis with the founding of the Institut in 1923; second, its period of exile in America when it developed into a critique of Western civilization; third, its postwar return to Frankfurt when it focused on "negative thinking" and an attempt to redefine the fate of reason in a new historical period; and fourth, the development of a "communication theory of society" with Habermas. For an excellent study of Habermas's thought, see Thomas McCarthy, *The Critical Theory of Jürgen Habermas* (Cambridge, Mass.: MIT Press, 1978). For a recent and most stimulating collection of essays on different aspects of Habermas's thought, including a lengthy reply to his critics by Habermas himself, see John B. Thompson and David Held, eds., *Habermas: Critical Debates* (Cambridge, Mass.: MIT Press, 1982). See also Held, *Introduction to Critical Theory: Horkheimer to Habermas* (London: Hutchinson, 1980); and Thompson, *Critical Hermeneutics: A Study in the Thought of Paul Ricoeur and Jürgen Habermas* (Cambridge: Cambridge University Press, 1981).

66. See Habermas, *Legitimation Crisis,* and see, for an example of his attempt to revise traditional marxist categories and concepts, his "Towards a Reconstruction of Historical Materialism," *Theory and Society,* no. 2 (1975): 287–300. See also Bernstein's comments in *The Restructuring of Social and Political Theory,* 188–89.

67. See Habermas, *Theory and Practice,* 242; and *Knowledge and Human Interests,* 45. See also Wellmer, *Critical Theory of Society,* chap. 2. On this see also Shapiro, "The Dialectic of Theory and Practice," 291–92.

68. See my discussion of this process in chapter 2 above.

69. See Habermas, *Knowledge and Human Interests,* 28–29, 43.

70. See ibid., 43ff.

71. See ibid., 42. In defense of Marx on this point, see the arguments in Ollman, *Alienation,* for example, 6.

72. Habermas, *Knowledge and Human Interests,* 52–53.

73. Ibid., 53.

74. See the comments in Schroyer, *The Critique of Domination,* 143.

75. Habermas, *Knowledge and Human Interests,* 55.

76. Ibid.

77. Ibid., 62.

78. Ibid., 63.

79. See Schroyer, *The Critique of Domination,* 140.

80. See Habermas's summary in *Knowledge and Human Interests,* 67–69.

81. Habermas's reconstruction of this movement forms part 2 of *Knowledge and Human Interests,* 71–186. See his summary, 189.

82. I shall deal with this concept momentarily. For the present, one can take knowledge-constitutive interest and cognitive interest to mean the same thing. Habermas's brilliant summary of this process in Peirce and Dilthey is found in ibid., 190–98.

83. See ibid., 198ff. In relation to this notion see my discussion of Kant's transcendental dialectic in chapter 2 above.

84. Ibid., 204–6.

85. Ibid., 208.

86. Ibid., 209.

87. Ibid. (Habermas's emphasis).

88. Ibid., 210.

89. Ibid., 210ff.

90. Bernstein, *The Restructuring of Social and Political Theory,* 191. See also my discussion of Hegel in chapter 2 above.

91. See Habermas, *Knowledge and Human Interests,* 301–2.

92. This is the argument in ibid., 302–4.

93. Habermas argues this in *Theory and Practice,* 41–81.

94. See the essay "On Theory and Praxis in Our Scientific Civilization," in ibid., 254–55.

95. See Habermas, "The Scientization of Politics and Public Opinion," in *Toward a Rational Society,* esp. 75.

96. Bernstein, *The Restructuring of Social and Political Theory,* 188.

97. Habermas, *Knowledge and Human Interests,* 196–97.

98. Ibid., 197.

99. See ibid., 306–17.

100. It should be mentioned that Habermas sets forth his scheme of work and interaction in a sociological manner in "Technology and Science as Ideology," in *Toward a Rational Society,* 81–122.

101. Habermas, *Knowledge and Human Interests,* 197.

102. See ibid., e.g., 133, 308.

103. Ibid., 308.

104. See ibid., 191.

105. Ibid., 192–93.

106. Ibid., 309–10.

107. See Schroyer's comments in *The Critique of Domination,* 149ff.

108. Habermas, *Knowledge and Human Interests,* 308.

109. Bernstein, *The Restructuring of Social and Political Theory,* 198.

110. Habermas, *Knowledge and Human Interests,* 310.

111. See ibid., 196, 310, 314.

112. Ibid., 314. For Habermas's discussion of critique see also the essay "Between Philosophy and Science: Marxism as Critique," *Theory and Practice,* 195–252.

113. See Habermas, *Knowledge and Human Interests,* 314–15. See also, his "Toward a Theory of Communicative Competence," in H. P. Dreitzel, ed., *Recent Sociology No. 2: Patterns of Communicative Behavior* (New York: Macmillan Co., 1970); and "The Communication Theory of Society: A Brief Introduction," trans. and rev. J. J. Shapiro (unpublished copy). This entire interest is developed more fully by Habermas in *Communication and the Evolution of Society* (Boston: Beacon Press, 1979). For reasons of space and relevance, I shall not endeavor here to deal with this dimension of Habermas's thought. For some commentary, see McCarthy, *The Critical Theory of Jürgen Habermas,* 272–357; Bernstein, *The Restructuring of Social and Political Theory,* 205–13; and Schroyer, *The Critique of Domination,* 158–64. See also a number of the essays in Thompson and Held, *Habermas.* Finally, I should

mention at this point that I have not undertaken to examine in detail, also for space limitations, another important dimension of Habermas's thought related to communication: psychoanalysis as a model of critique and emancipatory, self-reflective knowledge. See, for example, *Knowledge and Human Interests,* 214–300. See also the recent discussion in Russell Keat, *The Politics of Social Theory: Habermas, Freud, and the Critique of Positivism* (Chicago: University of Chicago Press, 1981).

114. Habermas, *Knowledge and Human Interests,* 311–15.

115. Ibid., 315.

116. Ibid., 317.

117. See Bernstein, *The Restructuring of Social and Political Theory,* 220ff. See also the excellent discussion in Dallmayr, *Beyond Dogma and Despair,* 246–69.

118. A central work for this development in philosophy of science is, of course, Kuhn's *Structure of Scientific Revolutions.*

119. Bernstein, *The Restructuring of Social and Political Theory,* 221–25.

120. Ibid., 224.

121. Habermas, *Knowledge and Human Interests,* 314.

122. Bernstein, *The Restructuring of Social and Political Theory,* 225.

123. Jeremy Shapiro, a major translator of Habermas (including *Knowledge and Human Interests*) and author of articles on culture, technology, and the Frankfurt School, suggested to me in a conversation this tendency and hazard of Critical Theory to be obsessed with continual self-reflective reconstruction.

Chapter Seven

1. Lee C. McDonald, "Private Ethics and Civic Virtue" (Paper presented to the annual meeting of the American Political Science Association in New York, 3 September 1978), 37. McDonald is working on a forthcoming book on political ethics. For another stimulating attempt to reorient current political inquiry from within a broadened classical tradition of political theory, see the engaging argument of Dante Germino, *Political Philosophy and the Open Society* (Baton Rouge: Louisiana State University Press, 1982). I should add that apart from the work of Bernstein and Jung, one finds another argument for a reconstituted political science informed by phenomenology and critical theory in Dallmayr's *Beyond Dogma and Despair.* For similar efforts emerging out of the tradition of more clearly sociological, rather than political, inquiry, see John O'Neill, *Sociology as a Skin Trade* (New York: Harper and Row, 1972); and Barry Smart, *Sociology, Phenomenology, and Marxian Analysis* (London: Routledge and Kegan Paul, 1976).

2. See, for example, Kant, "Fundamental Principles of the Metaphysics of Morals," in *Kant's Critique of Practical Reason and Other Works on the Theory of Ethics,* 6th ed., trans. T. K. Abbot (London: Longmans, Green and Co., Paternoster-Row, 1909), 30.

3. Although this assumption is evident in all of Strauss's work, it strongly underlines his argument in *Natural Right and History.*

4. This view permeates the entire effort of Voegelin's four-volume *Order and History;* see, for example, volume 2, *The World of the Polis* (1957), 2.

5. Lukács, *History and Class Consciousness,* 205.

6. See Eugene Miller, "Positivism, Historicism, and Political Inquiry," *American Political Science Review* 66 (September 1972): 814.

7. Merleau-Ponty, "The Battle over Existentialism," *SNS,* 81.

8. On historicism's objectivistic and positivistic forms, see Habermas's critique of Dilthey in *Knowledge and Human Interests,* chap. 8, esp. 179.

9. See Miller, "Positivism, Historicism, and Political Inquiry." This article is nonetheless helpful in many other ways, especially in terms of drawing some of the major battle lines in political epistemology. For a recent and provocative collection of essays regarding the general sources and issues in the broader realm of relativism in human inquiry, see Martin Hollis and Steven Lukes, eds., *Rationality and Relativism* (Cambridge, Mass.: MIT Press, 1982).

10. Merleau-Ponty, Preface to *Phenomenology of Perception,* xiv.

11. Jung, *The Crisis of Political Understanding,* 171.

12. Bloch, *On Karl Marx,* 103.

13. Merleau-Ponty, Preface to *Phenomenology of Perception,* xx.

14. Bloch, *On Karl Marx,* 86.

15. Merleau-Ponty, "Marxism and Philosophy," *SNS,* 134.

16. Habermas, *Knowledge and Human Interests,* vii.

17. Merleau-Ponty, "Concerning Marxism," *SNS,* 119.

18. Merleau-Ponty, *In Praise of Philosophy,* trans. John Wild and James M. Edie (Evanston: Northwestern University Press, 1963), 41.

19. Gunnell, *Political Theory,* 10.

20. Merleau-Ponty, *Adventures of the Dialectic,* 233.

Bibliography

Books

Adorno, Theodor W. *Negative Dialectics*. Translated by E. B. Ashton. New York: Seabury Press, 1973.

————. *Prisms*. Translated by Samuel Weber and Shierry Weber. London: Neville Spearman, 1967.

————. *Zur Metakritik der Erkenntnistheorie: Studien über Husserl und Phänomenologischen Antinomien*. Frankfurt am Main: Suhrkamp Verlag, 1970.

Althusser, Louis. *For Marx*. Translated by Ben Brewster. New York: Random House, 1970.

Anderson, Perry. *Considerations on Western Marxism*. London: New Left Books, 1976.

Archard, David. *Marxism and Existentialism: The Political Philosophy of Sartre and Merleau-Ponty*. Belfast: Blackstaff Press, 1980.

Arendt, Hannah. *Between Past and Future: Eight Exercises in Political Thought*. New York: Viking Press, 1968.

Avineri, Shlomo. *The Social and Political Thought of Karl Marx*. Cambridge: Cambridge University Press, 1968.

Ayer, A. J. *Language, Truth, and Logic*. 2d ed. London: Gollancz, 1958.

Benjamin, Walter. *Illuminations: Essays and Reflections*. Edited with an Introduction by Hannah Arendt and translated by Harry Zohn. New York: Schocken Books, 1968.

Bernstein, Richard J. *The Restructuring of Social and Political Theory*. New York: Harcourt Brace Jovanovich, 1976.

Bloch, Ernst. *On Karl Marx*. Translated by John Maxwell. New York: Herder and Herder, 1971.

Bochenski, I. M. *Europäische Philosophie der Gegenwart*. Munich: Francke Verlag, 1951.

237

Bologh, Roslyn Wallach. *Dialectical Phenomenology: Marx's Method*. London: Routledge and Kegan Paul, 1979.

Brecht, Arnold. *Political Theory: The Foundations of Twentieth-Century Political Thought*. Princeton: Princeton University Press, 1959.

Bronowski, Jacob. *The Common Sense of Science*. New York: Random House, 1959.

Buck-Morss, Susan. *The Origin of Negative Dialectics: Theodor W. Adorno, Walter Benjamin, and the Frankfurt Institute*. New York: Macmillan Publishing Co., Free Press, 1977.

Carnap, Rudolf. *The Unity of Science*. London: Routledge and Kegan Paul, 1934.

Chiodi, Pietro. *Sartre and Marxism*. Translated by Kate Soper. New York: Humanities Press, 1976.

Cooper, Barry. *Merleau-Ponty and Marxism: From Terror to Reform*. Toronto: University of Toronto Press, 1979.

Crick, Bernard. *The American Science of Politics*. Berkeley: University of California Press, 1959.

Dahl, Robert A. *Modern Political Analysis*. Englewood Cliffs, N.J.: Prentice-Hall, 1963.

Dallmayr, Fred R. *Beyond Dogma and Despair: Toward a Critical Phenomenology of Politics*. Notre Dame, Ind.: University of Notre Dame Press, 1981.

Dallmayr, Fred R., and McCarthy, Thomas A., eds. *Understanding and Social Inquiry*. Notre Dame, Ind.: University of Notre Dame Press, 1977.

Davidson, Alastair. *Antonio Gramsci: The Man, His Ideas*. Australian Left Review Publications, 1968.

————. *Antonio Gramsci: Towards an Intellectual Biography*. London: Merlin Press, 1977.

Dearden, R. F.; Hirst, P. H.; and Peters, R. S., eds. *Education and the Development of Reason*. London: Routledge and Kegan Paul, 1972.

De Beauvoir, Simone. *Force of Circumstances*. Translated by Richard Howard. New York: G. P. Putnam's Sons, 1965.

Desan, Wilfrid. *The Marxism of Jean-Paul Sartre*. New York: Doubleday, 1965.

————. *The Tragic Finale: An Essay on the Philosophy of Jean-Paul Sartre*. New York: Harper and Row, 1960.

Easton, David. *A Framework of Political Analysis*. Englewood Cliffs, N.J.: Prentice-Hall, 1965.

————. *The Political System: An Inquiry into the State of Political Science*. New York: Alfred A. Knopf, 1953.

Eulau, Heinz. *The Behavioral Persuasion in Politics*. New York: Random House, 1964.

Farber, Marvin. *The Foundations of Phenomenology: Edmund Husserl and the Quest for a Rigorous Science of Philosophy.* Cambridge: Harvard University Press, 1943.

Feyerabend, Paul. *Against Method.* London: New Left Books, 1975.

———. *Science in a Free Society.* London: New Left Books, 1978.

Findlay, J. N. *Hegel: A Re-Examination.* London: George Allen and Unwin, 1958.

Fiori, Giuseppe. *Antonio Gramsci: Life of a Revolutionary.* Translated by Tom Nairn. New York: Schocken Books, 1972.

Foster, Michael. *The Political Philosophies of Plato and Hegel.* Oxford: Clarendon Press, 1935.

Gadamer, Hans-Georg. *Hegel's Dialectic.* Translated by Christopher Smith. New Haven: Yale University Press, 1976.

———. *Truth and Method.* New York: Seabury Press, 1975.

Garaudy, Roger. *The Crisis in Communism.* Translated by Peter Ross and Betty Ross. New York: Grove Press, 1969.

Germino, Dante. *Beyond Ideology: The Revival of Political Theory.* New York: Harper and Row, 1967; reprint ed., Chicago: University of Chicago Press, 1976.

———. *Machiavelli to Marx: Modern Western Political Thought.* Chicago: University of Chicago Press, Phoenix Books, 1979.

———. *Political Philosophy and the Open Society.* Baton Rouge: Louisiana State University Press, 1982.

Gould, Carol. *Marx's Social Ontology.* Cambridge, Mass.: MIT Press, 1978.

Graham, George Jr., and Carey, George, eds. *The Post-Behavioral Era: Perspectives on Political Science.* New York: David McKay Co., 1972.

Gramsci, Antonio. *The Modern Prince and Other Writings.* Translated by Louis Marks. New York: International Publishers, 1957.

———. *Selections from the Prison Notebooks.* Translated and edited by Quinton Hoare and Geoffrey Nowell Smith. New York: International Publishers, 1971.

Gunnell, John G. *Philosophy, Science, and Political Inquiry.* Morristown, N.J.: General Learning Press, 1975.

———. *Political Theory: Tradition and Interpretation.* Cambridge, Mass.: Winthrop Publishers, 1979.

Habermas, Jürgen. *Communication and the Evolution of Society.* Translated and with an Introduction by Thomas McCarthy. Boston: Beacon Press, 1979.

———. *Knowledge and Human Interests.* Translated by Jeremy J. Shapiro. Boston: Beacon Press, 1971.

———. *Legitimation Crisis.* Translated by Thomas McCarthy. Boston: Beacon Press, 1975.

———. *Theory and Practice.* Translated by John Viertel. Boston: Beacon Press, 1973.

————. *Toward a Rational Society: Student Protest, Science, and Politics.* Translated by Jeremy J. Shapiro. Boston: Beacon Press, 1970.

Hartmann, Klaus. *Sartre's Ontology: A Study of "Being and Nothingness" in the Light of Hegel's Logic.* Evanston: Northwestern University Press, 1966.

Hartnack, Justus. *Kant's Theory of Knowledge.* Translated by M. Holmes Hartshorne. New York: Harcourt, Brace and World, 1967.

Hegel, G. W. F. *The Encyclopedia of Philosophical Sciences.* Translated by Gustav Emil Mueller. New York: Philosophical Library, 1959.

————. *The Logic of Hegel.* Translated by William Wallace. Oxford: Clarendon Press, 1892.

————. *The Phenomenology of Mind.* 2d ed. Translated by J. B. Baillie. London: George Allen and Unwin, 1931.

————. *Reason in History.* Translated by R. S. Hartman. Indianapolis: Bobbs-Merrill, Liberal Arts Press, 1953.

Heidegger, Martin. *Being and Time.* Translated by J. Macquarrie and E. Robinson. Oxford: Basil Blackwell, 1962.

Held, David. *Introduction to Critical Theory: Horkheimer to Habermas.* London: Hutchinson, 1980.

Hollis, Martin, and Lukes, Steven, eds. *Rationality and Relativism.* Cambridge, Mass.: MIT Press, 1982.

Horkheimer, Max. *Critical Theory: Selected Essays.* Translated by Matthew J. O'Connell et al. New York: Herder and Herder, 1972.

————. *Critique of Instrumental Reason.* Translated by Matthew J. O'Connell et al. New York: Seabury Press, 1974.

————. *Eclipse of Reason.* New York: Oxford University Press, 1947.

Horkheimer, Max, and Adorno, Theodor W. *Dialectic of Enlightenment.* Translated by John Cumming. New York: Herder and Herder, 1972.

Howard, Dick. *The Development of the Marxian Dialectic.* Carbondale: Southern Illinois University Press, 1972.

Howard, Dick, and Klare, Karl E., eds. *The Unknown Dimension: European Marxism since Lenin.* New York: Basic Books, 1972.

Hughes, H. Stuart. *The Obstructed Path: French Social Thought in the Years of Desperation, 1930–1960.* New York: Harper and Row, 1968.

Husserl, Edmund. *The Crisis of European Sciences and Transcendental Phenomenology: An Introduction to Phenomenological Philosophy.* Translated by David Carr. Evanston: Northwestern University Press, 1970.

————. *The Idea of Phenomenology.* Translated by W. P. Alston and G. Nakhnikian. The Hague: Martinus Nijhoff, 1964.

————. *Ideas: General Introduction to Pure Phenomenology.* Translated by W. R. Boyce Gibson. London: George Allen and Unwin, 1931.

————. *Logical Investigations.* 2 vols. Translated by J. N. Findlay. London: Routledge and Kegan Paul, 1970.

Isaak, Alan C. *Scope and Methods of Political Science: An Introduction to the Methodology of Political Inquiry*. Homewood, Ill.: Dorsey Press, 1969.

Israel, Joachim. *Alienation from Marx to Modern Sociology: A Macrosocial Analysis*. Boston: Allyn and Bacon, 1971.

Jacoby, Russell. *Dialectic of Defeat: Contours of Western Marxism*. New York: Cambridge University Press, 1981.

Jay, Martin. *The Dialectical Imagination: A History of the Frankfurt School and the Institute of Social Research, 1923–1950*. Boston: Little, Brown and Co., 1973.

Jung, Hwa Yol. *The Crisis of Political Understanding: A Phenomenological Perspective in the Conduct of Political Inquiry*. Pittsburgh: Duquesne University Press, 1979.

————, ed. *Existential Phenomenology and Political Theory: A Reader*. Chicago: Henry Regnery Co., 1972.

Kant, Immanuel. *Critique of Pure Reason*. Translated by Norman Kemp Smith. London: Macmillan and Co., 1929.

————. *Kant's Critique of Practical Reason and Other Works on the Theory of Ethics*. 6th ed. Translated by T. K. Abbot. London: Longmans, Green and Co., Paternoster-Row, 1909.

Keat, Russell. *The Politics of Social Theory: Habermas, Freud, and the Critique of Positivism*. Chicago: University of Chicago Press, 1981.

Kockelmans, Joseph. *A First Introduction to Husserl's Phenomenology*. Pittsburgh: Duquesne University Press, 1967.

Kojève, Alexandre. *Introduction to the Reading of Hegel*. Edited by Allan Bloom and translated by James H. Nichols, Jr. New York: Basic Books, 1969.

Kolakowski, Leszek. *Main Currents of Marxism*. 3 vols. New York: Oxford University Press, 1978.

————. *Toward a Marxist Humanism: Essays on the Left Today*. Translated by Jane Zielonko Peel. New York: Grove Press, 1968.

Korsch, Karl. *Marxism and Philosophy*. Translated by Fred Halliday. New York: Monthly Review Press, 1971.

Kuhn, Thomas. *The Structure of Scientific Revolutions*. 2d ed. Chicago: University of Chicago Press, 1970.

Lakatos, Imre. *The Methodology of Scientific Research Programmes*. Cambridge: Cambridge University Press, 1978.

Laslett, Peter, ed. *Philosophy, Politics, and Society*. First series. New York: Barnes and Noble, 1957.

Laslett, Peter, and Runciman, W. G., eds. *Philosophy, Politics, and Society*. Second series. New York: Barnes and Noble, 1962.

Lasswell, Harold D., and Kaplan, Abraham. *Power and Society*. London: Routledge and Kegan Paul, 1952.

Lauer, Quentin, S.J. *Essays in Hegelian Dialectic*. New York: Fordham University Press, 1977.

————. *The Triumph of Subjectivity: An Introduction to Transcendental Phenomenology*. New York: Fordham University Press, 1958.

————, ed. *Edmund Husserl: Phenomenology and the Crisis of Philosophy*. New York: Harper and Row, 1965.

Lichtheim, George. *From Marx to Hegel*. New York: Seabury Press, 1974.

Livergood, Norman D. *Activity in Marx's Philosophy*. The Hague: Martinus Nijhoff, 1967.

Louch, A. R. *Explanation and Human Action*. Berkeley: University of California Press, 1966.

Lukács, Georg. *History and Class Consciousness: Studies in Marxist Dialectics*. Translated by Rodney Livingstone. Cambridge, Mass.: MIT Press, 1971.

McCarthy, Thomas. *The Critical Theory of Jürgen Habermas*. Cambridge, Mass.: MIT Press, 1978.

Mallin, Samuel B. *Merleau-Ponty's Philosophy*. New Haven: Yale University Press, 1979.

Marcuse, Herbert. *The Aesthetic Dimension: Toward a Critique of Marxist Aesthetics*. Boston: Beacon Press, 1978.

————. *Eros and Civilization: A Philosophical Inquiry into Freud*. New York: Random House, Vintage Books, 1962.

————. *An Essay on Liberation*. Boston: Beacon Press, 1969.

————. *Negations: Essays in Critical Theory*. Translated by Jeremy J. Shapiro. Boston: Beacon Press, 1968.

————. *One-Dimensional Man: Studies in the Ideology of Advanced Industrial Society*. Boston: Beacon Press, 1964.

————. *Reason and Revolution: Hegel and the Rise of Social Theory*. London: Oxford University Press, 1941.

Marias, Julian. *Reason and Life: The Introduction to Philosophy*. Translated by K. S. Reid and E. Sarmiento. New Haven: Yale University Press, 1956.

Marković, Mihailo. *From Affluence to Praxis*. Ann Arbor: University of Michigan Press, 1974.

Marković, Mihailo, and Petrović, Gajo, eds. *Praxis: Yugoslav Essays in the Philosophy and Methodology of the Social Sciences*. Translated by Joan Coddington et al. Boston Studies in the Philosophy of Science, ed. Robert S. Cohen and Marx W. Wartofsky, vol. 36. Dordrecht: D. Reidel Publishing Co., 1979.

Marx, Karl. *Capital*. 3 vols. Translated by Samuel Moore and Edward Aveling. Moscow, 1957–1959.

————. *Grundrisse: Foundations of the Critique of Political Economy*. Translated by Martin Nicolaus. New York: Random House, Vintage Books, 1973.

————. *Karl Marx: Early Writings*. Edited and translated by T. B. Bottomore. New York: McGraw-Hill, 1964.

————. *Karl Marx: Selected Writings*. Edited by David McLellan. Oxford: Oxford University Press, 1977.

Marx, Werner. *Hegel's Phenomenology of Spirit*. Translated by Peter Heath. New York: Harper and Row, 1975.

Matson, Floyd. *The Broken Image*. New York: Braziller, 1964.

Meehan, Eugene J. *The Foundations of Political Analysis: Empirical and Normative*. Homewood, Ill.: Dorsey Press, 1971.

————. *The Theory and Method of Political Analysis*. Homewood, Ill.: Dorsey Press, 1965.

————. *Value Judgment and Social Science: Structures and Processes*. Homewood, Ill.: Dorsey Press, 1969.

Merleau-Ponty, Maurice. *Adventures of the Dialectic*. Translated by Joseph Bien. Evanston: Northwestern University Press, 1973.

————. *The Essential Writings of Merleau-Ponty*. Edited by Alden Fischer. New York: Harcourt, Brace and World, 1969.

————. *Humanism and Terror*. Translated by John O'Neill. Boston: Beacon Press, 1969.

————. *In Praise of Philosophy*. Translated by John Wild and James M. Edie. Evanston: Northwestern University Press, 1963.

————. *Phenomenology of Perception*. Translated by Colin Smith. London: Routledge and Kegan Paul, 1962.

————. *Primacy of Perception and Other Essays*. Edited by James M. Edie. Evanston: Northwestern University Press, 1964.

————. *Sense and Non-Sense*. Translated by H. L. Dreyfus and P. A. Dreyfus. Evanston: Northwestern University Press, 1964.

————. *Signs*. Translated by Richard C. McCleary. Evanston: Northwestern University Press, 1964.

————. *The Structure of Behavior*. Translated by Alden Fisher. Boston: Beacon Press, 1963.

————. *Themes from the Lectures at the College de France, 1952–1960*. Translated by John O'Neill. Evanston: Northwestern University Press, 1970.

————. *The Visible and the Invisible*. Edited by Claude Lefort and translated by Alphonso Lingis. Evanston: Northwestern University Press, 1968.

Nagel, Ernest. *The Structure of Science*. New York: Harcourt, Brace and World, 1961.

Natanson, Maurice. *A Critique of Jean-Paul Sartre's Ontology*. 1951. Reprint ed. The Hague: Martinus Nijhoff, 1973.

————. *Edmund Husserl: Philosopher of Infinite Tasks*. Evanston: Northwestern University Press, 1973.

Odajnyk, Walter. *Marxism and Existentialism*. New York: Anchor Books, 1965.

Ollman, Bertell. *Alienation: Marx's Conception of Man in Capitalist Society*. 2d ed. Cambridge: Cambridge University Press, 1976.

O'Malley, J. J.; Algozin, K. W.; and Weiss, F. G., eds. *Hegel and the History of Philosophy*. The Hague: Martinus Nijhoff, 1974.

O'Neill, John. *Sociology as a Skin Trade*. New York: Harper and Row, 1972.

Oppenheim, Felix. *Moral Principles in Political Philosophy*. New York: Random House, 1968.

Paci, Enzo. *The Function of the Sciences and the Meaning of Man*. Translated with an Introduction by Paul Piccone and James E. Hansen. Evanston: Northwestern University Press, 1972.

Papineau, David. *For Science in the Social Sciences*. New York: St. Martin's Press, 1978.

Petrovíc, Gajo. *Marx in the Mid-Twentieth Century*. Garden City, N.Y.: Anchor Books, 1967.

Pitkin, Hannah. *Wittgenstein and Justice*. Berkeley: University of California Press, 1972.

Pivcevic, Edo. *Husserl's Phenomenology*. London: Hutchinson, 1970.

Poster, Mark. *Existential Marxism in Postwar France: From Sartre to Althusser*. Princeton: Princeton University Press, 1975.

———. *Sartre's Marxism*. Cambridge: Cambridge University Press, 1982.

Psathas, George, ed. *Phenomenological Sociology: Issues and Applications*. New York: John Wiley and Sons, 1973.

Rabil, Albert. *Merleau-Ponty: Existentialist of the Social World*. New York: Columbia University Press, 1967.

Ricoeur, Paul. *Husserl*. Translated by E. G. Ballard and L. E. Embree. Evanston: Northwestern University Press, 1967.

Roche, Maurice. *Phenomenology, Language, and the Social Sciences*. London: Routledge and Kegan Paul, 1973.

Ryle, Gilbert. *The Concept of Mind*. London: Hutchinson, 1949.

Salvan, Jacques. *The Scandalous Ghost: Sartre's Existentialism as Related to Vitalism, Humanism, Mysticism, Marxism*. Detroit: Wayne State University Press, 1967.

———. *To Be and Not To Be: An Analysis of Jean-Paul Sartre's Ontology*. Detroit: Wayne State University Press, 1962.

Sartre, Jean-Paul. *Being and Nothingness: An Essay on Phenomenological Ontology*. Translated by Hazel Barnes. New York: Philosophical Library, 1956.

———. *Critique of Dialectical Reason*. Translated by Allan Sheridan-Smith. London: New Left Books, 1976.

———. *Search for a Method*. Translated by Hazel Barnes. New York: Alfred A. Knopf, 1967.

———. *Situations*. Translated by Benita Eisler. New York: Braziller, 1965.

———. *The Transcendence of the Ego*. Translated by Forrest Williams and Robert Kirkpatrick. New York: Noonday Press, 1957.

———. *The Words*. Translated by Bernard Frechtman. New York: Braziller, 1964.

Schroyer, Trent. *The Critique of Domination: The Origins and Development of Critical Theory*. Boston: Beacon Press, 1973.

Schutz, Alfred. *Collected Papers I: The Problem of Social Reality.* Edited by
Maurice Natanson. The Hague: Martinus Nijhoff, 1962.

————. *The Phenomenology of the Social World.* Translated by George Walsh
and Frederick Lehnert. Evanston: Northwestern University Press, 1967.

Shell, Susan. *The Rights of Reason: A Study of Kant's Philosophy and Politics.*
Toronto: University of Toronto Press, 1979.

Smart, Barry. *Sociology, Phenomenology, and Marxian Analysis.* London:
Routledge and Kegan Paul, 1976.

Smith, Norman Kemp. *A Commentary to Kant's "Critique of Pure Reason."*
2d ed. London: Macmillan and Co., 1923.

Spaeth, Howard, ed. *The Predicament of Modern Politics.* Detroit: University
of Detroit Press, 1964.

Spiegelberg, Herbert. *Doing Phenomenology: Essays on and in Phenomenology.* The Hague: Martinus Nijhoff, 1975.

————. *The Phenomenological Movement: A Historical Introduction.* 2 vols.
The Hague: Martinus Nijhoff, 1960.

Spurling, Laurie. *Phenomenology and the Social World: The Philosophy of
Merleau-Ponty and Its Relation to the Social Sciences.* London: Routledge
and Kegan Paul, 1977.

Stojanović, Svetozar. *Between Ideals and Reality: A Critique of Socialism and
Its Future.* Translated by Gerson S. Sher. London: Oxford University Press,
1973.

————. *In Search of Democracy in Socialism: History and Party Consciousness.* Translated by Gerson S. Sher. Buffalo, N.Y.: Prometheus Books, 1981.

Storing, Herbert, ed. *Essays on the Scientific Study of Politics.* New York:
Holt, Rinehart, and Winston, 1962.

Strauss, Leo. *Natural Right and History.* Chicago: University of Chicago
Press, 1953.

————. *On Tyranny: An Interpretation of Xenophon's Hiero.* New York: Free
Press, 1948.

Taylor, Charles. *Hegel.* Cambridge: Cambridge University Press, 1975.

Thévenaz, Pierre. *What Is Phenomenology? and Other Essays.* Edited by
James M. Edie and translated by James M. Edie, C. Courtney, and P.
Brockelman. Chicago: Quadrangle Books, 1962.

Thompson, John B. *Critical Hermeneutics: A Study in the Thought of Paul
Ricoeur and Jürgen Habermas.* Cambridge: Cambridge University Press,
1981.

Thompson, John B., and Held, David, eds. *Habermas: Critical Debates.* Cambridge, Mass.: MIT Press, 1982.

Voegelin, Eric. *Anamnesis: Zur Theorie der Geschichte und Politik.* Munich:
Piper Verlag, 1966.

————. *From Enlightenment to Revolution.* Edited by John Hallowell. Dur-
ham, N.C.: Duke University Press, 1975.

————. *The New Science of Politics*. Chicago: University of Chicago Press, 1952.

————. *Order and History*. 4 vols. Baton Rouge: Louisiana State University Press, 1956–1975.

Welch, E. Parl. *The Philosophy of Edmund Husserl: The Origin and Development of His Phenomenology*. New York: Columbia University Press, 1941.

Weldon, T. D. *The Vocabulary of Politics*. London: Penguin Books, 1953.

Wellmer, Albrecht. *Critical Theory of Society*. Translated by John Cumming. New York: Seabury Press, 1971.

Wolff, Robert Paul. *Kant's Theory of Mental Activity*. Cambridge: Harvard University Press, 1963.

Young, Roland, ed. *Approaches to the Study of Politics*. Evanston: Northwestern University Press, 1958.

Zaner, Richard M. *The Way of Phenomenology: Criticism as a Philosophical Discipline*. New York: Pegasus, 1970.

Articles

Bay, Christian. "A Critical Evaluation of Behavioral Literature." *American Political Science Review* 59 (March 1965): 39–61.

Catlin, George E. G. "Political Theory: What Is It?" *Political Science Quarterly* 72 (March 1957): 1–29.

Cobban, Alfred. "The Decline of Political Theory." *Political Science Quarterly* 68 (September 1953): 321–37.

Dahl, Robert. "Political Theory." *World Politics* 11 (October 1958): 89–102.

Dallmayr, Fred. "Beyond Dogma and Despair: Toward a Critical Theory of Politics." *American Political Science Review* 70 (March 1976): 64–79.

————. "Phenomenology and Marxism: A Salute to Enzo Paci." In *Phenomenological Sociology*, edited by George Psathas. New York: John Wiley and Sons, 1973.

Deutsch, Karl. "The Limits of Common Sense." *Psychiatry* 22, no. 2 (May 1959): 105–12.

Easton, David. "The Decline of Modern Political Theory." *Journal of Politics* 13 (February 1951): 36–58.

Factor, Regis A., and Turner, Stephen P. "The Critique of Positivist Social Science in Leo Strauss and Jürgen Habermas." *Sociological Analysis and Theory* 7 (October 1977): 185–206.

Germino, Dante. "Eric Voegelin's Framework for Political Evaluation in His Recently Published Work." *American Political Science Review* 72 (March 1978): 110–21.

————. "The Fact-Value Dichotomy as an Intellectual Prison." *Modern Age* (Spring 1979): 140–44.

Habermas, Jürgen. "Toward a Theory of Communicative Competence." In *Recent Sociology No. 2: Patterns of Communicative Behavior*, edited by H. P. Dreitzel. New York: Macmillan Co., 1970.

———. "Towards a Reconstruction of Historical Materialism." *Theory and Society* 2 (1975): 287–300.

Jung, Hwa Yol. "The Political Relevance of Existential Phenomenology." *Review of Politics* 33 (October 1971): 538–63.

Marcuse, Herbert. "Contributions to a Phenomenology of Historical Materialism." *Telos,* no. 4 (Fall 1969): 3–34.

Miller, Eugene. "Positivism, Historicism, and Political Inquiry." *American Political Science Review* 66 (September 1972): 796–817.

Miller, Warren. "The Role of Research in the Unification of a Discipline." *American Political Science Review* 75 (March 1981): 9–16.

Nagel, Ernest. "Problems of Concept and Theory Formation in the Social Sciences." *Science, Language, and Human Rights*. Papers for the symposia held at the annual meeting of the Eastern Division of the American Philosophical Association. Philadelphia: University of Pennsylvania Press, 1952.

Ranney, Austin. " 'The Divine Science': Political Engineering in American Culture." *American Political Science Review* 70 (March 1976): 140–48.

Rovatti, Pier Aldo. "Critical Theory and Phenomenology." *Telos,* no. 15 (Spring 1973): 35–40.

Sabine, George. "What Is a Political Theory?" *Journal of Politics* 1 (February 1939): 1–16.

Shmueli, Efraim. "Can Phenomenology Accommodate Marxism?" *Telos,* no. 17 (Fall 1973): 164–80.

———. "Consciousness and Action: Husserl and Marx on Theory and Praxis." In *Analecta Husserliana V: The Crisis of Culture,* edited by Anna-Teresa Tymieniecka. Dordrecht: D. Reidel Publishing Co., 1976.

Strauss, Leo. "An Epilogue." In *Essays on the Scientific Study of Politics,* edited by Herbert Storing. New York: Holt, Rinehart, and Winston, 1962.

———. "Philosophy as Rigorous Science and Political Philosophy." *Interpretation* 2 (Fall 1971): 1–9.

———. "Political Philosophy and the Crisis of Our Time." In *The Predicament of Modern Politics,* edited by Howard Spaeth. Detroit: University of Detroit Press, 1964.

———. "What Is Political Philosophy?" *Journal of Politics* 19 (August 1957): 343–68.

Index

Absolute, the: and dialectical theory, 84–85; discussed in Hegel, 38–40; lure of, 186; and Sartre, 128

Absolute knowledge, 35; and dialectical theory, 47; in Hegel, 33–48 passim; Marx's view of, 53

Abstraction, 186; and concreteness, in Hegel, 45–46; problem of, in political science, 4, 183–84, 188

Action, 117, 122, 168; behavioralism's deficient view of, 131; and existential phenomenology, 130, 132; instrumental, 156, 158, 161–71; and knowing, 185; and praxis, 148–49; in Sartre, 101

Action systems, 171

Activity: in Kant's philosophy, 29, 32, 33; and human nature, 108

Adorno, Theodor, 144, 160; on negative dialectics, 231 n.60

Alienation, 131, 209 n.95; and dialectical marxism, 69; importance for political science, 69–70; and knowledge, in Marx, 51–60

Althusser, Louis, 85, 87–88

Ambiguity, 81, 83, 84, 88–89, 188; and commitment, 194–95, 197; nature of, 129

American political science, 189

Analytic-synthetic distinction, 204–5 n.5; in Hume and Kant, 29

Anglo-American philosophy, 26, 91, 150

Application of theory, as nondialectical, 139–40

Archimedean standpoint, 106, 124

Arendt, Hannah, 3, 16

Aristotle, 24; and classical *theoria,* 166–67; and the dialectic, 42; on nature of political theory, 16; philosopher of community, 134; and theory and practice, 135

Art, and Marx, 63

Atheism: meaning of, for Marx, 57; in Sartre, 101

Atam bomb, 67

Atomism, 45, 108

Aufhebung (Aufheben), 161, 174, 180, 210 n.116, 221 n.95; absence of, in Heidegger, 98; defined, 37; and dialectical theory, 192; and Hegel, 45; in Marx's theory, 57, 60

Augustine, Saint, 42

Austin, John, 26, 216 n.2

"Authentic existence," in Heidegger, 99

Axiological positivism, 10, 19